Conversations with
the Confessions

Conversations with the Confessions

Dialogue in the Reformed Tradition

JOSEPH D. SMALL, EDITOR

Geneva Press
Louisville, Kentucky

Book design by Sharon Adams
Cover design by Night & Day Design

First edition
Published by Geneva Press
Louisville, Kentucky

This book is printed on acid-free paper that meets the American National Standards Institute Z39.48 standard. ∞

PRINTED IN THE UNITED STATES OF AMERICA

06 07 08 09 10 11 12 13 — 10 9 8 7 6 5 4 3 2

Library of Congress Cataloging-in-Publication Data

Conversations with the confessions : dialogue in the reformed tradition / Joseph D. Small, editor.—1st ed.
   p. cm.
   Includes bibliographical references.
   ISBN-13: 978-0-664-50248-5 (alk. paper)
   ISBN-10: 0-664-50248-2 (alk. paper)
   1. Presbyterian Church (U.S.A.). Book of confessions.   2. Presbyterian Church (U.S.A.)—Creeds.   3. Reformed Church—Creeds.   I. Small, Joseph D.

BX8969.5.C67   2005
238'.5—dc22   2005041394

Contents

Contributors

John P. Burgess, James Henry Snowden Associate Professor of Systematic Theology, Pittsburgh Theological Seminary

Margit Ernst-Habib, Reformed theologian living in Germany, formerly on the faculty of Columbia Theological Seminary

Willie James Jennings, Assistant Research Professor of Theology and Black Church Studies and Academic Dean, Duke Divinity School

Clifton Kirkpatrick, Stated Clerk of the General Assembly, Presbyterian Church (U.S.A.); President of the World Alliance of Reformed Churches

Thomas G. Long, Bandy Professor of Preaching, Candler School of Theology, Emory University

Martha L. Moore-Keish, Assistant Professor of Theology, Columbia Theological Seminary

Kevin Park, Pastor, Bethany Presbyterian Church, Bloomfield, New Jersey

Cynthia L. Rigby, W. C. Brown Associate Professor of Theology, Austin Presbyterian Theological Seminary

Joseph D. Small, Coordinator of the Office of Theology and Worship, Presbyterian Church (U.S.A.)

Laura Smit, Dean of the Chapel, Calvin College

Sheldon W. Sorge, Associate for Theology, Office of Theology and Worship, Presbyterian Church (U.S.A.); Adjunct Professor, University of Dubuque Theological Seminary

John L. Thompson, Professor of Historical Theology, Fuller Theological Seminary

Leanne Van Dyk, Professor of Reformed Theology and Academic Dean, Western Theological Seminary

Charles A. Wiley, Associate for Theology, Office of Theology and Worship, Presbyterian Church (U.S.A.)

Preface

Clifton Kirkpatrick

Second only to the Bible, the foundational witness to Jesus Christ in the Presbyterian Church (U.S.A.) is *The Book of Confessions*. Although it is the first part of the church's constitution, it is less well known than the second part, the *Book of Order*. *The Book of Confessions* is clearly our greatest constitutional treasure, a wonderful source of wisdom to deepen our faith in Christ and inspire our faithfulness. *Conversations with the Confessions* offers us a fresh invitation to life-giving dialogue with these treasures. I hope many Presbyterians (and others!) will take advantage of this opportunity for renewed conversation.

One of the identifying marks of Reformed Christians is the use of confessions to state foundational commitments of faith. Confessions declare faith both to the church and to the world in which the church lives. Confession making was a hallmark of the sixteenth-century Reformation. In a time of religious crisis, John Knox and five colleagues drafted the Scots Confession to state boldly what they believed. Reformed communities in the Netherlands, Germany, and Hungary drew strength from the Heidelberg Catechism, while the Swiss found guidance in the Second Helvetic Confession.

The Presbyterian Church (U.S.A.) is unique in that we do not have a single confession of faith, but rather a *collection* of confessions. Each one was written in a particular time and place to express the eternal faith of the church in a specific context. In the early centuries of the church, the Nicene and Apostles' Creeds were composed to make clear the faith of the church in the midst of a pagan world. In the Reformation era, six confessions and catechisms were written to make clear the witness to the gospel of Reformed Christians in an era of theological and ecclesial upheaval. In the twentieth century, three confessions responded to emerging issues: The Theological Declaration of

Barmen affirmed the lordship of Christ over against the claims of the Nazis, the Confession of 1967 called the church to a ministry of reconciliation in the face of pressing social divisions, and A Brief Statement of Faith affirmed the faith of the reunited Presbyterian Church in beautiful and poetic language.

The importance of *The Book of Confessions* does not lie in every specific article, admonition, or prohibition. What is important are the common themes that express the central verities of the Christian faith in all the different contexts in which the church lives and moves and has its being. These common themes—expressed in different historical and cultural contexts—provide the contemporary church with rich material for significant conversation about the shape of Christian faith and life today.

This broad, rather than narrow, way of understanding our confessions is not new to Presbyterians. In the "Adopting Act" of 1729, the church made it clear that officers were not required to subscribe to every articulation in the Westminster Confession and Catechisms (then the church's sole confessional standard) but rather to uphold its "essential and necessary articles." Our church's adoption of a *Book of Confessions* is itself an expression of theological breadth and an invitation to theological dialogue in the best spirit of the Presbyterian tradition. It is also a wonderful way to enable diverse Christians to discover the fullness of shared affirmations such as Trinity, incarnation, and justification by grace through faith that ring true throughout the confessions and throughout Christian experience in every age.

I welcome you as you join in a fresh "conversation with the confessions." You will discover in the pages of this book many of the riches of theological truth that can be found in our confessions, strengthening faithfulness in our time just as they did when first composed. The opening essay sets out the need for the church's conversation with the confessions and illustrates ways in which the conversation can proceed. The remaining essays engage the confessions in two ways. First, conversations are held with confessions from different periods of the church's life: early church creeds, Reformation confessions, the Westminster Standards, and twentieth-century confessions. Next the full range of confessions is brought into conversation around common, basic questions such as "Who is God?" "Who are we?" "Why the church?" and "How shall we worship?" These conversations with the confessions are not self-contained, for they are intended to include you and to inaugurate an ongoing conversation throughout the church.

I want to initiate the conversation by highlighting for you my perspective on some parts of our confessional heritage, the challenges facing the church to which the confessions sought to respond, and the great affirmations of the Christian faith that they lifted up in their time and that they also lift up for our own. I invite you to join me in discovering again the rich insights of our confessions so that each of us and the whole church will be able to confess in our contemporary world the faith "once given to the saints."

THE ECUMENICAL CREEDS

The Nicene Creed was the first creed adopted by representatives of the entire church, and it is still the most widely affirmed confession of faith among all three major branches of the Christian church: Orthodox, Roman Catholic, and Protestant. As the creed known and used by the majority of Christians worldwide, the Nicene Creed has always represented a consensus of what the church believes.

The basic uncertainty in the early church concerned the nature and person of Jesus Christ. The Council of Nicea made it clear to all the world that Jesus Christ is both "the only Son of God" and "truly human," and that the Holy Spirit is "the Lord, the giver of life . . . who with the Father and the Son is worshiped and glorified." Thus, the Nicene Creed gave formal declaration to what we know today as the doctrine of the Trinity. The Nicene Creed gives powerful witness to the great truth that the one God created the world, redeemed it in Jesus Christ, and renews it through the power and presence of the Holy Spirit. The church's faith has been thoroughly trinitarian ever since.

I have always treasured the Nicene Creed's statement about the church: "We believe in one holy catholic and apostolic Church." In an age of rampant individualism and party spirit, it is important to be reminded anew of the great truths that the church is one (faithful Christians are always ecumenical), that the church is holy (it is God's church, not ours), that the church is catholic (the Christian community welcomes the broad diversity of the human family), and that the church is apostolic (it exists not for itself, but to share God's love, justice, and mercy with all the world). The Nicene Creed provided grounding and direction to Christian people faced with the turmoil of the fourth century. Sixteen centuries later its message provides that same grounding and direction in the things that truly matter for Christians.

As I travel across the church, I am pleased by how many congregations use the Apostles' Creed and by the large number of worshipers who have memorized it. Although the affirmations of the creed were surely accepted by the earliest followers of Jesus and the statements about God the Father, Son, and Holy Spirit were confessed in baptism for centuries, the creed as we have it did not become "official" in its present form until the reign of the Emperor Charlemagne in 814. The Apostles' Creed gets to the heart of the matter in just three paragraphs. The first paragraph makes a bold affirmation of the one God who is Creator with power and might. The central paragraph states the magnificent themes of Jesus the redeeming Christ. The final section on the Holy Spirit emphasizes the worldwide ecumenical community of all believers in all ages. As a creed so dear to so many Christians, it appropriately ends with the simple word "Amen" (So be it). To these great truths of the Christian faith, we should all give a loud "Amen!"

THE REFORMATION ERA CONFESSIONS

The Book of Confessions leaps from the early creeds to confessions written during the Protestant Reformation. In one decade came the Scots Confession (1560), which virtually made Scotland Presbyterian, the Heidelberg Catechism in Germany (1563), and the Second Helvetic Confession in Switzerland (1566). These Reformation confessions were followed in the next century by the Westminster Confession of Faith and its two catechisms in England (1647). These strong and vigorous documents must be seen against the background of the medieval Roman Catholic Church, for the Reformers stated what they believed in distinction from much Roman Catholic teaching and practice at that time. The watchwords of the Reformation—*sola gratia, sola fide, sola scriptura* (grace alone, faith alone, scripture alone)—characterize these confessions.

For me, these ardent defenses of the faith have an enduring quality that is expressed in the opening questions and answers in two Reformation catechisms:

> **Q. What is the chief end of man [*sic*]?**
> A. Man's chief end is to glorify God, and to enjoy him forever. (Westminster Shorter Catechism)
> **Q. What is your only comfort, in life and in death?**
> A. That I belong—body and soul, in life and in death—not to myself but to my faithful Savior, Jesus Christ. (Heidelberg Catechism)

These are great and abiding truths of the Christian faith—in the twenty-first century as well as in the sixteenth!

TWENTIETH-CENTURY CONFESSIONS

It is spine tingling to reflect upon the courage of stalwart Christians who proclaim Christ as Lord in times of intense struggle. Upon becoming chancellor of Germany in early 1933, Adolf Hitler promoted the so-called "German Christians," who subordinated the gospel to an anticommunist, anti-Jewish, anti-Masonic, and anti-internationalist racial purity ideology. But the revolutionary character of the good news does not permit acceptance of alien ideologies. A Pastors' Emergency League was formed and the First Confessing Synod of the Evangelical Church was held in 1934 in Barmen, a small city in northern Germany. "The Theological Declaration of Barmen" called upon Christians to stand against Nazi efforts to capture the church, and to proclaim the gospel's enduring evangelical truths. Germany and the world had to endure ten more years of Hitler's tyranny, but the church's witness was not futile. Albert Einstein stated, "Only the church stood across the path of Hitler's campaign for suppressing the truth. . . . I am forced to confess that what I once despised, I now praise unreservedly."[1] Einstein saw the power of the gospel to enable the church to stand against the forces of oppression in his time. May we once again reclaim this confession, not to promote one "side" over another in our church, but as a rallying cry for the church of Jesus Christ to be stalwart in the cause of God's justice in our time and place!

In contrast to the other creeds in *The Book of Confessions*, many Presbyterians remember vividly the crafting of the Confession of 1967 and A Brief Statement of Faith. "C67," as it is informally called, was not meant to be a comprehensive creed for all time, but a confession of faith for its own time, based on 2 Corinthians 5:19: "In Christ God was reconciling the world to himself." Trinitarian in structure, the confession deals with God's work of reconciliation, the ministry of reconciliation, and the fulfillment of reconciliation. C67 is forceful in its emphasis on the reconciling work of Christ and the church's calling to live out that reconciling work in all areas of personal and societal life. The Confession of 1967 was written and adopted during a turbulent period of rapid social change in both society and church.

A Brief Statement of Faith was written to provide a newly reunited church with a common confession of faith that could be used in congregational worship. The Articles of Agreement at the time of the 1983 reunion called for the appointment of "a committee representing diversities of points of view and of groups within the reunited church to prepare a Brief Statement of the Reformed Faith." Some wondered if a diverse committee could prepare a common statement that would be approved by a diverse church, but the committee wrote an innovative and well-received document that was approved overwhelmingly and is used widely throughout the church.

Our confessions give voice to common affirmations that define the shared faith of the church catholic and that I believe are shared by the vast majority of Presbyterians. Chapter 2 of the Form of Government, drafted at reunion, does an excellent job of highlighting the major themes of our common faith as Presbyterians:

the mystery of the triune God
the incarnation of the eternal Word of God in Jesus Christ
salvation by grace alone
salvation by faith alone
the authority of Scripture
the sovereignty of God
election for service as well as salvation
covenant life together in the church
faithful stewardship that shuns ostentation
seeking justice and living in obedience to the Word of God

These are the core theological convictions that unite Presbyterians. We need to affirm this confessional tradition and continually reappropriate it for our time. The biggest problem with our *Book of Confessions* is that it is so little known and studied in the PC(USA). While the *Book of Order* may be a "best seller," *The Book of Confessions* surely is not. Without shared faith in Jesus Christ, however, no polity can renew the church. One of our first priorities for the renewal of our church as a New Testament church in a new century is the reclaiming of our *Book of Confessions* as the foundation of our life together. The first step toward that renewal is a serious, sustained conversation with our confessions, and that is exactly what this helpful volume offers.

NOTE

1. Quoted in Arthur C. Cochrane, *The Church's Confession under Hitler* (Philadelphia: Westminster Press, 1962), 40.

1

The Church's Conversation with the Confessions

Joseph D. Small

The confessions of our church: Presbyterians are supposed to sincerely receive and adopt the essential tenets they express, and we are to be instructed, led, and guided by them. Presbyterian ministers of the Word and sacrament, elders, and deacons have even taken vows to do all these things. Yet there are many among us who would be hard pressed to name all the documents in *The Book of Confessions*, let alone speak about their settings, emphases, or relationships to our time and place. We know too well that there is a slip between the formal place of confessions in our ecclesiology and the way things are in sessions, presbyteries, and our own offices and homes. To the extent that we pay attention to them at all, it is often as museum pieces—as mildly interesting historical artifacts—or, increasingly, as rule books to identify bad faith or bad life in other people.

Perhaps that is too harsh. The Apostles' Creed is confessed in the worship of many of our congregations, although the Nicene Creed—the premier ecumenical creed of the church catholic—is only beginning to be used by Presbyterians. Many of us have discovered the liturgical and catechetical possibilities of A Brief Statement of Faith, and some of us retain a deep regard for the Confession of 1967. But other documents in *The Book of Confessions* are neglected. The origin of the Second Helvetic Confession is known only to stamp collectors, and both the adjective and the noun turn us away from the Larger Catechism. Moreover, the explicit intention of a *confessional collection* is ignored. *The Book of Confessions* as a whole, as a creedal compendium of explicit ecclesial integrity, is not much honored among us.

The capacity of *The Book of Confessions* to aid in the formation of shared faith, or to assist us in the resolution of conflicts among us, is severely limited. Although I regret that, I know that it is not enough to say that we *should* honor

1

the confessions' guidance; most of us have promised that already. What is needed is some indication of *why* and *how* we could honor their guidance. Our task is to explain to ourselves the confessions' place and function among us.

UNBEARABLE LIGHTNESS

The beginning of an explanation may lie in an odd place: not in the confessions themselves but in a novel by the Czech writer Milan Kundera. In *The Unbearable Lightness of Being*, Kundera contrasts the myth of eternal return with the reality of life's ephemeral, transitory nature. Do events recur over and over again in an endless cycle, he asks, or is each event a singular, fleeting point in time? If every event in history, every act of ours, were repeated endlessly, life would place an unbearable weight upon us, for eternal return would make every event "a solid mass . . . its inanity irreparable."[1] Kundera muses, "If every second of our lives recurs an infinite number of times, we are nailed to eternity as Jesus Christ was nailed to the cross. It is a terrifying prospect. In the world of eternal return the weight of unbearable responsibility lies heavy on every move we make. That is why Nietzsche called the idea of eternal return the heaviest of burdens."[2]

Milan Kundera is not the only writer to ponder the myth of eternal return. In a lighter vein, Kurt Vonnegut's 1997 novel *Timequake* imagines that a sudden glitch in the space-time continuum causes the reality of "temporary return." Vonnegut imagines that a timequake zapped the universe back from February 2001 to February 1991, making everybody and everything repeat exactly what they had done during that decade, for good or ill:

> It was déjà vu that wouldn't quit for ten long years. There was absolutely nothing you could say during the rerun, if you hadn't said it the first time through the decade. You couldn't even save your own life or that of a loved one, if you had failed to do that the first time through. . . . Only when people got back to when the timequake hit did they stop being robots of the past. As the old science fiction writer Kilgore Trout said, "Only when free will kicked in again could they stop running obstacle courses of their own construction."[3]

Could any of us imagine the unbearable burden of having to relive every moment of the past ten years of our life!

But we do not live in an endless cycle of eternal return or in an occasional cycle of repeated decades. We live in a world where events occur only once, so that each act, each decision, is unique. Throughout Kundera's novel his characters decide and act without, of course, prior experience of those decisions and acts and the results of their decisions and acts. Do they decide wisely and act well? Is there any answer to that question? Kundera's character Tomas thinks the thought we already know: "Human life occurs only once, and the reason we cannot determine which of our decisions are good and which is bad is that in a given situation we can make only one decision; we are not granted a second, third, or fourth life in which to compare various decisions."[4]

So life is lightness. The heavy burden of reliving life is not one we have to bear. While it may be amusing to ask what we would have done differently if we had our lives to live over again, the question is mercifully rhetorical. Our lives are lighter than air; the weight of the repeated past is not placed upon us.

And yet the very lightness of our being is unbearable. Should Tomas have allowed Tereza to stay in his flat, where he fell in love with her? Should he have followed her back to Russian-occupied Czechoslovakia, throwing away his medical practice in safe Switzerland? Should they have moved from Prague into the countryside, where they met their deaths—crushed by the weight of an overturned truck? Weighty questions, but there are no answers, and so the lightness of our being becomes unbearably heavy as we must decide and act without the prior experience of those decisions and actions that would enable us to know how to decide, how to act.

Of course we do not live in absolutely isolated moments of time. Each of us has a past, a stream of experience that provides a context for the decisions and actions of our present. We "learn from experience," do we not? Perhaps. But what does experience have to teach us when a person shows up at the door of our flat? When a person we love has gone to a place of uncertainty and danger? When we must decide whether to leave the city for the countryside? Individual lives are light, not heavy with the burden of the past. And yet the lightness of our being can become unbearable as we find ourselves weighed down with the necessity of deciding and acting in the unrepeatable and therefore unknowable now.

WE RATHER THAN *I*?

Our task is not to muse about the innumerable personal decisions we have to make every day, however, but to talk about the confessions and about theology. Theology and confessions of faith are not the province of the individual, but of the community of faith—the church. Does it make a difference to our deciding and acting when it is *we* who decide and act rather than *I*? Perhaps not, for just like individuals we do not have the benefit of a second, third, or fourth life with which to compare our present. Or do we?

We are not isolated theological individuals. We live within the church—one holy catholic and apostolic—within the "communion of saints," which is a community of time as well as space. So the decisions *we* make about the content of *our* beliefs, the focus of *our* proclamation, and the direction of *our* service are not of the same order as an individual deciding whether to let another person stay. Each decision at the door of a flat is unique, but decisions and actions about the shape of our thinking, praying, and living the faith are not unique, at least not in the same way. Our theological thinking, deciding, and acting can be made within the context of two, three, four, and more other moments in the church's life over the course of centuries and the span of the globe. We are not alone (at least, we need not be alone). As we think and decide and act, we are in the company of sisters and brothers who have lived and died the faith before us and who are living it now throughout the world. We have other lives to which we can compare our own, other thoughts and other choices that correlate with ours. We have the benefit of other lives—unless we turn our backs on those who have gone before us.

It is when we think the faith without reference to the previous experience and thought of our forebears in the faith that we become weighed down by the unbearable lightness of our being, the unbearable lightness of our theology. Each moral choice we make becomes as free floating as a decision about letting someone stay in our flat. Each theological judgment is as immune from critical appraisal as the decision of Tomas and Tereza to move from the city into the countryside. That is why Kundera speaks of "the profound moral perversity of a world which rests essentially on the nonexistence of return, for in this world everything is pardoned in advance and therefore everything is cynically permitted."[5]

I hope readers have not become impatient with this talk about an obscure novel by a Czech writer. I have spent time with *The Unbearable Lightness of Being* because Kundera skillfully uses narrative to prompt reflection on the widespread view among us that the past—particularly tradition—is a burden that must be shed if we are to live freely in the present. It is a popularized inheritance from the Enlightenment, of which we are all heirs, that tradition is the enemy of free inquiry, a jailer that prevents the free exercise of rational thought and reasonable choice. The past, tradition, and dogma must be abandoned if we are to attain genuine intellectual and moral maturity.

The church, true child of the Enlightenment in its evangelical as well as its liberal form, believes that it must free itself from the weight of the past. Evangelicals imagine that we must shed the burden of centuries as we return to the pristine Christian community of the New Testament, while liberals imagine that we must shed centuries of racism, patriarchy, and Eurocentrism in order to construct the pristine Christian community of a new era. Little wonder that we are unsure what to do with confessions of faith from past centuries, thinking them a heavy load to carry around the church. Little surprise that we discover the lightness of our theology unbearable as we become weighed down by the present without the means of building up shared faith and faithfulness.

Perhaps we can begin to unburden ourselves by pondering a historian's distinction between tradition and tradition*ism*. Jaroslav Pelikan says, "Traditionalism is the dead faith of the living. Tradition is the living faith of the dead."[6] Traditional*ism* is an uncritical repetition of an accumulated past, while tradition is a lively conversation with those who have lived and died the faith before us. We are part of a communion of saints, sisters and brothers in the faith who have lived within the grace of the Lord Jesus Christ, the love of God, and the communion of the Holy Spirit. Their experience and their wisdom are not inferior to our own; we do not stand at the apex of the history of God's Way in the world.

There is a danger in any age, surely including our own, of arrogance toward those who have preceded us. Perhaps it only seems that our arrogance is particularly overweening, but we are not content merely to dismiss past centuries, for we now snub Christian thought and life from bare decades ago. It is what C. S. Lewis called "chronological snobbery, the uncritical acceptance of the intellectual climate common to our own age and the assumption that whatever has gone out of date is on that account discredited."[7] Do we really imagine that the issues and problems we face are unique to our time and place? Do we really think that those who have lived and died the faith before us have nothing to tell us? Do we really believe that our thoughts and actions are at the pinnacle of human achievement, superior to all that has preceded us?

If we recognize the arrogance of turning a deaf ear to the voices of our forebears, we can, in Lewis's words, "pass to the realization that our own age is also a 'period,' and certainly has, like all periods, its characteristic illusions. They are likeliest to lurk in those widespread assumptions which are so ingrained in the age that no one dares to attack or feels it necessary to defend them."[8] Tradition, the living faith of those who have gone before us, need not be a weight that we must shed in order to be free and faithful in Christ. Tradition itself can be liberating, freeing us from captivity to the limited perspective of our time and place. Without the capacity to transcend the taken-for-granted assumptions of twenty-first-century North America, we become prisoners in the tiny cell of "here and now." Ignoring the church's tradition because we fear that the past may oppress us only subjects us to the tyranny of the present. *The Book of Confessions*' Brief Statement of Faith calls upon the church "to hear the voices of people long silenced."[9] Among the long-silenced voices we need to hear are the voices of all who have gone before us in the living of Christian faith.

THE PRESENCE OF THE PAST

The Book of Confessions, a central part of our heritage, makes present to us our brothers and sisters who have struggled to be faithful. Through the confessions of our church we are privileged to hear their wisdom—and some of their fool-ishness—as we struggle to be faithful. Their questions are not identical to ours, but there are times when their different questions enable us to understand our own questions better. Their answers may not be the same as ours, yet there are times when their answers startle us into new apprehensions of the truth. At times we may conclude that their questions and answers are dead wrong, but even that determination serves to sharpen our own perceptions of the possi-ble shape of our faithfulness.

Presbyterians are Reformed Christians, and this makes us heirs to a partic-ular view of the contemporary church's relationship to its tradition. We do not understand tradition as an evolutionary "development of doctrine" in which the church's apprehension of the gospel becomes fuller in each succeeding age. Neither do we identify a particular period in the tradition with a purer under-standing of the gospel, whether the early church or the sixteenth-century Reformation. Instead, we Reformed Christians are called to understand our-selves as participants in a continuous theological and doctrinal conversation that endures through time and space.

Perhaps a set of images will be helpful. Imagine that all Christians through-out history are gathered in one place. If we thought of tradition as a progres-sive development of doctrine, the gathered Christians would be marching forward in a column, with us at its head. Although we contemporary Chris-tians might benefit from the wisdom of those behind us in line, we would think of our doctrinal formulations as more developed, better expressed, embody-ing fuller truth. In this arrangement, those of us in the vanguard would pay some attention to those in our wake, but we would understand ourselves as building upon their foundation in order to construct a more developed expres-sion of faith and faithfulness.

On the other hand, if we thought that some periods in the church's life were purer and more faithful than most, we would still see gathered Christians stretched out in a line. Only now we would think of it as a broken line of detours and wrong turns. We would have to leap back over most of those in the line in order to reach an authoritative point in the past, a model to which we would strive to conform. Most voices in the past would be expressions of error; only in heeding the true word from the faithful moment could we restore our church's fidelity.

But as Reformed Christians we are invited to picture the great gathering of Christians as arranged, not in a line, but in a circle. Believers from every time and place face one another, carrying on a continuous conversation. The col-loquy occurs through Christ, the circle's center. Today's church brings its insights into an ongoing discussion with those who have gone before; all voices are necessary to the conversation. Ancient voices are not honored merely because of their proximity to Christian beginnings, sixteenth- and seventeenth-century voices are not heeded simply because they stand at the beginnings of the Reformed tradition, and contemporary voices are not privileged because they have access to the intellectual tools of modernity.

As part of the great circle, the Presbyterian Church (U.S.A.) plays an active role, both as a speaker and as a listener. We give voice to recent convictions in the Confession of 1967 and A Brief Statement of Faith (1991). Yet we are attentive to voices from other times and places, even listening to them before we speak. As we listen, we overhear conversations among our forebears as well as carry on our own conversation with them. There are times when we listen in on their discussion, times when we pay particular attention to one of their voices, and times when we participate actively. At least that is how we are invited to understand ourselves as part of the "communion of saints."

Christian conversation across time and space is more than a casual exchange of opinion. The conversation is a consultation about the gospel, a discussion about the shape of our proclamation and the form of our mission. It is now a discussion about *our* proclamation and *our* mission, of course, but our proclamation and mission are rescued from solipsism by the voices of our forebears. Throughout the centuries, Christians throughout the world have had to decide how they would speak and live the gospel. Their witness, available to us in creeds, confessions, and catechisms, is indispensable to our faithful witness. There is a sense in which they speak to us in scriptural cadence:

> We declare to you what was from the beginning, what we have heard, what we have seen with our eyes, what we have looked at and touched with our hands, concerning the word of life—this life was revealed, and we have seen it and testify to it, and declare to you the eternal life that was with the Father and was revealed to us—we declare to you what we have seen and heard so that you also may have fellowship with us; and truly our fellowship is with the Father and with his Son Jesus Christ. We are writing these things so that our joy may be complete. (1 John 1:1–4)

THE AUTHORITY OF THE PAST

The confessions of our church—the living faith of our forebears—have a certain authority over us. After all, these creeds, confessions, and catechisms have received the approbation of generations as well as the ecclesial recognition and approval of our own church. We are accountable to this tradition. Our first task is to be questioned by the confessions, not as an exercise in servitude but precisely as a liberating denial of the tyranny of the present. Being questioned by the tradition is not our only responsibility; we must also subject the tradition to our own questions. We are not traditionalists, so we can be utterly honest about crusades and inquisitions, easy acceptance of Christendom and easy dismissal of the leadership of women, neglect of evangelistic mission and excess of missionary zeal. But if we listen to our forebears we will also hear their hard questions addressed to us. Perhaps then we can be utterly honest about our own accommodations to the culture, our indifference to the proclamation of the gospel, our abandonment of shared conviction and community in easy acquiescence to the individualism, localism, particularism, and privatism of our time.

The eleven creeds and confessions in *The Book of Confessions* are not the only voices in the ongoing conversation. Individuals also participate—from Clement to Calvin to Barth to Jürgen Moltmann and Ellen Charry. Yet the confessions have an authority that individuals do not, precisely because they are the voice of the church, the articulated convictions of the community of faith in various times and places. The creeds and confessions were all adopted by councils of the church, whether by an ecumenical council or the assembly of a particular church. As the voice of the church adopted by the Presbyterian Church (U.S.A.), the confessions have a prior claim on individual conviction. Each one of us is answerable to the confessions before they are answerable to us.

The confessions are not freestanding authorities. The *Book of Order* makes it clear that confessional statements are subordinate standards, "subject to the authority of Jesus Christ, the Word of God, as the Scriptures bear witness to him."[10] This serves to locate confessional authority, however, not to diminish it. We do not have direct access to Christ; our knowledge is always mediated, most reliably by the witness of Scripture. The witness of Scripture is not given separately to each individual; the confessions provide reliable guidance to reading and receiving the witness of Scripture. Thus, the *Book of Order* is clear that while confessions are subordinate standards, "they are, nonetheless, standards. They are not lightly drawn up or subscribed to, nor may they be ignored or dismissed."[11]

But why these eleven? In addition to the ecumenical creeds, there are hundreds of Reformed confessions and catechisms. Reformed churches have always been confession-making churches; in different times and various contexts they have believed it necessary to give present testimony to their faith and action. In the sixteenth century alone more than sixty confessions were produced by Reformed churches. The World Alliance of Reformed Churches has published a representative collection of more than twenty-five Reformed confessions from the twentieth century. The great variety of Reformed confessions is not simply an accident of history and geography. Reformed emphasis on the sovereignty of God leads to acute awareness of the dangers of idolatry, including the idolatry of creeds. Thus, Reformed churches rarely identify a particular historic confession as the authoritative expression of Christian faith.

The Reformed stance toward confessions is illustrated by the statement of Heinrich Bullinger at the signing of the First Helvetic Confession:

> We wish in no way to prescribe for all churches through these articles a single rule of faith. For we acknowledge no other rule of faith than Holy Scripture. . . . We grant to everyone the freedom to use his own expressions which are suitable for his church and will make use of this freedom ourselves, at the same time defending the true sense of this Confession against distortions.[12]

Although there have been times when a Reformed church has required allegiance to a single confession—often the Westminster Confession of Faith—Westminster itself attests that "all synods or councils . . . may err, and many have erred; therefore they are not to be made the rule of faith or practice, but to be used as a help in both" (6.175).

Reformed aversion to "a single rule of faith" has not led to the avoidance of confessional statements because it has been coupled with freedom to use expressions that are suitable to particular churches. Thus, alongside Westminster's acknowledgment of confessional error and its relegation of confessions to subordinate status is its conviction that "for the better government and further edification of the Church, there ought to be such assemblies as are commonly called synods or councils: and it belongeth to the overseers and other rulers of the particular churches . . . to appoint such assemblies; and to convene together in them, as often as they shall judge it expedient for the good of the Church" (6.173). Distrust of a single confession, coupled with freedom to express the truth of the gospel in various ways, focused in the particular needs of churches in different contexts, leads to the continuing Reformed practice of confession making.

The Reformed tradition understands the formulation of confessions as part of the mandate of proclamation entrusted to the church. Thus, churches belonging to the Reformed family have been inclined to state their deepest convictions in every generation. All of this is stated succinctly in the Presbyterian Church (U.S.A.)'s Confession of 1967. The preface begins with the conviction that "the church confesses its faith when it bears a present witness to God's grace in Jesus Christ." The need for present witness has always been a feature of ecclesial existence, for "in every age, the church has expressed its witness in words and deeds as the need of the time required. . . . No one type of confession is exclusively valid, no one statement is irreformable" (9.02, 9.03).

Presbyterians do not limit their theological attention to the documents contained in *The Book of Confessions*. The church continues to confess its faith in statements that are not included among its confessional standards. For example "A Declaration of Faith," written in the early 1970s, has been commended to the church for use in education and liturgy, churchwide study of the South African "Belhar Confession" is encouraged, and the church has approved three contemporary catechisms. The church also listens to voices from the past that are not part of *The Book of Confessions*. A new translation of the "French Confession of 1559" has been approved for educational use by the church. So why do the particular eleven documents comprise the church's confessional standards?

The Presbyterian Church (U.S.A.) has identified these creeds, confessions, and catechisms as statements that declare to the church and to the world "who and what it is, what it believes, and what it resolves to do."[13] The church is clear that the contents of *The Book of Confessions* are the result of ecclesiastical judgment: The church chose these confessions and not others. Yet the church's judgment is not arbitrary or capricious. The eleven were chosen by the church as witnesses that transcend their own time and place, expressing doctrinal and moral standards that shape current faith and witness. The *Book of Order* declares, "In its confessions, the Presbyterian Church (U.S.A.) gives witness to the faith of the Church catholic[,] . . . identifies with the affirmations of the Protestant Reformation . . . [and] expresses the faith of the Reformed tradition. . . .Thus, the creeds and confessions of this church reflect a particular stance within the history of God's people. They are the result of prayer, thought, and experience within a living tradition."[14]

The historical particularity of the creeds, confessions, and catechisms situates them, but it does not confine them or weaken their voices. While each reflects "a particular stance within the history of God's people," their distinctiveness gives their voices timbre and resonance. It is not inconsequential that the Nicene Creed was the first formal creed of the church, and that it remains the only creed used ecumenically by the majority of Christians throughout the world. The Apostles' Creed, while restricted to churches that emerged from the Latin West, nevertheless gives voice to the baptismal unity that overarches the fragmentation of the churches. Sixteenth- and seventeenth-century confessions and catechisms articulate not only the affirmations of the Reformation but the foundational perspectives of the Reformed tradition in which we stand. Twentieth-century confessions are expressions of the Reformed conviction that the church is called to bear a present witness to the gospel in every time and place.

The particularity of creeds, confessions, and catechisms does not create a hierarchy or a weighting system, but it does modulate each of their voices so that we hear distinct tones and characteristic inflection in the words they speak. As we listen to the discrete accents of the confessions, we become attuned to features that help us to hear and respond.

The Nicene Creed occupies a singular place among all the confessional statements of the churches. It is not simply age or ubiquity that has set it apart, although these are significant attributes. Instead, Nicea presents us with a certain "dogmatic irreversibility." The church at a particular time in its history was presented with a dramatic choice in which it determined that fidelity to the gospel required one articulation rather than another. The choice made at Nicea gave expression to the fundamental trinitarian and christological witness of the church, and so decisively determined the future of Christian thinking, professing, and confessing the faith. The affirmations of the Nicene Creed shape the affirmations of the creeds, confessions, and catechisms that follow. There is a sense in which later confessions can be seen as contextualized implementations of the Nicene (and Apostles') Creed. Its voice resonates deeply throughout *The Book of Confessions* and within the church's ongoing conversation with the confessions.

The Confession of 1967 also occupies a special, although more modest, place among the confessional statements of the Presbyterian Church (U.S.A.). C67 acknowledges that "no one type of confession is exclusively valid" and that the church is "aided in understanding the gospel by the testimony of the church from earlier ages and from many lands." These insights made *The Book of Confessions* possible, initiating a new era of enriched confessional conversation. In this conversation, timbre and tone provide nuance as the conversation ranges through various questions, problems, and possibilities.

Confessions are not timeless abstractions. Their historical particularity does not seal them in time capsules, however. Rather, as time and place give specific witnesses to the grace of the Lord Jesus Christ, the love of God, and the communion of the Holy Spirit, they open a free arena for lively conversation about the shape of present witness to the gospel.

SAYING YES AND SAYING NO

When we listen to that part of the tradition given voice in *The Book of Confessions*, what do we hear? We hear expressions of the search for distinguishing marks of faithful Christian community. Those who have gone before us asked and answered questions about where to draw identifying lines between faithful and unfaithful confession of God, between faithful and unfaithful living out of that confession. Christians in Nicea and Rome, in Geneva, Heidelberg, and Edinburgh, in Barmen and Portland, shaped Christian faith and faithfulness by saying Yes to some things and No to others. Genuine confession of faith is always both affirmation of truth and denial of untruth. "If the Yes does not in some way contain the No," said Karl Barth, "it will not be the Yes of a confession. . . . If we have not the confidence to say *damnamus* [what we refuse], then we might as well omit the *credimus* [what we believe]."[15]

In the church's self-understanding throughout the centuries, it is only the call of God that constitutes a Christian community's true identity as the *ekklesia*, the "called forth ones." The identity of a community as *Christian* entails renunciation of what is not from God as well as affirmation of God and God's new Way, as does the identity of an individual Christian, expressed in the baptismal liturgy's "renunciation and confession." Sometimes the No is explicit, as with Barmen and the Confession of 1967; at other times it is implicit, as with the Apostles' and Nicene Creeds. But always, in the community's struggle to define itself in fidelity to the grace of the Lord Jesus Christ, the love of God, and the communion of the Holy Spirit, it must say Yes to its perception of God's way in the world and No to the ways of the world apart from God.

Barmen says Yes to something that the church too often forgets:

> The church's commission, upon which its freedom is founded, consists in delivering the message of the free grace of God to all people in Christ's stead, and therefore in the ministry of his own Word and work through sermon and sacrament.

We may hear those words and nod casually, "Of course." Until we are confronted with Barmen's accompanying No:

> We reject the false doctrine, as though the church in human arrogance could place the Word and work of the Lord in the service of any arbitrarily chosen desires, purposes, and plans. (8.26–.27)

Can it be that an institutionalized church—our institutionalized denomination and its institutionalized congregations—places the gospel in the service of our own desires, purposes, and plans? Is it possible that our rhetoric about the primacy of the church's mission is a justification for pushing the Word and work of Christ aside in a rush to promote our own purposes and achieve our own plans? Is it conceivable that our "seeker friendly" worship submerges Word and sacrament in our desire to become attractive once again? Those are not questions with simple answers, but our attention to the wisdom of our forebears may awaken us to the reality that we cannot say Yes to everything, and that if we say Yes to our Lord it will mean saying No to the wishes of our chosen desires, purposes, and plans.

The Nicene Creed calls us to confess our belief in

> one Lord, Jesus Christ
> the only Son of God,
> eternally begotten of the Father,

God from God, Light from Light,
true God from true God,
begotten, not made,
of one Being with the Father;
. . . .
[and in]
the Holy Spirit, the Lord, the giver of life,
    who proceeds from the Father and the Son,
    who with the Father and the Son is worshiped and glorified.

To say Yes to these central affirmations of Christian faith is to do far more than recite a comfortable liturgical orthodoxy. Does it mean saying No to an understanding of God as one who is "creator, redeemer, sustainer" in sequential or alternating modes? Does it mean refusing a picture of Jesus as the tragic hero or moral exemplar of pop historicism? Does it rule out a generalized Spirit who bypasses the embarrassment of christological particularity? Does all of this say No to the monistic deity of bourgeois Protestantism by proclaiming Holy Trinity?

The church's confessional tradition is more than a mildly interesting survey of the past. The confessions confront us at a deeper level than documentaries on the History Channel. A Brief Statement of Faith gives clear voice to a theme that runs throughout Reformed confessions when it affirms that the Holy Spirit gives us courage "to unmask idolatries in Church and culture" (10.4). Our confessions are one instrument of the Spirit's work, for their Yes and No challenge us to say our own Yes and No, calling us away from easy acquiescence to cultural realities and from lazy conformity to churchly assumptions.

The task of defining the appropriate center of Christian faith and faithfulness, and their appropriate boundaries, is not unique to some generations while absent from others. Rather, it is an ever present and continuous process that draws from the past experience of the church as it presses toward hope in the future that God is bringing to be. Christopher Morse puts it well: "Memory and hope, story and promise, occur inseparably in the apostolic tradition. To keep the memory from blocking the hope (the temptation of conservatives), and to keep the hope from severing itself from the memory (the temptation of liberals) is the task of all dogmatics that seeks to be attentive to apostolic tradition."[16] Christian tradition, and particularly that part of the tradition expressed through *The Book of Confessions*, is the memory and the hope of our parents in the faith as they tried to determine the proper shape of a Christian community that proclaims the gospel, nurtures the faithful, worships, preserves the truth, promotes social righteousness, and displays to the world the coming reign of God.

When we listen to the tradition as it is expressed in the confessions of our church, we are struck by the interplay of universality and particularity. The ancient formula "What is held everywhere, always, and by all is what is to be believed [*quod ubique, quod semper, quod ab omnibus creditum est*]" expresses the necessary catholicity of the church's belief. Clearly, this is not an objective statement of empirical fact. However, it does express the truth that some elements of faith and faithfulness are essential to Christian identity—that without which no community would be identifiably Christian. There are certain elements of faith that are common to all our confessions, the discernible shape of Christian identity across time and space. But there are particular elements in the confessions as well. Some of these elements mark a form of Christian identity that is distinctly Reformed, a particular expression of catholic faith. Other particularities in the confessions are clearly tied to times and places that are not our own, what Calvin called *adiaphora*: acceptable convictions and practices that are changeable, not essential, elements of Christian identity. It is the theological task of the community of faith to distinguish between the catholic and the particular, and to make distinctions between those particularities that are important to the Reformed tradition and those that are indifferent, changeable, matters of pastoral discretion. All of this is part of our conversation with the confessions—and their conversation with us.

The conflicts among us—both the big and the little ones—are evidence of our struggle to define the character of Christian community. What will we say Yes to, and what will we say No to? What is essential if community is to be Christian? What is important if Christian community is to be identifiably Reformed? What is a matter of pastoral and ecclesial discretion? We don't agree about these things, of course. But we are not the first people to ask the questions. We do not have to bear the weight of these problems alone.

The confessions may be particularly important at times when the church faces pressures from the culture, raising questions of identity distinct from the culture, or when the church faces conflict within, raising questions about the shape of evangelical identity, for these are precisely the situations that gave rise to most of our confessional standards. Since we are challenged by the same issues that challenged the confessions' framers, we can listen and learn from the ways they understood the crises, and the ways they responded. And as we listen to those who have gone before us, we may even discover that we are able to listen more openly to those who are with us now.

> Since we are surrounded by so great a cloud of witnesses, let us also
> lay aside every weight and the sin that clings so closely, and let us run
> with perseverance the race that is set before us, looking to Jesus the
> pioneer and perfecter of our faith. (Heb. 12:1–2)

NOTES

1. Milan Kundera, *The Unbearable Lightness of Being* (New York: Harper & Row, 1984), 4.
2. Ibid., 5.
3. Kurt Vonnegut, *Timequake* (New York: G. P. Putnam's Sons, 1997), xii–xiii.
4. Kundera, *Unbearable Lightness of Being*, 222.
5. Ibid., 4.
6. Jaroslav Pelikan, *The Vindication of Tradition* (New Haven, CT: Yale University Press, 1984), 65.
7. C. S. Lewis, *Surprised by Joy* (San Diego: Harcourt Brace Jovanovich, 1955), 207.
8. Ibid., 208.
9. *The Constitution of the Presbyterian Church (U.S.A.)*, Part I, *The Book of Confessions* (Louisville, KY: Office of the General Assembly, 2002), A Brief Statement of Faith, 10.4. Hereafter, all confessional references will appear in parentheses within the text, according to the numbering system in *The Book of Confessions*.
10. *The Constitution of the Presbyterian Church (U.S.A)*, Part II, *Book of Order* (Louisville, KY: Office of the General Assembly, 2004), G-2.0200.
11. *Book of Order*, G-2.0500b.
12. Philip Schaff, *Creeds of Christendom* (New York: Harper & Brothers, 1877), 1:389–90.
13. *Book of Order*, G-2.0100.
14. *Book of Order*, G-2.0300–.0500.
15. Karl Barth, *Church Dogmatics*, I/2 (Edinburgh: T. & T. Clark, 1956), 631, 630.
16. Christopher Morse, *Not Every Spirit* (Valley Forge, PA: Trinity Press International, 1994), 48.

2

A Conversation with the Ecumenical Creeds

Leanne Van Dyk

Strangely, when we approach the New Testament, we instinctively think that old is good, but when it comes to creeds and confessions, we tend to assume that old is bad. We respect the fact that the Gospel of Mark is old, probably older than the other Gospels. In certain circles, Mark (and perhaps the enigmatic Q) have an extra quota of authenticity due to their age. The older Letter to the Galatians seems to carry more authority with some people than the later epistles to Timothy and Titus. But the Apostles' Creed and the Nicene Creed are routinely dismissed by some because they are so old. How can such old documents, so the argument goes, have anything to say to us in our contemporary setting? For these people, A Brief Statement of Faith and the Confession of 1967 seem much more relevant.

Kathleen Norris tells the story of a seminary student and an Orthodox priest-theologian at Yale Divinity School. It is a story that has been quoted widely because it so perfectly captures the contemporary suspicion of creeds. The theologian had come as a guest speaker to lecture on the history of the creeds in the Christian tradition. In a time for questions after the lecture, a student asked, "What can one do when one finds it impossible to affirm certain tenets of the Creed?" The priest answered by saying, "Well, you just say it. With a little practice and effort, most can learn it by heart."

The student apparently felt misunderstood and so asked a follow-up question: "What am I to do if I find I cannot affirm parts of the Creed, like the Virgin Birth?" The answer was the same, "You just stand with the congregation and say it. You keep saying it. Eventually it will come to you, with practice and time." Once more the student, this time in a raised voice, said, "How can I say a creed that I do not believe?" Then the priest said, "It is not *your* creed, it is *our* creed. It may come to you, in time. For some, it takes longer than for others."[1]

The frustrated student was voicing an assumption that many in the church have—that ancient creeds are subject to individual scrutiny. If one agrees with them, fine. If one does not, then the creeds may be, perhaps even must be, discarded. The Orthodox theologian was operating with an entirely different assumption—that the ancient creeds are the treasures of the whole church that shape and form us slowly over time. We place ourselves under their tutelage, in trust and confidence, because they have been the patient teachers of countless believers who have gone before us. Now we too are in the procession of believers who stand after the proclamation of the Word and confess in one voice what we believe. Kathleen Norris's story is illuminating because we can place our own attitudes toward the ancient creeds with either the student or the priest—or perhaps we find sympathy with both.

We find sympathy with the student in the story because, deep in our bones, we are children of the Enlightenment. We have all grown up assuming that we are the arbiters of our own destiny, that each of us individually decides what to buy, whom to marry, what our political convictions are, and what we believe. Yet we sympathize with the priest in the story because, deep in our hearts, we are lonely and anxious. We have discovered that the ideal of the "lone individual" of our culture is frequently isolating and dividing. On the one hand, we resist the notion of standing together with the generations of believers who have come before us to confess the great creeds of the faith—we want to *choose!* On the other hand, we long to join our voice with the great chorus of voices proclaiming a common faith—we want to *belong!*

In our consideration of the Apostles' and the Nicene Creeds, then, it is helpful to realize the ambiguity that many contemporary people sense when they rise to profess their faith in the words of one of these great ecumenical creeds. The uneasiness they may feel is seldom analyzed, of course. Few people say, "I am the heir of a confused Enlightenment inheritance. I long both for autonomy and connection. The words of the creeds raise this ambiguity in my mind."

Other cultural factors conspire against glad acceptance of the ancient creeds as well. The dominant cultural attitudes of the West are strikingly individualistic and autonomous. Although Asian and African cultures are more sensitive to family and community contexts, even these traditional cultures are being pressured by the segmenting forces of global economies and cultural influences from the West.

In this dominant global cultural model, each person is the sole arbiter of his or her own set of beliefs, opinions, and decisions. There are multiple ironies in this dominant cultural model, however. In spite of the claims of individual autonomy and freedom, it is no secret that adolescents are loathe to stand out from their peers and will carefully moderate their behavior to fit in with the crowd. This behavior does not disappear even among mature adults. The pressures of the group are powerful factors in consumer habits, a fact that advertisers are quick to exploit in their advertising campaigns. In spite of the fact that we like to think we make up our own minds about everything, our behavior in the marketplace, at least, betrays the deeper truth that we move with the crowd and have a profound need to fit in.

The pervasive antiauthoritarianism of contemporary culture also impacts attitudes toward worship and creeds. In a May 23, 2004, *Los Angeles Times* article, "Religion; the Do-It-Yourself Doctrine," journalist Charlotte Allen notes that a common attitude among contemporary Christians is that no one should tell anyone how to practice his or her faith, or even what the faith is. Interestingly, this attitude characterizes both progressive and evangelical sectors of the denominational spectrum. Allen notes that along with this attitude is an additional assumption that the ancient creeds crushed vibrant and diverse spiritualities in the early Christian communities, that they destroyed a flourishing of lively faith. What is common to these contemporary marks of American religion is a deep assumption that each person has an indubitable right to craft a tailor-made relationship with their own faith.

The ecumenical creeds do not fare well in this cultural climate. It is not difficult to see that when it comes to creeds and confessions, we tend to assume that old is bad. Some Christian observers, however, believe that the creeds are not a "take 'em or leave 'em" proposition. New Testament scholar Luke Timothy Johnson puts in a good word for the ancient creeds, pointing out that they did not oppressively crush other flourishing spiritualities. Rather, they grew up in very early Christian communities as a way of defining *who* the people of faith were so that it could become clear *what* it meant to live by the faith. Johnson comments in Allen's article, "But nowadays it's amazing how many people believe that the creeds were foisted on Christianity. There's this belief that structure and spontaneity are opposites, and that traditional Christianity is incompatible with mysticism and with communal and egalitarian experience. That's never been true. It's a sociological fantasy of the 1960s." Johnson would not deny that politics played a part in the formation of the creeds, especially the Nicene Creed and, later still, the fifth-century Chalcedonian Definition. But the basic impulse to formulate creeds is not to dominate and oppress; rather, it is to express a fundamental identity in Christian faith. That identity sometimes came in the midst of persecution and opposition, a reality some Christian communities still experience in the world today.

THE FUNCTION OF CREEDS

Because reciting a creed creates ambiguities for contemporary believers, it might be helpful to remind ourselves how creeds function and what their potential is for strengthening and nurturing Christian faith.[2] First of all, creeds *identify* Christian believers in the faith. This is exactly how the Apostles' Creed was used in the early history of the church. The roots of the Apostles' Creed go back deep into the early church, to the instruction of converts into the Christian faith.[3] After a period of instruction in the faith, often lasting for weeks or months, converts were ready for the sacrament of baptism. In the early church, baptism was a ceremony of drama and symbolism, highlighting the great change of identity that was about to happen to the convert, to be joined with the body of Christ and the community of believers. Each convert was asked a series of questions by the minister or priest. In an important third-century document, the church father Hippolytus records detailed instructions for baptism using an early form of the Apostles' Creed. Here we can see how the creed is used as a tool for shaping basic Christian identity.

> And [when] he [who is to be baptized] goes down to the water, let him who baptizes lay [his] hand on him saying thus:
> Dost thou believe in God the Father Almighty?
> And he who is being baptized shall say: I believe.
> Let him forthwith baptize him once, having his hand laid upon his head.
> And after this let him say:
> Dost thou believe in Christ Jesus, the Son of God,
> Who was born of the Holy Spirit and the Virgin Mary,
> Who was crucified in the days of Pontius Pilate,
> and died,
> And rose on the third day living from the dead
> And ascended into the heavens,
> And sat down at the right hand of the Father,
> And will come again to judge the living and the dead?
> And when he says: I believe, let him baptize him the second time.
> And again let him say:
> Dost thou believe in the Holy Spirit in the Holy Church,
> and the resurrection of the flesh?
> And he who is being baptized shall say: I believe. And so let him baptize him the third time.[4]

Second, the ecumenical creeds *educate* persons in their Christian beliefs. One of my professors once commented that young Christian minds do not naturally come fully furnished with the content of the faith. Teachers are needed to bring in the "furniture"—the tables, sofas, and carpets of the major doctrines. That is why the Trinity, Jesus Christ, and the Holy Spirit are included in the Apostles' Creed and the Nicene Creed, but precise lists of divine attributes are not. Smaller "decorative objects," say, the curtains and candlesticks of the room, the theory of divine inspiration and the doctrine of the intermediate state, can come at a later time. But the creeds furnish the minds of new Christians with the basic furniture of faith.

This is why John Calvin insisted that the people in his congregation in Geneva memorize the Apostles' Creed. Most people in that city of refugees were illiterate tradespeople and merchants who had never received an education. Neither had they ever learned, in their spoken language, the Lord's Prayer and the Apostles' Creed. One of the reforms that Calvin brought to Geneva was worship services in the French language, the language of most of the people in the city. Calvin required that church members memorize the Lord's Prayer and the Apostles' Creed as a basic minimum of literacy in the faith. The creed functioned as a tool of education.

The records of the Genevan church consistory, only recently available in English translation, show that individuals who were brought before the consistory for matters of disciplinary action were often reminded to practice their memorization of the creed. The record reads in one case, "Summoned to render an account of his faith. He responded that he had a little progress and said the *Pater*, 'Our Father, etc.,' and a few words of the creed. The Consistory advise, having given him proper admonitions, that he find a teacher who will instruct him in the faith and explain what the words mean and make him understand what concerns God."[5] Dozens of examples similar to this appear in the volume. Clearly, the church leadership took memorization of the creed with utmost seriousness. Are we to conclude that rote memorization was a tool of oppression and domination? Hardly. In a time and place where literacy was scarce, the creed was a means of educating the people in the faith, of furnishing their hearts and minds with the content of the gospel.

Third, the ecumenical creeds *unify* Christian believers. This can be seen most simply by the very first word of the Nicene Creed: the word "We." The purpose of the Nicene Creed was to unify a painfully divided Christian community over a dispute that had been brewing between two factions in the church. These factions had all the markings of political parties, with political maneuverings, followers, gifted speakers, smear campaigns, and genuine issues of importance.

Some people have said that the Nicene Creed is the creed of bishops. Although the list of bishops who gathered in Nicea in the summer of 325 is not known, the council included approximately three hundred bishops, together with their assistants and secretaries. A historian of that day remarked wryly that the highways were filled with the dust of "galloping bishops." The details of this doctrinal skirmish were complex and philosophically freighted, but the fundamental issue went to the very heart of the Christian gospel: Who is Jesus Christ? This basic question was then, and still is, of fundamental importance to Christians. Simply stated, the matter before the bishops of Nicea had to do with the identity of Jesus Christ. Is Jesus Christ truly God? Or is Jesus Christ a "junior-level deity"?

The Council of Nicea concluded with a vigorous affirmation of Jesus Christ's full divinity, of the fully divine nature of the incarnate Christ. The creed of Nicea, then, was formulated to state the faith of the whole church, the faith of what "we" believe. Yes, it was written by bishops, the teachers of the church, based on existing regional creeds already in use. But this creed, more than any other, has been received by the many diverse Christian traditions. Millions of Christian people stand each Sunday after the proclamation of the Word to say "We believe" in the affirmations of the Nicene Creed. This has been occurring for over fifteen hundred years in countless languages on every continent. When we express our faith in the words of the Nicene Creed, we stand with the "cloud of witnesses" that goes before us in the faith that unites us.

The capacity of creeds to unite believers is not limited to ancient creeds. The catechisms and confessions of the Reformation were also written in times of controversy and danger, and functioned to draw people together. The best contemporary example of the unifying role of creeds is the 1934 Barmen Declaration, now one of the confessional documents of the PC(USA). In the 1930s, the witness of the Christian church in Germany was co-opted by the official ideology of the Nazi regime. Pastors were required to pledge their allegiance to Adolf Hitler; swastika flags were hung in church sanctuaries, and pastors who spoke out in protest against the increasing Nazi control over both church and society were removed from their posts. A small resistance movement of Lutheran, Reformed, and United Church pastors organized the "Confessional Synod" of the German Evangelical Church to oppose the "German Christian" accommodation to National Socialism. A representative group of pastors drafted the Barmen Declaration as an appeal to the church to proclaim the lordship of Jesus Christ and resist the state's pretensions to lordship. In a context of threat to the integrity of the gospel and danger to the church, the Theological Declaration of Barmen brought the Confessing Church together, gave it an identity, and clarified its Christian call in that particular time and place.

Fourth, creeds have an *apologetic and polemical* function. This is perhaps the most difficult function for us to accept in a cultural context that is multiethnic, multicultural, and multireligious. We live in a society that requires of us tolerance and acceptance for peoples of other cultures and other faiths. This reality was illustrated in a recent community dispute in Detroit over a newly built mosque. Muslim practice requires that the call to prayer be sounded five times a day. When the permit for the mosque's loudspeaker was filed, however, there was resistance at the local level. Why, some residents thought, should they have to listen to the Muslim call to prayer when they were not Muslim? Yet it did not seem to occur to them that their Muslim neighbors had lived with Christian church bells, Christian Christmas crèches, and other Christian symbols for a long time. As America becomes more religiously diverse, Christian communities will be faced with challenging opportunities for hospitality toward persons of other religious traditions.

Nevertheless, when Christians state what they believe, they also mark off what they do not believe. When we say the familiar words of the Apostles' Creed, for example, we are clearly indicating many alternatives that we do not affirm. Imagine saying the Apostles' Creed, declaring what you do believe and then silently declaring what you are rejecting. In our contemporary context, the primary affirmations of the Apostles' Creed might come with these accompanying rejections:[6]

> I believe in God, the Father Almighty, Maker of heaven and earth.
>   (*not in the stock market or military might*)
> And in Jesus Christ, his only Son our Lord
>   (*not in the many false lordships of the world that tempt me to turn away from Jesus Christ, or that offer themselves as alternatives to Christ*)
> I believe in the Holy Ghost
>   (*not in my spirit as the final measure of reality*).

In a religiously diverse culture, we sometimes get the mistaken impression that we must not reject *anything*, that it is somehow impolite to state clearly what we believe and, likewise, what we do not believe. But this is not the case. As our communities and neighborhoods become ever more diverse and multicultural, it is even more important to find clarity and identity in our baptism and in the creed that was spoken at our baptism.

Fifth, creeds have a *doxological* function. They are one of the ways we praise God, because the words of the creed give voice to our faith and trust in the one triune God whom we worship and glorify. This creedal way of praising God has long been practiced by the church as it has used the Apostles' Creed in celebrations of baptism and the Nicene Creed in the Eucharistic liturgy. When we think of the creeds as a gift of praise to God, as an offering of the best words the Christian tradition has produced to express its faith, the creeds can become a doxology rather than an act of rote memorization.

Sixth, the creeds *edify* Christians. The first meaning of the word "edify" in the dictionary is to "instruct," but this is not the meaning I have in mind. The second dictionary meaning of "edify" is to "enlighten." This points to the "aha" moments that sometimes occur when a new insight flashes or a fresh perspective dawns—or what happens, every once in a while, when a Christian believer recites the Apostles' Creed or the Nicene Creed. It may not happen often. But the creeds can edify; they can enlighten. So it pays to be alert. It even pays to study the creeds, to learn their unique language, their history, the issues at stake in their writing, for a fresh insight or new perspective may emerge from this process of study.

Consider an example. One particularly lovely line in the Nicene Creed is the first line about the Holy Spirit. "We believe in the Holy Spirit, the Lord, the giver of life." This is a line that can be repeated dozens, hundreds of times, perhaps, until that one time when the sheer wonder of "the Lord, the giver of life" lights up the interior space of your soul. You see that all the pulsing hearts, breathing lungs, and firing synapses in all the creatures of this planet and all the fiery gaseous planets of all the galaxies in the universe owe their very existence to the life-giving Holy Spirit. And the size of that thought is so immense that you have to hang on to the pew in front of you for a minute. That is the edification that the creeds offer now and then, if you pay attention to the words and what they mean.

Seventh, the creeds can *comfort* Christians. At times, the creeds may put broken believers back together again. Gordon MacDonald imagines that creeds are like the nails in his New Hampshire home. The clapboards work loose during the long, hard winters and need to be renailed each spring. "One of the great joys of repeating the Christian creed is that it gives us an opportunity to reaffirm the central truths of God's revelation," MacDonald writes. "As we say, 'I believe,' . . . we begin to hammer back the nails of our convictions and commitments."[7]

Our daughter recently witnessed a winter blast of harsh experience in her middle school. At the lunchroom table, often the scene of social humiliations small and large, one girl taunted another about her Christian belief, reducing her to tears. I don't know if reciting the Nicene Creed brought comfort to that middle school student the next Sunday. I like to think that it might have—that she, standing with the congregation that promised to support her at her baptism, recited with them, "We believe in one God, the Father, the Almighty." I like to think that the great creed of the church helped her to put her shattered self back together again.

Even that most dense and abstract creedal word of all, the famous Greek word *homoousios*, had a pastoral intent. This precise philosophical word, which refers to Christ's full divine nature with the Father—"of one Being with the Father"— was also a model for the unity that ought to characterize the Christian. Thus, *homoousios*, the mysterious oneness between Father and Son, is the standard of mutuality and reciprocity within the Christian community as well. The ancient line in the Nicene Creed, "of one Being with the Father," might serve as a pastoral reminder of the kind of unity that ought to characterize relationships in our churches, our marriages, our social structures, and our friendships.

PAST MEETS PRESENT

When the bishops of Nicea issued their creed in the late summer of 325, and when the Council of Constantinople expanded and reaffirmed it in 381, did they understand it the same way we understand it today? When early converts to the Christian faith recited the Apostles' Creed as a summary of their new faith, did they mean then what we mean now when we say the words of this ancient creed? These are interesting and puzzling questions. The fact that the church is centuries old puts this question before us: Do ancient words mean today what they meant in their original context? Humanly speaking, the church's longevity is a thing of wonder. When we consider the obstacles and challenges to the church over the centuries, it is amazing that the church has survived through time and place in spite of so many crises. Our faith, of course, gives us the additional perspective of seeing the hand of God guiding and protecting and leading the church, but questions of historical context and meaning still remain.

Would it be possible for a fourth-century Christian believer—say, one of the bishops of the Council of Nicea—and a twenty-first-century Christian believer—say, a Presbyterian from Charlotte, North Carolina—to carry on a meaningful conversation about their faith? I am convinced that such a conversation would be possible. There would be moments of genuine puzzlement, of course, and there would be contextual confusions. But the core of Christian faith would unite these Christians, separated by centuries but not by convictions. The core beliefs expressed in the Nicene Creed and the Apostles' Creed would unite them as brothers and sisters in the faith. A conversation would certainly be possible.

The very first article of the Nicene Creed would be one topic of conversation: "We believe in one God, the Father, the Almighty, maker of heaven and earth, of all that is, seen and unseen." The bishop of Nicea might explain why this article was particularly important for inclusion in the creed. Fourth-century Christians had to contend with multiple rivals to their faith. Pagan religions proposed that the material world was infused with divinities, that groves of trees were sacred, that natural beauty spots, caves, and springs were sacred, and that all the gods and spirits of nature were to be worshiped. In addition to pagan religions, Gnosticism was a widely diverse movement that threatened the Christian church from within. One church historian sees Gnosticism as an "insidious" adversary in the early centuries of the church's life, when it was still forming its fundamental doctrines.[8] "Gnostic groups functioned *inside* the church and on its fringes, and it was subtly attractive. That was what made it so subversive, and that was what led to the efforts to suppress it."[9] Although there was variety among the many gnostic groups, there were common features.

Gnosticism posited a split in God between the god who created and the Father god. It also understood the material world as the result of accident or sin, believing that the world we know is second-class, inferior to the spiritual realm. Gnostics divided humans into two categories: the elite few who could be initiated into the secrets of spiritual knowledge, and the multitude who could not know about God and had to depend on the spiritual elite.

The bishop might then explain how important it was to begin the creed with a strong affirmation of the one true God, not a pantheon of deities and not a divided God! It was also important to begin the creed with an affirmation that God is our Creator God, the Creator of all things that exist. Thus, the world is *good*, not bad. Our Father in heaven, with all the goodness and care of a gracious heavenly parent, creates for us a world of splendor and wonder. This is what the compact first article of the Nicene Creed affirms, says our fourth-century bishop.

The Presbyterian from Charlotte might jump in at this point. Yes, she would say. I can see that. Even though Gnosticism doesn't exist in the twenty-first century (or does it?), we too need to hear that God created the world and all that is in it. We are also confronted with cultural forces that are operating against this basic faith affirmation. In the twenty-first century, Christians need to clarify their belief that creation is the good work of a good Creator, for this means that the earth is worthy of our protection and preservation for our children and grandchildren. All creatures on the earth are God's good creation, and so are valued and worthy of our protection. Our own bodies are good and worthy of our care, as are the bodies of other people.

Our Charlotte Presbyterian might have more to say. Because she is a physicist, she would find the phrase "visible and invisible" particularly interesting. Of course, her brothers from the fourth century knew nothing of the tiny particles called quarks and leptons. They were thinking of the angelic hosts when they confessed that God is the creator even of things invisible. But a twenty-first-century believer could have a renewed and expanded appreciation of the "visible and invisible" phrase in the Nicene Creed. The vast reaches of the outer galaxies, the microcosmos of atoms and electrons, and the subparticles of quantum physics—these too are all creatures of God.

The conversation between a fourth-century person and the twenty-first-century person about each article of the Nicene Creed and the Apostles' Creed would be fruitful. Certainly the article on Jesus Christ, the big middle of both ecumenical creeds, would be an important place to compare shared commitments as well as different cultural insights. The Nicene Creed's famous section, "We believe in one Lord, Jesus Christ, the only Son of God, eternally begotten of the Father, God from God, Light from Light, true God from true God," tends to attract the exasperation of some contemporary Christians who are more interested in the earthy Jesus of the Gospels, the Jesus who healed the sick and befriended those whom society considered marginal. But Christians of the third and fourth centuries would assure us today that these phrases from the creed are not abstract and disconnected from the Jesus of the Gospels—far from it. These phrases are intended to declare that Jesus, the same Jesus who lived among his friends and ate with outcasts and sinners, is the one unique Savior, the truly divine Immanuel, God-with-us Redeemer. Jesus Christ was no junior-grade god, no merely exceptional human, but God in the flesh, God taking on our human condition so that in Christ we might be reconciled with God.

So much is at stake here in these phrases, our friends from long ago would eagerly say, that we too should treasure them. As the only Son of God, eternally begotten of the Father, God from God, Light from Light, true God from true God, Jesus' true home is in trinitarian union with God. Although fully divine, he took on human form and became one of us. The disciples did not have the words to articulate all of this, but the church gradually came to an awareness of this truth, passing on the depth of faith in the words of the Nicene Creed. These have been the ecumenical treasure of the church ever since.

One contemporary theologian says, "Confessing that Jesus is 'of the same essence as the Father' should cause a catch in our breath and a quickening of our pulse."[10] He is referring, of course, to the famous Greek word *homoousios*, the word around which the fiercest arguments raged at the Council of Nicea. What is it about this word that might cause one's pulse to race? When the Nicene assembly said that Jesus Christ was *homoousios*, of one Being with the Father, they were making a claim of such enormous theological magnitude and practical implication that it should make a believer's pulse race and knees wobble. It means that the Jesus who tenderly gathered children to him, who hung around with the dispossessed and ostracized, who touched the untouchable, who cared nothing for the comforts of power and prestige, that *this Jesus* was, in fact, *God*. This means, then, that God is like Jesus in all these things. If Jesus acted this way, and Jesus is God, then we know what the heart of God is like. This is why *homoousios* should make our hearts race. Because Jesus is fully God, we have true and reliable knowledge of God—an astonishing thought!

But *homoousios* also means that when we minister to homeless people in our neighborhoods, undocumented migrant workers crossing our borders, people living and dying with HIV/AIDS, and countless others who need acts of love and kindness, we are carrying on the ministry of Christ. When we act as Jesus acted, we are living Christlike lives, and when we act like Christ we act, in a real sense, like God.

In all likelihood, our Presbyterian physicist from Charlotte had never thought of these phrases in the Nicene Creed like that before, although she had recited "of one Being with the Father" hundreds of times. She was interested in hearing from the Nicene bishop why *homoousios* was so important in his context, but she is astonished to realize how that ancient word might function as a way to signal Christ's concern for hurting and helpless people in inner cities and how it might summon her to take up Christ's work.

This phrase in the Nicene Creed, "of one Being with the Father," boldly claims that Jesus Christ and God are, together with the Holy Spirit, united in a Trinity of divine love and communion. The Nicene assembly was fully aware of the weight of this claim. Luke Timothy Johnson says, "What they saw as essential to faith is to deny that the Son is simply an improved version of ourselves. . . . Is it God who saves us in Jesus or not?"[11] The bishops fought so vigorously over that single Greek word *homoousios* because it was key to the audacious claim that Jesus, the sage from Nazareth, was truly God.

It is a claim that we still need to hear today. Both the Apostles' Creed and the Nicene Creed give a disproportionately large amount of text to the death and resurrection of Jesus and its meaning for us. This places the creeds in very good company. The Gospels move quickly from the birth to the adulthood of Jesus, and then skip months, perhaps even years, at a time through the ministry of Jesus. But the pace radically slows in the last days of Jesus' life. Then each moment counts. The creeds, too, pause at the sufferings, the cross, the death of Jesus. Real life and real death are recounted in such precision that even the name of Pontius Pilate appears in both the Apostles' Creed and the Nicene Creed. The Nicene Creed subsumes its recitation of suffering and death under the phrases "for us and for our salvation" and "for our sake." Jesus suffered, died, rose again, and ascended into heaven for a purpose. He did all these things for us and for our salvation.

Remarkably, a group of Christians of the fourth century and the twenty-first century could sit together and have a conversation about what their salvation through Jesus Christ means to them. They would be baffled by many things in each other's lives, but they would find common ground in their salvation. The physicist from Charlotte might say, "I am rescued from my sin and hopelessness through the death of Jesus. He saves me because he has joined himself to me and given me new life." A child in the group might say, "Jesus loves me. That's why I'm saved." A participant in the conversation from either century might say, "Christ has taken up into his own person all the darkness of evil and all the weight of sin and overcome it all by his perfect obedience and love. He has conquered all the powers of death. We are free!" A believer from the Nicene bishop's congregation might say, "We have all gone astray from God's law. Jesus' death satisfied perfectly God's law, so that we will not have to bear the consequences."

What if a skeptic or an agnostic were sitting in on that conversation? What if such a person were to say, "Yes, but what does all this actually mean? You all are talking in metaphors here! What difference does this so-called salvation make?"

It is a fair question. What difference does salvation make in the lives of Christians, whether in the fourth century or the twenty-first century? Luke Timothy Johnson points out that first-century Christians would not have had a hard time answering that question. Salvation was an immediate and real experience. "The powerful sense of present experience can be detected simply from the New Testament's use of the simple word 'now,'" Johnson says. "In the single letter to the Romans, for example, Paul declares that *now* God's righteousness is being revealed (3:21, 26), *now* they have been made righteous (5:9), *now* they have been reconciled to God (5:11), *now* they are freed from sin (6:22), *now* they are discharged from the law (7:6), *now* there is no condemnation for God's people (8:1), and *now* the mystery of God is being revealed (16:26)."[12] Salvation was wonderfully immediate and present to the earliest Christian communities. It was expressed in terms of forgiveness of sins, freedom from principalities and powers, new life, peace, hope, perseverance in suffering, and joy.

Some contemporary Christians make the mistake of thinking that salvation is a reality only in a future life. Salvation is not in the here and now, they think; it is only in the by-and-by. Other contemporary Christians make the mistake of thinking that salvation is limited only to this present life. They limit salvation to reclamation projects in this world—ecological projects, economic projects, social justice projects. Both mistakes limit the true reach of the gospel. Salvation is a reality that embraces both our earthly existence now and the promise of a future life with God. "For us and for our salvation" Jesus Christ became incarnate, lived, died, rose, and ascended in order to bring us a new way of living now and into eternal life with God.

Understandings of Jesus' death that are drawn from various places in Scripture and expressed throughout the Christian tradition are numerous. But all share the fundamental conviction expressed in the Nicene Creed: For us and for our salvation, Jesus Christ came down from heaven and lived the life that he did, a life that ended in his death and then his glorious resurrection and ascension. It is this "for us" that summarizes the middle articles of both the Apostles' Creed and the Nicene Creed and that unites the Christian believers from the first to the twenty-first centuries.

In our imaginary conversation between one of the bishops of the Nicene assembly and a Presbyterian from Charlotte, surely one of the most puzzling articles of the Nicene Creed for exploration would be, "He will come again in glory to judge the living and the dead, and his kingdom will have no end." Some Christians of former times, as do some Christians today, assumed that the judgment would begin when Christ appeared visibly to all people on earth, signaled by an audible trumpet blast. Not all Christians then or now share this assumption, of course. Because differing interpretations may divide us, it is important to clarify the core theological concepts of this most puzzling article of the creed.

The creeds are clear that the Jesus of the Gospels—the same Jesus who cured the sick, suffered execution, rose victorious from the grave to conquer sin and death, and walked with the Emmaus disciples and explained the Scriptures—will be our judge. Our Savior is our Judge. It is a core theological conviction that we do not know the exact details of the return of Christ and the final judgment, yet we do have confidence that God's kingdom will finally come, so that "God may be all in all" (1 Cor. 15:28). The details are not known, but this confident vision unites Christians across the centuries and through differences of interpretation over the particulars.

Perhaps only the final phrase of the Nicene Creed can match words about the final judgment for producing furrowed brows on contemporary Christians: "We look for the resurrection of the dead, and the life of the world to come." And yet this declaration ought to bring sighs of relief or shouts of joy to believers. The resurrection of the dead is God's resounding affirmation of the creation, a promise of final restoration for the broken creation that will heal all wounds, stitch together ripped seams, and reconcile all shattered relationships. The resurrection of the dead is God's resounding affirmation of our bodies, bodies that suffer from arthritis, diabetes, cancer, and Alzheimer's disease. These same bodies will rise to eternal life with God, restored in a way that is appropriate for eternal life with God, and also in a way appropriate for creaturely life.

Again, we do not know the details. But what we do know is cheerfully expressed in the last line of the Nicene Creed: "[We look for] the life of the world to come." The world to come has life! And we are looking forward to it. This lovely blend of confidence and "agnosticism"—confidence in God's goodness and sovereignty while not knowing the details of exactly how this will be—ought to characterize the Christian affirmation of the resurrection of the dead and eternal life. In the meantime, we take up our life of witness and service in this life, following Jesus, bearing one another's burdens, worshiping, rejoicing with those who rejoice and weeping with those who weep.

SERVANTS AND STEWARDS

In his first letter to the church in Corinth, the apostle Paul included a short self-description: "Think of us in this way, as servants of Christ and stewards of God's mysteries" (1 Cor. 4:1). The great ecumenical creeds have also proven themselves to be servants of God and stewards of God's mysteries throughout the centuries. They are not the *only* word that can be spoken about God's revelation to us and they are not the *last* word that can be spoken about God's revelation to us. But they are faithful servants and stewards and, as such, join us in the work of servanthood and stewardship.

If we recognize the creeds as fellow workers in the common task of serving God, we will be able to study them and puzzle through them, yet consider them to be trusted guides and teachers, sages in the faith. Once we have listened well, we will have the freedom and confidence to bring our questions to them. Rainer Maria Rilke once advised a young poet, "I want to beg you, as much as I can, dear sir, to be patient towards all that is unsolved in your heart, and try to love the questions themselves."[13] Hasty conclusions about deep mysteries of the faith often short-circuit opportunities for growth. Perhaps the Orthodox priest was on to something: "Well, you just say it. With a little practice and effort, most can learn it by heart."

NOTES

1. Kathleen Norris, *Amazing Grace: A Vocabulary of Faith* (New York: Riverhead Books, 1998), 64–65. See Ron Byars's chapter on the creeds in *A More Profound Alleluia: Theology and Worship in Harmony* (Grand Rapids: Eerdmans, 2005), for a treatment of this story and a discussion of the creeds in our culture.
2. I am indebted to Scott Hoezee's helpful study guide *Speaking as One: A Look at the Ecumenical Creeds* (Grand Rapids: CRC Publications, 1997), 12–13.
3. See Joseph D. Small, "The Spirit and the Creed," in *Fire and Wind: The Holy Spirit in the Church Today*, ed. J. Small (Louisville, KY: Geneva Press, 2002), 4–8.
4. *The Treatise on the Apostolic Tradition of St. Hippolytus of Rome, Bishop and Martyr*, ed. Gregory Dix and Henry Chadwick (London: Alban Press, 1991), 20.1–2, pp. 30–31.
5. Robert Kingdon, ed., *Registers of the Consistory of Geneva in the Time of Calvin*, vol. 1, 1542–1544 (Grand Rapids: Eerdmans, 1996), 26.
6. I learned this polemical function of the affirmations of the creed from John D. Witvliet, who develops a similar approach to the use of doxology and praise in his article "Isaiah in Christian Liturgy: Recovering Textual Contrasts and Correcting Theological Astigmatism," *Calvin Theological Journal* 39, no. 1 (April 2004): 135–56.
7. Gordon MacDonald, *Ordering Your Private World* (Nashville: Thomas Nelson, 1984), 168, quoted in Marianne Micks, *Loving the Questions* (Valley Forge, PA: Trinity Press International, 1993), 9.
8. Frances Young, *The Making of the Creeds* (Philadelphia: Trinity Press International, 1991), 19.
9. Ibid., 18.
10. Hoezee, *Speaking as One*, 40.
11. Luke Timothy Johnson, *The Creed: What Christians Believe and Why It Matters* (New York: Doubleday, 2003), 131–32.
12. Johnson, *Creed*, 146.
13. Rainer Maria Rilke, *Letters to a Young Poet* (New York: W. W. Norton & Co., 1934), 33–34.

3

A Conversation with
the Reformation Confessions

John L. Thompson

When we describe the Nicene Creed and the Apostles' Creed as *ecumenical*, we acknowledge a contrast between them and every other document in *The Book of Confessions*. The creeds that follow, it would seem, are *not* ecumenical, not catholic. Indeed, there is a sense in which the confessions and catechisms of the sixteenth century are the exact opposite. They document not a coming together, but a breaking apart. They are the record of a relationship gone awry, a conversation broken off in anger.

A conversation with the Reformation confessions and their framers is not likely to be a sweet and sentimental journey. To the contrary, any remembrance of the Reformation and any serious conversation with the Reformers will be bittersweet. Vicariously, we ought to feel something of the tragedy and pain of their (our) reluctant break with Rome, as well as their open tensions with Lutherans and Anabaptists. But we should also absorb some sense of the emancipation and relief that these first Protestants felt when they rediscovered the pure and liberating power of the gospel. By their own accounts, this restoration of the gospel changed their lives—and saved their souls. The break with Rome was excruciating, yet urgent; there was loss, yet much was gained.

Both aspects—what was gained and what was lost—are at the heart of what we might learn from a conversation with Reformation confessions. On the one hand, if we are to understand the legacy of Presbyterian beliefs and practices, we need to ask them about the *urgency* of the Reformation. What was the point? What did Calvin, along with his colleagues represented in our *Book of Confessions*—John Knox, Zacharias Ursinus, Heinrich Bullinger—wish to achieve? Did they mean to found a new church or denomination? On the other hand, we should also ask about the *limits* of the Reformation critique. Granted, harsh words and even lethal deeds were exchanged by Catholics and Protestants, but were these new confessions meant to put an end to all further conversation? Did they mean to burn all bridges behind them? Had Christian tradition strayed so far that they intended to forget the past altogether?

These questions are important, because they are still our own. Presbyterians have not reunited with Roman Catholics, but we continue to have serious ecumenical conversations; an appendix to the *Book of Order* contains the text of our 1997 agreement with three other denominations.[1] These confessions may once have fixed the boundaries of Reformed identity, but our own sense of identity is not identical with that of our sixteenth-century forebears. We have taken up conversations and reopened arguments that were once seen as settled. Our own perspective on the gospel has changed *our* lives too. Accordingly, conversation with our Reformed ancestors should prompt us to ask questions not only about the past but also about the present and the future. In other words, as Presbyterians and Christians, who are we, and how did we get here? And how should we chart our course in days to come?

Our conversation will take place in three stages. We will begin with a brief discussion of where our three sixteenth-century confessions came from and how they found their way into *The Book of Confessions*. Then we will turn to the *urgency* of these confessions, and finally to their *limits*. (One might say that we will look at what these confessions thought was broken in the theology of their day, and what was not.)

WHY *THESE* THREE CONFESSIONS?

Reformed Christians have never been like the Lutherans in their writing of confessions. The followers of Martin Luther quickly rallied around a few confessional documents—Luther's two catechisms (1529) and the Augsburg Confession (1530)—to which they added only three or four other writings, culminating in the Book of Concord in 1580.[2] In contrast, Reformed Christians had produced at least three dozen confessions by the end of the sixteenth century, each with varying provenance and constituency.[3] This multitude of confessions reflects Reformed Christianity's multiple origins, for even though we claim to pay special attention to John Calvin, neither he nor any other single figure can be said to have "founded" the Reformed churches. "Reformed" Christianity arose as a gradual coalescence of many churches and leaders in Europe, most of whom admired Luther yet found reason to dissent from Lutherans on important matters.

Of course, American Presbyterians once embraced only the Westminster Confession of Faith and its two catechisms. But in the same year that the church ratified the Confession of 1967 it also adopted a *Book of Confessions*—nine separate documents in all. Although the newly included Reformation confessions were clearly among the most important and revered writings of their day, they were not the only contenders. Some would have preferred the Belgic Confession of 1561, which is still part of the constitution of the Christian Reformed Church; some wanted to include the French Confession of 1559; still others expressed a preference for Calvin's Geneva Catechism.[4] To be sure, the process that led to adding these confessions was not without political implications. For some, adding these other confessions was a way of diluting and decentering the authority and tenor of the Westminster documents.[5] In the minutes of the General Assembly, however, other reasons are cited, including the desire to communicate that Presbyterians see themselves "in a wider historic context than that of the British Churches of the 1640s."[6] As Edward A. Dowey, Jr., put it, "The Westminster Confession, standing alone, is not modern enough to guide the present, nor is it ancient enough to represent the past."[7]

Out of the wide array of Reformed confessions, then, the C67 task force—known officially as the Special Committee on a Brief Contemporary Statement of Faith—chose to supplement the Westminster Confession with these three. For our purposes, we might say that they chose to invite three old friends into a renewed conversation.

1. *The Scots Confession.* Written in the space of four days in 1560 at the request of the Scottish Parliament and published early in 1561, it was the product of a committee of six, including John Knox.[8] It emerged abruptly at a moment when Protestant insurgents saw their English defenders leave the Scots to themselves, after having driven French and Catholic forces from the country. The C67 task force praised the Scots Confession as "a fresh, vigorous, sometimes vituperative manifesto of reformation," and commended it as fruitful for study and historically important "as an English language document of the Reformation."[9]

2. *The Heidelberg Catechism.* Written in 1563 at the behest of Frederick III, ruler of a German province known as the Palatinate, it has been variously credited over the years to Caspar Olevianus and/or Zacharias Ursinus, as well as to a committee drawn from the theology faculty at Heidelberg that surely included both Olevianus and Ursinus.[10] Whatever the authorship, Frederick wanted a catechism that would promulgate a consistent account of (Protestant) Christian beliefs so as to benefit not only the young, but also "pastors and schoolmasters."[11] At the same time, it served as Frederick's apology for his Reformed beliefs in a province dominated by often hostile Lutherans. The C67 task force recognized this catechism for its literary and theological excellence, its importance for Reformed churches in Europe and the United States, and especially for an approach to the Decalogue that stressed gratitude rather than legalism.[12]

3. *The Second Helvetic Confession.* This was originally Heinrich Bullinger's personal confession, composed in 1561 when he was gravely ill. (He also led in writing the First Helvetic Confession in 1536.) Bullinger's confession was well received by his colleagues in Zurich and was sent to Frederick III, who had requested some tutoring in the Reformed faith prior to his defense of the Heidelberg Catechism before the imperial assembly in 1566.[13] Reporting it as "the most widely received and adopted Reformed confession of its time," the C67 task force went on to praise the Second Helvetic for its "irenic tone" and "catholic comprehensiveness." It is unique in its heavy orientation to "practical church life," yet it typifies Reformed confessions of the sixteenth century in the way it develops the doctrine of election "in close conjunction with the doctrine of Christ." And it offers "a remarkably strong teaching about the sermon: 'The preaching of the word is the word of God.'"[14]

Careful reading of the 1965 *Minutes* can disclose, even at forty years' remove, the hopes and fears of the C67 task force. For them, the seeming rigidity and scholastic dogmatism of the seventeenth-century Westminster Confession needed to be offset by the supposedly kinder, gentler, less legalistic, more christocentric affirmations of the previous century.[15] While there are contrasts to be drawn between the confessions, it is open to question whether the sixteenth century ever was all it was hoped to be in 1965. Recent scholarship has been inclined to find continuity rather than contrast between the "scholastic" Protestants of the seventeenth century and their own Calvinist forebears. Though we need not pass judgment on the values or process that drove this selection, it is instructive for us to reflect on the interests expressed by the C67 task force. Some of the same themes will probably interest us as well. And we can also appreciate the effort to draw Presbyterians into a broader conversation with these confessions, as well as broadening the church itself through a greater awareness of our history and tradition.

In reflecting on the choice of these three Reformation creeds, we may add two other observations. First, it has often been noted, sometimes with surprise or dismay, that none of these writings comes directly from the hand of John Calvin. This is one of the reasons that some have wished to include or substitute the Geneva Catechism or the French Confession. Yet, however highly one may regard Calvin, there is no reason to be greatly disappointed. Traces and echoes of the French Reformer abound in these works, even in the Heidelberg Catechism, whose sponsor, Frederick III, claimed never to have read Calvin's writings! Knox and Olevianus studied with Calvin in Geneva; the Heidelberg Catechism probably drew on Calvin's own Geneva Catechism; and some passages of the Second Helvetic Confession carry a verbatim resemblance to the *Institutes.*

It is also worth noting that all three of our documents date from the 1560s. That decade saw the death of Calvin, as well as the final session of the Council of Trent, the council that formulated the Roman Catholic response to Protestantism. By this date, the Reformation was well into its second or third generation (figuring from the posting of Luther's Ninety-five Theses in 1517). The split between Protestants and Catholics was a well-established fact, as were the divisions between Lutherans, Anabaptists, and Reformed (the preferred self-designation of "Calvinist" churches since the 1540s[16]). Yet not all these boundaries were impermeable. Calvin regarded Luther as virtually an apostle of the Reformation. Despite the sharp tensions between Lutherans and Calvinists over the Lord's Supper, Calvin and his Reformed colleagues represented here recognized that Luther's initial call for reform and his exposition of justification had blazed a path for them too.

THE URGENCY OF THE REFORMATION CONFESSIONS

The theology of these confessions leads us into a land of stark contrasts in which there seem to be no shadows or shades of gray, but only bright light and deep darkness. People often find sunshine in Heidelberg's well-known opening question and answer: "What is your only comfort, in life and in death? That I belong—body and soul, in life and in death—not to myself but to my faithful Savior, Jesus Christ." These *are* words of comfort, and it is significant that our 1991 Brief Statement of Faith opens with an homage to this question and answer. Indeed, the Heidelberg Catechism is often depicted as a catechism of comfort from start to finish, in view of its stress on the gifts and benefits our gracious God bestows. But when we read past question 1, we immediately find that all this comfort comes at a price! Among the trio of things one must know in order to "live and die in the blessedness of this comfort," the first is this: "the greatness of my sin and wretchedness" (4.002).

Finding Good News in Our Indictment as Sinners

The greatness of our sin and wretchedness (such unpopular terms today!) is elaborated concisely but insistently by these early questions. Thus, as the law teaches us, we are "by nature . . . prone to hate God and . . . neighbor" (4.005). Our first parents are blamed for "poisoning" our lives with original sin, and "unless we are born again through the Spirit of God," we are indeed "so perverted that we are altogether unable to do good and [are] prone to do evil" (4.007–.008).

I have read these lines of the Heidelberg Catechism with my family, and the severity of expression caught us all up short. Are we really so prone to *hate* God, we wondered? Can we do *nothing* good at all? What about kindly neighbors, philanthropists, defenders of human rights, public servants? This is a great place to engage the Reformers in conversation: Why so much emphasis on human underachievement? Why this obsession with sin?

For the Reformers, the answer lay in the conjunction of two factors: first, their vision of who *God* is; second, their understanding of who *we* are not. This dual line of inquiry is embedded in Heidelberg's second question and answer, which juxtaposes knowing our own sin and knowing the source of our deliverance. Perhaps just as famous an instance of this duality, however, are the opening lines of Calvin's *Institutes* (which was itself created to be a catechism of sorts):

> [T]rue and sound wisdom consists of two parts: the knowledge of God and of ourselves. But . . . which one precedes and brings forth the other is not easy to discern. In the first place, no one can look upon himself without immediately turning his thoughts to the contemplation of God, in whom he "lives and moves" . . . Indeed, our very poverty better discloses the infinitude of benefits reposing in God. . . . Thus, from the feeling of our own ignorance, vanity, poverty, infirmity, and—what is more—depravity and corruption, we recognize that the true light of wisdom, sound virtue, full abundance of every good, and purity of righteousness rest in the Lord alone. To this extent we are prompted by our own ills to contemplate the good things of God; and we cannot seriously aspire to him before we begin to become displeased with ourselves. . . . Accordingly, the knowledge of ourselves not only arouses us to seek God, but also, as it were, leads us by the hand to find him.[17]

Calvin was not one to tickle the ears of his hearers. It is true that self-knowledge is a good thing and a worthy pursuit. But Calvin is confident, as is the Heidelberg Catechism, that if we know ourselves truly, we will know ourselves as broken. We are not what we are meant to be, and only the deceived can manage such complacency. If we truly know ourselves, we will know how much we lack. If we truly know God, we will know how far we have sinned and fallen short. Thus, the knowledge of God is likely to be found not among the smug but among the meek: it is not those who are well who need a physician, but those who are sick.

Although the Protestant Reformation had many causes, one touchstone for Luther and Calvin, shared by these confessional documents, was their fervent conviction that what made the gospel "good news" was its gift of peace to the conscience burdened by sin. Romans 5:1, "Therefore, since we are justified by faith, we have peace with God," was an axiom that could be used to test one's theology: Does your theology bring your conscience peace? On the eve of the Reformation, there were some Roman Catholic theologians for whom peace was not the goal. To the contrary, they thought that the church should keep its members in a state of anxiety, on a pendulum constantly swinging between hope and fear. Too much hope, like too much peace, could threaten to become presumption. It was far better for people to remain in anxious striving, for it motivated them to work and so please God![18]

For Luther, Calvin, and virtually all their colleagues, this sort of medieval theology represented an embezzlement of the gospel. The catastrophe was twofold. The peace of conscience that is the birthright of everyone who trusts in Christ was replaced with fear and anxiety. And such proclamation led Christians to place their trust not in the adequacy of Christ but in the efficacy of their own good works. Consequently, Luther and Calvin saw such theology as nothing less than deadly to the soul.

An insistence on the thoroughgoing sinfulness of human beings is central to all Reformation confessions. It appears in the Scots as an assertion of our hostility to God, our slavery to Satan, and the utter defacement of the image of God (3.03). The Second Helvetic is no softer: "Full of all wickedness, distrust, contempt and hatred of God, we are unable to do or even to think anything good of ourselves" (5.037). Although the Reformers asserted that our indictment as sinners is an essential part of the gospel, we should understand that they saw themselves not as masochists but as realists. The oft maligned and much misunderstood Calvinist doctrine of "total depravity" never meant that every human being is as bad as he or she could possibly be, as if all of us were constantly on an unbridled but secret spree of sin and perversion. Rather, it means that no part of our being is untainted by self-interest, and even acts of supposed self-sacrifice run the risk of an inappropriate or prideful self-regard.

We have to think carefully about this tenet of Reformed theology, for in our day this teaching can be very hard to sell. It is common to hear parishioners complain about being called *sinners*—if they even hear this "s-word" mentioned. Yet the Reformers regarded a strong acknowledgment of sin as necessary both for salvation and for the well-being of the Christian life. To know oneself as a sinner is truly to know oneself as the lost sheep whom the Shepherd sought to rescue. To know oneself as a sinner is also to know the *relief* of dropping the most disabling pretense a person can have. If we are to have a gospel that holds forth the promise of redemption, it is essential to know ourselves as in need of redemption. If we do not know ourselves as such, then we have much to learn from these confessions.

Worship as Imperative and Necessity

The Reformation obsession with sin (if that's what it is) is thus a testimony to the duality between God's holiness and human mediocrity, between God's righteousness and human injustice and self-absorption. It would be hard to imagine a Reformed theology that did not maintain the poles of divine goodness and human brokenness, sharpening them against one another. Surely this is the logic that drives worship: a recognition of the "worthship" of God,[19] and a recognition by those who are not God that we belong to Another.

In her journal, Annie Dillard once summed up a day like this: "All day long I feel created."[20] This wonderful line captures something of what it means to belong to God: to know that you are not supposed to play the role of Deity— not designed to be omniscient or omnipotent, not expected to go through a day without mistakes, not intended to be anything other than a *creature*: finite, mortal, and grateful. Something like this is at work in the opening line of the Scots Confession, which uses four verbs to describe our relationship to God: It is God alone to whom we must *cleave*, whom we must *serve, worship,* and *trust.* The Westminster Shorter Catechism makes the same point when it describes "the chief end of man" as "to glorify God, and to enjoy him forever" (7.001). Unfortunately, there is little in our society that prepares us to find joy in service or subordination. When we do manage to take pleasure in the glory of another, more often than not it is a misplaced fascination with the rich and famous, film stars and sports heroes. The Reformers remind us that only God is worthy of such glorification.

"Glory" is one of those words that is somewhat foreign to the modern vocabulary, however. The notion of *God's* glory—of God acting to reveal that glory, or of human beings existing to give God glory—may seem particularly obscure. In brief, God's glory is God's self-revelation: a proclamation of God's worth, goodness, justice, beauty, and power. To know or proclaim God's glory is to tell the truth about God—the whole truth. God's glory is an important theme for these confessions, because the Reformers feared that God's glory was being eclipsed by false claimants to an honor that belongs to God alone. So the reform of the church in the sixteenth century entailed not only a renewed recognition that God desires our trust and cleaving rather than our random good works but also a renewed recognition that God wants us to "accept no substitutes," to recognize that only God is God.

The Reformation confessions derive an everyday orientation from the glory of God. Because it is God who inspires us to serve God and our neighbor, it is God (not ourselves) whom we seek to glorify through these good deeds (4.091; 5.117). God's glory is served when rulers govern well because they mirror God's justice (3.24). Even swearing an oath (a controversial topic in the sixteenth century) may add to God's glory insofar as it furthers the manifestation of fidelity and truth and protects the well-being of a neighbor (4.101). To belong to God is thus the reflex of glorifying God, living a life oriented to and by God—in other words, worshiping God in all of life. Properly understood, all of life leads us to worship as we *tell* the truth about who God is and *practice* that truth by cleaving, serving, and trusting God alone.

Finding God's Word and God's Church among Human Counterfeits

The Reformed confessions worried about many "broken" practices of worship in their day. One such practice was the worship of saints, their statues, or relics (5.020–.027). Another was worshiping Christ in or under the bread and wine of the Lord's Supper, which the Reformers regarded as idolatry (4.080, 4.098; 5.205). But these Roman Catholic practices were merely symptoms of a deeper malaise. A remarkable passage in the Second Helvetic Confession urges pastors to devote "the greatest part of meetings for worship . . . to evangelical teaching" and goes on to warn lest "the congregation [be] wearied by too lengthy prayers, . . . [so that] they either leave the meeting or, having been exhausted, want to do away with it altogether" (5.220). In the sixteenth century, Reformed churches were sometimes practically interchangeable with schools, so much did they stress the educative effect of the sermon. Why? Because the root cause of Catholic errors, as the Reformers saw it, lay in a clergy and laity who were uninformed about what the Bible said and misinformed about the Bible's authority.

Although the Reformers did not always state it in these terms, sound biblical teaching was for them virtually a "mark" of the church, a defining and essential characteristic. Actually, the Scots Confession lists three marks by which the church is known: "the true preaching of the Word of God, . . . the right administration of the sacraments of Christ Jesus, . . . and lastly, ecclesiastical discipline uprightly ministered, as God's Word prescribes, whereby vice is repressed and virtue nourished" (3.18).[21] These three are not enumerated as such in the Second Helvetic Confession, which instead looks especially to "the lawful and sincere preaching of the Word of God as it was delivered to us in the books of the prophets and the apostles, which all lead us unto Christ" (5.134). Both salvation and "right worship" (including sacraments and discipline) thus depend on the Word of God for their truth, rightness, lawfulness, and fidelity.[22]

The problem was multidimensional: Not only was the Bible relatively unknown by the laity (vernacular translations were a dangerous Protestant invention), but the Catholic Church had added law upon law to what the Bible taught. In other words, the Word of God—including the good news of salvation and any sense of how God ought to be worshiped—had been effectively obscured by made-up traditions. For the Reformers, allowing human inventions to displace the clear Word of God was foolish, ungrateful, or worse: "In religious matters and the worship of God," it is not a good work but an evil one to do "things which have no other warrant than the invention and opinion of man" (3.14). The Heidelberg Catechism makes the issue utterly simple:

"We must not try to be wiser than God" (4.098). Indeed, this issue dictates the early structure of the Second Helvetic Confession, which begins with chapters on the sufficiency of Scripture and on the lesser value (but not necessarily worthlessness!) of the writings of the church fathers, the decrees and canons of councils, and the "traditions of men" (5.014; cf. 5.116, 5.240).

We have to consider this tenet of Reformed theology carefully. On the one hand, we can see here how the Reformers used the Bible to clear away a mass of rules and ceremonies that had been made binding on the conscience. Christians were being led to believe that salvation was not merely a matter of trusting Christ, but that it also entailed a host of purportedly "apostolic" rules and advice that clearly contradicted Scripture (5.014). The return to "Scripture alone" was thus a blow on behalf of Christian freedom, and we too should welcome it as such. On the other hand, the framers of these confessions often held stronger opinions on just what was "clearly" biblical and therefore obligatory than many Christians would today. The stress on the sole authority of the Bible as a guide to acceptable worship soon evolved into the Reformed concept of Scripture as the "regulative principle" of worship—the notion that only what Scripture (or, better, the New Testament) commands by way of worship is normative. Anything not commanded is to be regarded as prohibited.

That conversation continues to this day within many Reformed churches. Because the exhortation to restrict our worship to what Scripture approves is embedded in our confessional heritage, we ought to be part of this conversation. As the Second Helvetic Confession reminds us, mixing up human traditions and divine commands is a bad idea, at least if we care to be faithful to Scripture as our authority: "Works and worship which we choose arbitrarily are not pleasing to God."[23] The "regulative principle," then, seems to be a good idea. But problems arise in deciding just what is and is not authorized by Scripture. Calvin approved singing the Psalter, but he abhorred instrumental music in church. Although one might find a precedent of sorts in, say, Psalm 149:3 ("Let them praise his name with dancing, making melody to him with tambourine and lyre"), Calvin insisted that musical instruments were authorized in worship only for the Old Testament people of God, who lived during the "infancy" of the church.[24] Similar reasoning has led some Presbyterians not to observe Christmas or Easter, because no warrant is found in Scripture. The Second Helvetic Confession allows such observances, however, including the Lenten fast and Pentecost, provided they are expressions of Christian liberty and "not . . . imposed on the faithful."[25] There is every reason to worry that we will rationalize our own tastes as somehow faithful to Scripture while critiquing the practices of others as too harsh or too lax. Nonetheless, as Reformed Christians, we Presbyterians should be careful and thoughtful about worship rather than prizing novelty and invention. Even as the Second Helvetic Confession urged pastors to extend teaching and shorten prayers, so should we scrutinize the content of our services. Is the point of our announcements, songs, choral offerings—not to mention our sermons and confessions and prayers—really to tell the truth about God, or do they try too hard to entertain? Are our services presented as ministering God's Word, or do they imitate the "human traditions" of our own media-conscious era, such as the "traditions" of chatty newscasters or talk-show hosts? Caution and conservatism here will probably enmesh us in the so-called worship wars, but that is just where the Reformation confessions say we belong.

Election, Not Perfection, and the Dangers of a False Anthropology

In the Presbyterian Church (U.S.A.) these days, it is unusual to hear much mention of predestination. A Presbyterian student of mine once interrupted a lecture on this topic: "Does anyone else know about this? I mean, I grew up Presbyterian, and I don't think my parents know anything about predestination!" The C67 task force was on the same emotional page when it suggested that sixteenth-century accounts of election are preferable to those of the seventeenth because they are more christocentric. But misgivings over Westminster were not new in 1965. The "Declaratory Statement" appended to that confession in 1903 (6.191–.193) addressed Presbyterian discomfort over too "high" a doctrine of predestination by declaring that all those dying in infancy (*all* infants, not just "elect" infants [so 6.066]) were assured of salvation.

Formally at least, the Reformation was not about predestination. Its chief concern was the doctrines of salvation by grace alone (*sola gratia*) and justification by faith alone (*sola fide*). But the doctrine of election was seen by all Protestants as a necessary implication of *sola gratia*: If we are truly saved by grace and not by our works, that means we are not saved by our strength of will or by a self-generated decision. Both Luther and Calvin rejected all attempts to depict faith as a good work, much less a work of which we are capable. The Second Helvetic Confession agrees: Faith is "a pure gift of God," which God gives "when, to whom and to the degree he wills" (5.113). It comes only when God "inwardly moves the hearts of his elect to faith by the Holy Spirit" (5.144). "By grace alone" is therefore truly radical, even scandalous, for it proclaims that God alone is sovereign over who comes to believe. It is a false view of humanity to suppose we can ever earn or deserve salvation, even by virtue of our faith. The only real difference between Luther and Calvin on this point is that Calvin felt it was important to teach the Bible's doctrine of election openly, while Luther demurred.

In picking up a conversation with the Reformers on this topic, three considerations are well worth pursuing. The first pertains to the *purpose* of the doctrine. Reformed Christians did not derive the doctrine of election from speculation, but from Scripture—from the Old Testament, from Jesus, from Paul. They believed that if the Bible taught a doctrine, there must be a reason, indeed, a blessing or benefit. Actually, if understood correctly, predestination is in some ways a fairly "useless" teaching, because it does not pretend to resolve all questions. Divine election does not destroy the human will (5.043–.049). It does not diminish the role of exhortation, striving, or prayer (5.058, 5.061, 5.144). It does not excuse us from preaching, or allow us to abandon hope for anyone (5.055). Predestination does remind us that God's *grace* is truly *God's* grace, and so teach us humility. It also frees us from fear by assuring us that our salvation is guarded by God.[26] The effect of the doctrine of election is both doxological and transforming: As we read in Ephesians 1:4–6, we are elected not because we are holy, but that we might be holy and thus magnify God's grace (5.054).

A second consideration pertains to misconceptions about free will. Often predestination and free will are presented as a paradox, as if they were polar opposites. In fact, the Second Helvetic Confession is at pains to preserve the human experience of willing and deciding (after all, what we have is called a *will*, not a *nil*![27]). What is at stake, however, is not whether we really will things or make choices. Of course we do. But *what* do we will or choose? Most Protestant Reformers endorsed Augustine's distinction between *choice* and *desire*. Human beings have the freedom to choose, indeed, to choose whatever delights them. The problem is that, apart from grace, we will find delight only in ourselves rather than in God.[28] The Second Helvetic Confession describes this as the *enslavement* of the will, whereby a sinner not only serves sin, but does so *willingly* (5.043). Truly, a miserable freedom! The miracle of regeneration, then, involves the illumination of our minds and the restoration of our wills (5.047). Yet Christians continue to need and benefit from God's internal working, for our wills remain infirm "until the end of our lives" (5.048–.049).

To recognize that our free will survives, but in a damaged condition, is a *pastoral* diagnosis. The human will is important, but it is neither absolute nor well controlled. Our choices are often wrong and self-serving, directed by habits and inscrutable impulses. Indeed, if our wills were as potent and precise as some believe, why do we ever sin? The mystery of our free will as it relates to election could be compared to the experience of falling in love. Is the act of loving another an experience of freedom? Most would say it is, yet can you stop loving someone by sheer force of will? Can you make yourself fall in love with someone, or make someone fall in love with you? How is it then that one person comes to love God while another does not? Is it a matter of choice and gritty determination, or does it require divine intervention? The Reformed tradition opts for the latter answer. Our confessions also recognize the weakness of the will in living the Christian life: our new obedience is at best "only a small beginning" (4.114).[29] In this life, even our fragile resolve is a gift from God, and at the end, Christ will become the sole keeper of our hearts and minds. This would be a good thing for the church to remember in times of persecution—or as you watch a loved one slide into Alzheimer's.

There is a third consideration to note. The C67 task force praised Bullinger's confession for its christocentrism, although Westminster is not really lacking on this score, as the litany of "in Christ" and "by Christ" in 6.018–.019 attests. Nonetheless, the Second Helvetic Confession does open a "back door" into the doctrine of election. That is to say, it recognizes that to be a Christian is to place one's faith and trust in Jesus Christ, not in a doctrine of election. Closely paraphrasing Calvin's 1539 *Institutes*, this confession therefore urges us to "let Christ . . . be the looking glass, in whom we may contemplate our predestination. We shall have a sufficiently clear and sure testimony that we are inscribed in the Book of Life if we have fellowship with Christ, and he is ours and we are his in true faith" (5.060).[30] In other words, election is not to be treated abstractly. We should not ask, "Am I elect?" but more simply, "Do I belong to Christ?" If you believe in Christ, if you are in Christ, "it is to be held as beyond doubt that . . . you are elected" (5.059). It may be a source of relief to hear that we don't need to *believe* in election to *be* elect! Our belief and trust are to be placed in Christ alone.

As usual, we have to think carefully about this topic. Reformed Christians have traditionally been among those most willing to talk about the Bible's teachings on election rather than ignore them. In our conversation with the confessions, the Reformers remind us that we cannot have it both ways. We cannot rejoice in God's sovereign grace only to turn around and claim we are saved by our own decision. The doctrine of election has serious implications for how we understand the grace of God, how we preach the gospel, how we understand ourselves and our brokenness, and, ultimately, where we place our trust.

THE LIMITS OF THE REFORMATION CRITIQUE

Some would say the Reformation got everything just right, and there is no need for anything but a return to that sixteenth- or seventeenth-century perfection. I do not think we can claim the Reformation's perfection as long as Christendom remains divided. One of the tragic ironies of the Reformation is indicated by an often overlooked characteristic of the Reformation confessions. Almost all of them acknowledge or presume the prior and greater authority of what we now call the ecumenical creeds, particularly the Apostles' Creed. (This authority is secondary to Scripture, of course, but not to the later confessions). Although the Apostles' Creed is not mentioned by the Scots Confession, it forms the substance of more than a quarter of the Heidelberg Catechism and is commended by the Second Helvetic in at least five places.[31] (It is also appended to the Westminster Shorter Catechism and recognized by the Confession of 1967.)

The Second Helvetic Confession is particularly strong in its acknowledgment of the Nicene Creed. Indeed, the Second Helvetic is more conscious of history and tradition than any of the other Reformation creeds, including Westminster. There are at least a dozen appeals to the corroborating authority of various church fathers, and a dozen catalogs of ancient heresies whose condemnation the Reformed church by no means wished to overturn.[32] Its expositions of the Trinity and Christ are adorned with passages that unmistakably draw on Nicea and Chalcedon (5.016–.017, 5.066–.067), and at the end of the chapter on Jesus Christ there is a wholesale endorsement of the creeds of Nicea, Constantinople, Ephesus, and Chalcedon, as well as the so-called Athanasian Creed (5.078). These references offer at least some qualification to the earlier warning, common also to the Scots Confession, that councils may err and their decrees must be tested by Scripture (3.20; 5.012–.013). The Reformers recognized that while many things in medieval theology needed to be fixed, not all was broken. They had no interest in revisiting the trinitarian or christological controversies, and they saw little need to improve on many of the old answers, even if they did not come directly from the apostles.

All of this suggests that whatever the Reformers meant to fix or accomplish, they did not want to forsake the church's past or its catholic character. They would have been much happier if they had been able to reform the church rather than merely resect it. The Second Helvetic Confession voices open resentment against the claim that "only the Roman Church" is catholic. Clearly, the Reformed churches were ready to argue for this birthright as their own (5.126). The Second Helvetic also presses the case that the true church might have members even where the marks of the church are not visible; sometimes the church even seems to be extinct, yet it is not (5.137–.138). Lines like these remind us that the Reformers too were in a conversation—albeit not a happy one—with their Roman Catholic rivals, formerly their brothers and sisters.

As this essay was being written, the 2004 Synod of the Christian Reformed Church took up the matter of whether to retain question 80 of the Heidelberg Catechism. This question-and-answer, added in the catechism's second edition and expanded in the third, is by all accounts Heidelberg's most polemical passage in its condemnation of "the papal Mass" as "fundamentally a complete denial of the once for all sacrifice and passion of Jesus Christ (and as such an idolatry to be condemned)" (4.080). The Christian Reformed Church's own conversations with the Heidelberg Catechism and with their Roman Catholic contemporaries led them to reconsider whether the Reformation got this particular point about the Mass "just right."

Sometimes the Reformation is caricatured as a classic Western, with brave and outnumbered Protestants who defended the faith against a corrupt and monolithic church and were ready to die in defense of the gospel. There were times when that is what happened,[33] but we do ourselves and our Protestant ancestors a disfavor if we accept that caricature as the whole truth. Remember, these three confessions appeared late in the game, straddling the final period of the Council of Trent. That council of the Catholic counter-Reformation met three times (in 1545–1547, 1551–1552, and 1562–1563), and each period proved more dismal to Protestant hopes. In response to the first period, Calvin wrote a rejoinder, *Acts of the Council of Trent, with an Antidote*. Despite his provocative title, Calvin treated Catholic arguments seriously and with discernment, suggesting he still hoped for rapprochement; the later periods of Trent elicited no such response. What could easily be missed, however, is that prior to the Council of Trent, Protestants and Catholics engaged in earnest conversations at numerous formal colloquies and through volumes of informal correspondence, hoping to avoid the split that we now take for granted. An older work by John T. McNeill chronicles this early ecumenism, in which persons of good faith clashed with political agendas, some worked for compromise while others stalled, and tentative understandings foundered upon intractable disagreements.[34]

Despite the failure of these early ecumenical conversations, we risk misconstruing the edginess of our own confessions if we forget that these attempts were made. It is proper to be overwhelmed by the existence of so many denominations today, especially when we know how much we have in common with them, including a common commitment to the ecumenical creeds. At the least, we ought to feel some discomfort or dissonance when we know there are walls between our church and other churches that share so much of our own "catholic" substance. Of course, this does not mean that the Reformation was much ado about nothing! But we need not pretend that the Reformers got everything right. Even the feisty Scots Confession admits that even a Reformed creed is only a subordinate authority: "If any man will note in our Confession any chapter or sentence contrary to God's Holy Word . . . we shall alter whatever he can prove to be wrong."[35]

Two weeks after the 2004 Synod of the Christian Reformed Church reconsidered that church's commitment to Heidelberg's question 80, the 216th General Assembly of the PC(USA) voted to qualify how passages in *The Book of Confessions* that denigrate the Catholic Church are to be regarded:

While these statements emerged from substantial doctrinal disputes, they reflect 16th and 17th century polemics. Their condemnations and characterizations of the Catholic Church are not the position of the Presbyterian Church (U.S.A.) and are not applicable to current relationships between the Presbyterian Church (U.S.A.) and the Catholic Church.[36]

The wording here is judicious and, happily, looks in two directions: The *doctrinal disputes* were and are substantial, but the *polemics* have not been helpful. Our Reformation confessions were all affected to some degree by the bitter climate that followed the Council of Trent. Four centuries later, we read them with different sensitivities, and in full awareness of the warming trend that followed the Second Vatican Council in the 1960s. The Reformers would not have expected this thaw in the 1560s, but they would undoubtedly have welcomed it. We still have disagreements with Roman Catholics, not to mention Lutherans and Anabaptists. Nevertheless, we may take it as a mark of our *ecclesia reformanda*—the church that continues to need and receive reform—that conversations once broken off have now resumed.

NOTES

1. *The Constitution of the Presbyterian Church (U.S.A.)*, Part II, *Book of Order* (Louisville, KY: Office of the General Assembly, 2004), appendix C: "A Formula of Agreement between the Evangelical Lutheran Church in America, the Presbyterian Church (U.S.A.), the Reformed Church in America, and the United Church of Christ: On Entering into Full Communion on the Basis of *A Common Calling*." The Formula of Agreement was approved by the 209th General Assembly (1997), affirmed by vote of the presbyteries, and declared by the 210th General Assembly (1998).
2. In addition to the Apology of the Augsburg Confession (1531), the Book of Concord added the Smalcald Articles (1537), Melanchthon's treatise "On the Power and Primacy of the Pope" (1537), and the Formula of Concord (1577).
3. For details, see Jan Rohls, *Reformed Confessions: Theology from Zurich to Barmen* (Louisville, KY: Westminster John Knox Press, 1998).
4. A few details of these alternative considerations are found in John Wilkinson, "On Being a Confessional Church," a presentation to the General Assembly Theological Task Force on Peace, Unity, and Purity of the Church (February 2003), 4–8. The document was accessed July 12, 2004, at http://www.pcusa.org/peaceunitypurity/resources/wilkinson0203.pdf.
5. See John Wilkinson, "The Making of the Confession of 1967," *Church and Society* 92, no. 5 (May–June 2002), 27–29.
6. See *Minutes of the 177th General Assembly (1965) of the United Presbyterian Church in the United States of America*, Part I, *Journal* (Philadelphia: Office of the General Assembly, 1965), 308; this passage originally appeared in the *Minutes* of 1959, Part I, 268–69.

7. Dowey's remark is on p. 318 of his article ("Confessions of the Church: Types and Functions") that was incorporated into the 1965 *Minutes*, Part I, 315–18. As chair of the C67 committee, he was probably responsible for much of the larger report in these minutes.

8. Historical summaries of the writing of these three confessions may be consulted most easily in *The Book of Confessions: Study Edition* (Louisville, KY: Geneva Press, 1996), 25–31, 51–58, 85–91. For more detail and bibliographical references, see the following articles in the *Oxford Encyclopedia of the Reformation* (hereafter, *OER*), 4 vols., ed. Hans J. Hillerbrand (New York: Oxford University Press, 1996): "Helvetic Confessions," by Timothy George (2:219–22); "Olevianus, Kaspar," by Mario Turchetti (3:174); "Scottish Confession," by James Kirk (4:33–36); "Ursinus, Zacharinus," by Derk Visser (4:202–3).

9. 1965 *Minutes*, Part I, 320.

10. On the issue of authorship, the jury is divided, if not hung. See Lyle D. Bierma's introduction to Caspar Olevianus, *A Firm Foundation: An Aid to Interpreting the Heidelberg Catechism* (Grand Rapids: Baker, 1995), xiii–xxviii.

11. See Frederick's preface to Heidelberg in *The Book of Confessions: Study Edition*, 57–58.

12. 1965 *Minutes*, Part I, 321.

13. George, "Helvetic Confessions," *OER* 4:220.

14. 1965 *Minutes*, Part I, 321.

15. For similar reasons, the task force recommended (successfully) that the Westminster Larger Catechism be omitted from the proposed collection as "unwieldy," "excessively legalistic," and unconscionable in its use of proof-texting; see 1965 *Minutes*, Part I, 322.

16. See Konrad Repgen, "Reform," *OER* 3:394.

17. John Calvin, *Institutes of the Christian Religion*, ed. John T. McNeill, trans. Ford Lewis Battles (Philadelphia: Westminster Press, 1960), 1.1.1 (LCC 1:35–37).

18. For an account of such preaching, with an eye to Luther's hostile response, see Heiko Augustinus Oberman, *The Harvest of Medieval Theology: Gabriel Biel and Late Medieval Nominalism* (reprint, Grand Rapids: Eerdmans, 1967), 222–24.

19. Our English word *worship* is literally the modern form of the antiquated *worthship*.

20. Annie Dillard, *Holy the Firm* (New York: Harper & Row, 1977), 25.

21. The first two of these were also marks of the church for Calvin in *Institutes* 4.1.9, but Calvin's desire for discipline in the church was scarcely less than that of John Knox. For Calvin, discipline was not so much a mark of the church per se as it was a mark of a church's *health*. As the "sinews" that hold the church together, discipline is necessary to keep the church "in proper condition" (*in recto statu*; *Institutes* 4.12.1). Although Bullinger did not name discipline as a mark of the church, he (like Calvin) regarded it as "an absolute necessity in the Church" (5.165).

22. Although "sincere" preaching in 5.134 translates the obvious cognate *syncera*, I have rendered it here as "faithful," which I think captures the intention better than the rather subjective sense of the English *sincere*. For the Latin, see Wilhelm Niesel, ed., *Bekenntnisschriften und Kirchenordnungen der nach Gottes Wort reformierten Kirche*, 3rd ed. (Zurich: Evangelischer Verlag, 1938), 251, lines 15–17. The same construction occurs in Calvin at *Institutes* 4.1.9 (*OS* 5:13.24), where the Battles translation (p. 1023) renders *syncere* as "purely [preached]."

23. The Second Helvetic Confession 5.116 goes on to cite two classic Scripture proofs for this doctrine: the injunction in Col. 2:23 against *ethelothrēskia*, or "self-devised worship," and the words of Jesus in Matt. 15:9: "In vain do they worship me, teaching as doctrines the precepts of men."

24. See Calvin's commentary on Psalm 149:2–3 (Calvin Translation Society edition 5:312): "The musical instruments he mentions were peculiar to this infancy of the Church, nor should we foolishly imitate a practice which was intended only for God's ancient people."

25. Second Helvetic Confession 5.226, 5.230. The first of these passages also offers a rule of thumb for which traditional feasts and fasts are lawful: "We do not approve of feasts instituted for men and for saints. *Holy days have to do with the first Table of the Law and belong to God alone.* Finally, holy days which have been instituted for the saints and which we have abolished, have much that is absurd and useless, and are not to be tolerated. In the meantime, we confess that the remembrance of saints, at a suitable time and place, is to be profitably commended to the people in sermons, and the holy examples of the saints set forth to be imitated by all" (emphasis added).

26. Compare 6.021 with Calvin's allusion to the "three benefits" of this doctrine in *Institutes* 4.21.1.

27. The Latin wordplay in 5.043 (*voluntas/noluntas*) survives in our English idiom "willy-nilly."

28. Westminster Shorter Catechism 1, "to glorify God and to *enjoy* him forever," embodies the same Augustinian echo.

29. The Scots Confession is under no illusion that we are likely to offer God our obedience in anything but an amateurish fashion: "Our nature is . . . corrupt, weak, and imperfect," yet God graciously accepts our "imperfect obedience" (3.15). Indeed, according to the Second Helvetic Confession, one of the marks of Christians is their quickness to "acknowledge their infirmity" (5.049).

30. For the Latin, see Niesel, *Bekenntnisschriften und Kirchenordnungen*, 235, lines 14–17; cf. Calvin, *Institutes* 3.24.5 (*OS* 3:416.3–9).

31. 5.018, 5.112, 5.125, 5.141, 5.233.

32. Patristic authors (especially Augustine) are cited at 5.022, 5.026, 5.029, 5.031, 5.041, 5.049, 5.058, 5.075, 5.161, 5.162, and 5.230. Ancient heresies are condemned in 5.008, 5.019, 5.030, 5.032, 5.040, 5.051, 5.068, 5.103, 5.126, 5.166, and 5.181.

33. No one should draw generalizations about the persecutors or victims during the Reformation without consulting Brad S. Gregory's comprehensive account, *Salvation at Stake: Christian Martyrdom in Early Modern Europe* (Cambridge, MA: Harvard University Press, 1999).

34. John T. McNeill, *Unitive Protestantism: The Ecumenical Spirit and Its Persistent Expression* (Richmond, VA: John Knox Press, 1964).

35. Preface to the Scots Confession, in *Book of Confessions: Study Edition*, 31.

36. This document can be found in the *Minutes of the 216th General Assembly (2004) of the Presbyterian Church (U.S.A.)*, Part I, *Minutes* (Louisville, KY: Office of the General Assembly, 2004), 424–28. As part of this action, material was added to the preface and notes of *The Book of Confessions*, and the church underscored its commitment to further conversations with the World Alliance of Reformed Churches and the United States Conference of Catholic Bishops.

4

A Conversation with
the Westminster Standards

John P. Burgess

CONVERSATION AND CONFESSION

In the midst of growing political crisis, Parliament called representatives of the Scottish and English Protestant churches to meet in Westminster Abbey in order to provide a new creed and form of government for the Church of England. The "Westminster divines" wanted to reform the Church of England and to unify British churches and the nation along the lines of the Calvinism that John Knox and other Reformers had introduced nearly a century before.[1] Meeting from 1643 to 1647, the assembly composed the Westminster Confession of Faith and the Larger and Shorter Catechisms, as well as a directory of worship and a form of church government, all of which the assembly hoped would impel a deeper living of the faith in church and society.

The Westminster Standards illustrate the principle that every confession is an ongoing historical conversation. In their immediate context, the Westminster divines debated the theologies held by various Protestant parties in the British Isles, especially Episcopalians, Presbyterians (from both Scotland and England, for each group had a distinctive historical experience), and Independents (present in America as New England Congregationalists). The Westminster Assembly was itself an extended conversation, meeting more than a thousand times over five years. The assembly also had to negotiate with Parliament, which reviewed the documents and asked that scriptural proofs be added.

A Conversation with the Past

The Westminster divines were in conversation with the past as well as the present. The Westminster Confession of Faith generally follows the order of the

51

classic Christian creeds, moving from God's work of creation (Father) to God's work of redemption (Son) to God's work of gathering and sustaining a holy church (Holy Spirit). While the two catechisms do not explicate the Apostles' Creed line by line, the Shorter Catechism does list it as a foundational document, and both catechisms carefully explicate the Ten Commandments and the Lord's Prayer, which Western churches have often used alongside the creed for catechetical purposes.[2] Further, the Westminster Standards mine the Scriptures and the great theological traditions that shaped the Reformation, drawing from insights of the major Reformed confessions of the sixteenth century.

As the Westminster documents develop these resources, they give particular attention to issues of the Christian life. The title of the second part of the Larger Catechism states, "Having Seen What the Scriptures Principally Teach Us to Believe Concerning God, It Follows to Consider What They Require as the Duty of Man." The Westminster divines were convinced that confessing the faith was not an exercise in intellectual abstraction but rather an encouragement to deeper, more faithful Christian living. The Presbyterian Church (U.S.A.)'s *Book of Order* continues to affirm this position in the "Historic Principles of Church Order," among which is the declaration that "truth is in order to goodness; and the great touchstone of truth, its tendency to promote holiness. . . . There is an inseparable connection between faith and practice, truth and duty. Otherwise, it would be of no consequence either to discover truth or to embrace it."[3]

A Continuing Conversation

Reflection on the Westminster Standards has continued through the church's subsequent history, a conversation that is reflected in the very format of the Confession of Faith in the current *Book of Confessions*. At points, the Confession is divided into two columns, one reflecting amendments introduced by the Presbyterian Church in the United States (the former "southern" church), the other, amendments of the United Presbyterian Church in the United States of America (the "northern" church). The practice of amending the Confession has deep roots in American Presbyterianism. The first Presbyterians in the colonies organized themselves as a synod and in 1729 adopted the Westminster Standards.[4] With the nation's independence, they organized a General Assembly, and in 1788, at the instigation of such church leaders as John Witherspoon, the Presbyterian minister who signed the Declaration of Independence, they altered the Confession's article on the civil magistrate.[5]

The Confession had originally entrusted civil rulers with the authority to preserve the church's peace and order, and to suppress "all Blasphemies and Heresies." The amendment now called on "civil magistrates to protect the church of our common Lord, without giving the preference to any denomination of Christians above the rest, in such a manner that all ecclesiastical persons whatsoever shall enjoy the full, free, and unquestioned liberty of discharging every part of their sacred functions, without violence or danger" (6.129). The distinctive American understanding of the separation of church and state became a confessional principle.

Other significant amendments came into the Confession in 1903, when the northern church, in reaction against interpretations of the Westminster standards that emphasized divine sovereignty at the expense of human freedom, added articles on "The Holy Spirit" (6.183–.186) and "The Gospel of the Love of God and Missions" (6.187–.190).[6] The church did not alter the original Confession's statement that God has predestined the elect to everlasting life and foreordained all other humans to everlasting death (6.016), but it argued that these assertions had to be held "in harmony with the doctrine of [God's] love to all mankind, his gift of his Son to be the propitiation for the sins of the whole world, and his readiness to bestow his saving grace on all who seek it. . . . God desires not the death of any sinner. . . . No man is condemned except on the ground of his sin" (6.192). The southern church later adopted these changes too and—further emphasizing their importance—placed them immediately after the articles on Christ rather than at the end of the Confession.[7]

In the 1950s, both churches, again responding to changes in church and society, made amendments to the Confession's article on "Marriage and Divorce." In the 1960s, the northern church formed a theological commission to consider additional revisions to the Confession, in response to new understandings of biblical authority and interpretation and to the turbulent social changes that American society was experiencing. The result was a new kind of conversation with the Westminster Standards.

Rather than making more piecemeal amendments to Westminster, the church adopted a contemporary statement of faith, the Confession of 1967. "C67," as it came to be called, did not claim to be a comprehensive system of doctrine in the spirit of the Westminster Confession of Faith. However, in calling the church "to that unity in confession and mission which is required of disciples today" (9.05), C67 implicitly asserted that the Westminster Standards were no longer an adequate confessional basis for the church's life. Some critics of Westminster went so far as to accuse it of having fallen away from the vitality of Calvin's theology.[8] Along with the adoption of the new confession, the church created a *Book of Confessions* that included representative documents from all ages of the church. No longer would the church's confessional conversation take place within the parameters of the Westminster Standards alone; rather, Westminster was set into conversation with seven other confessional documents (and an eighth, with the adoption of A Brief Statement of Faith in 1991).

The Westminster divines had been in conversation with the church's confessional heritage. *The Book of Confessions* now altered the terms of the confessional conversation. The church would no longer attempt to adjudicate theological differences by amending Westminster but, rather, agreed to let these differences stand. The emphasis no longer fell on one set of standards for one church but, rather, on a diversity of theologies and the need to submit all of them to the continuing, reforming work of the Holy Spirit, "which enables the church to hear the Word of God through Scripture in every new time and situation."[9]

A Conversation with the Church Today

The church's conversation about the status of *The Book of Confessions* includes continuing debate about the authority of the Westminster Standards. At the time of its adoption, *The Book of Confessions* included only two of the Westminster documents, the Confession of Faith and the Shorter Catechism. Critics had rejected the Larger Catechism as too ponderous and moralistic, especially in its detailed explication of the Ten Commandments. Nevertheless, as one of the confessional standards of the southern church, the Larger Catechism again became a Presbyterian confessional standard at the time of reunion in 1983. For better or worse, the Westminster Standards today represent nearly half of the material in *The Book of Confessions*, and they call for our thoughtful consideration.

In this essay, we can only begin a conversation with the Westminster Standards. Three of their insights, however, are of particular interest for the church today: the authority and interpretation of *Scripture*, the nature and process of *sanctification*, and the eternal destiny of the *self*. Whether we finally agree or disagree with the particular positions that Westminster stakes out, its confession and catechisms can help us ask better questions of ourselves. We will see along the way that the three Westminster documents hold a conversation among themselves. Each was composed for a different purpose: the Confession of Faith as a comprehensive statement of belief, the Larger Catechism to guide catechetical preaching, and the Shorter Catechism for children. Each of them has a slightly different emphasis and interest within a shared theology.

SCRIPTURE

How Should the Conversation Begin?

Two people meet on the street. Will they exchange pleasantries or berate each other? Will they speak of noisy neighbors, international politics, the weather, or changes in American society? They can begin with any one of these topics and later take up the others, but the starting point is significant. Where they begin their conversation says something about who they are and what they care about. Even their opening words are revealing: "Hi," "Hello," "Good morning," "Pardon me," or "Hey, get out of my way!" How we begin a conversation communicates formality or informality, friendship or enmity, a connection to the past or an opening to the future.

Similarly, the composition of every creed, confession, and catechism requires a decision about which article of belief should come first, for the church's faith does not have a single starting point. Questions in one area inevitably lead to questions in another. Matters of Christology (the doctrine of Christ), for example, soon lead to ecclesiology (the doctrine of the church): The church is the body of Christ, and who Christ is determines what the church is. Alternatively, we can begin with ecclesiology and move to Christology: Because we are a church, we want to know more about the One to whom we belong. No order of confessional articles is perfect, no order is without possible merit. Nevertheless, how a confessional conversation begins says something about the particular concerns of an era.

The ancient creeds have a trinitarian structure: They begin with God the Father Almighty, move to God the Son, and conclude with God the Holy Spirit. From the outset they say clearly who the Christian God is and how the Scriptures testify to him. In contrast, the three twentieth-century documents in *The Book of Confessions* start with Jesus Christ, emphasizing that in Christ God has revealed himself to humanity most clearly. The Reformation confessions adopt yet other starting points. The first article of the Scots Confession proclaims God as the only one whom we must serve and worship, to whom we must cleave, and in whom we must trust. This doxology to the one true God vividly reminds us that earthly rulers must never command our ultimate allegiance. The opening words of the Heidelberg Catechism have a very different tone: "What is your only comfort, in life and in death? That I belong—body and soul, in life and in death—not to myself but to my faithful Savior, Jesus Christ, who at the cost of his own blood has fully paid for all my sins." For Heidelberg, all theology flows from the personal assurance of salvation in Christ.

The Second Helvetic Confession and the Westminster Confession of Faith begin with an article on Scripture. Scripture did not command separate attention in the ancient creeds, for they were understood as summaries of the biblical story beginning with creation ("We believe in one God, the Father, the Almighty, maker of heaven and earth" [1.1; cf. 2.1]) and proceeding to the end of time ("We look for the resurrection of the dead, and the life of the world to come" [1.3; cf. 2.3]). Where the Nicene Creed does speak explicitly of the

Scriptures, it links them to Christ ("On the third day he rose again in accordance with the Scriptures" [1.2]) and to the Holy Spirit ("who has spoken through the prophets" [1.3]).

The Reformers believed that the authority of Scripture had become obscured, however. They reacted against the claims of the Catholic Church that it alone could rightly interpret the Bible, and they worried that the Scriptures had suffered neglect at its hands. The great Protestant motto *sola scriptura*—Scripture alone—declared that the church does not stand above the Bible but beneath it; that it is given not only to the church's authoritative teachers but also to every member of the church; and that it is more than a record of the church's past, for it is the means by which God speaks a living Word to the church today. Reformation leaders translated the Bible into the language of the people, promoted literacy so that the people could read the Scriptures for themselves, and trained ministers to preach and teach the Word. The church's life was to revolve around the Scriptures and their testimony to God's gracious purposes in Jesus Christ.

By placing an article on Scripture at the beginning, the Second Helvetic and the Westminster Confessions emphatically affirm these Reformation insights. The Scriptures should guide the church's life, and its confession of faith should flow from the biblical witness. Whether we speak of the Trinity, God's self-revelation in Jesus Christ, God's authority above all principalities and powers, or personal assurance of faith, everything that we know and say must be based on the authoritative testimony of the Bible. By putting Scripture first, the Second Helvetic and the Westminster Confessions tell us that unless the biblical foundations are secure, the house of faith will eventually totter and fall.

Westminster makes these foundations especially firm. Whereas the Second Helvetic Confession merely refers to the "canonical Scriptures" (5.001), Westminster lists each book of the Old and New Testaments (6.002). The Second Helvetic Confession notes that the apocryphal books are not of canonical authority but have been used profitably by the church (5.009); Westminster dismisses them altogether, arguing that they "are of no authority in the Church of God, nor to be any otherwise approved, or made use of, than other human writings" (6.003). Westminster makes clear from the outset that Scripture is God's gift to fallen humanity; there is no better place to begin a conversation about God and our lives before God.

Inspired, Infallible, and Inerrant?

Critics have sometimes accused Westminster of setting the stage for an incipient fundamentalism that treats the Bible as a collection of inspired, infallible, and inerrant propositions, as though Christians must simply accept the Bible, no questions asked—"God said it. I believe it. That settles it." *Inspiration* refers to the idea that the words of Scripture are not merely human but divine, the work of the Holy Spirit. God "breathed" these words into speech. *Infallibility* emphasizes that the Scriptures are authoritative in every matter that they address, including history and science. If the Bible says that God created the world in seven days, it means seven days—likewise if it says that Moses really parted the Red Sea and Jesus actually walked on water.[10] *Inerrancy* refers to the notion that the Scriptures are without error; there are no internal contradictions, and all parts harmonize. Inspiration, infallibility, and inerrancy are all ways of saying that the Bible is utterly reliable in every respect, having authority greater than any other book.

In the nineteenth and early twentieth centuries, some defenders of inspiration, infallibility, and inerrancy appealed to Westminster's doctrine of Scripture. Among them were such theological giants as Charles Hodge and Benjamin B. Warfield, professors at Princeton Theological Seminary. Westminster states, "The Old Testament in Hebrew (which was the native language of the people of God of old), and the New Testament in Greek (which at the time of the writing of it was most generally known to the nations), being immediately inspired by God, and by his singular care and providence kept pure in all ages, are therefore authentical" (6.008). The Princeton school built on Westminster by arguing that the "original autographs" of the Scriptures were without error. Any apparent errors in our Bibles today, any discrepancies between ancient manuscripts, were the result of scribal errors that occurred as the Scriptures were passed down from one generation to the next. The Princeton school believed that if we could find the original Hebrew and Greek manuscripts, all problems would be cleared up. Unfortunately, they acknowledged, the original manuscripts have been lost to the ages, but minor errors and discrepancies in the received biblical texts should not undermine our confidence that Scripture is ultimately of God.

But there are other ways of looking at Westminster, and a different conversation is possible. The Confession of Faith does affirm that the Scriptures are inspired of God, but it is cautious in its references to infallibility and does not use the term "inerrancy" at all. It never asserts that the Scriptures are historically or scientifically reliable in every detail, and it never asks that we accept the Scriptures "on faith," without struggle or interpretation. Rather, the Confession speaks of inspiration in order to refer us to Scripture's reliability as "the rule of faith and life" (6.002). The Bible's primary interest is not giving us historical or scientific information. Rather, it tells us who God is and who we are as God's creation and children; it is concerned with matters of salvation (6.001; cf. 6.006). The Scriptures are "authentical" in the sense that "in all controversies *of religion* the Church is finally to appeal unto them" (6.008, my emphasis). The Bible refers first of all to spiritual realities; it tells us of God's relationship to humankind and invites us to know the living God for ourselves today.

The Confession of Faith mentions "infallibility" three times. The first reference is to Scripture's "infallible truth" (6.005). The Confession immediately clarifies that this truth refers to "all things necessary for [God's] own glory [and] man's salvation, faith, and life" (6.006). The second reference is to "the infallible rule of interpretation of Scripture, [which] is the Scripture itself" (6.009). In the end, we should test every interpretation of the Bible against the Bible itself, not against church tradition or personal perspective. As the Confession reminds us, "When there is a question about the true and full sense of any scripture . . . , it may be searched and known by other places that speak more clearly" (6.009). This clarity emerges when we approach the Bible not as a collection of disconnected quotations from which we pick or choose for our own purposes but, rather, as the grand story of God's relations with the world from the beginning to the end of time, and of God's work in the history of Israel and the church. The sure rule of biblical interpretation is to keep the larger message of salvation in sight.

The third reference to infallibility occurs in the 1903 amendment on "The Holy Spirit": "By [the Holy Spirit] the prophets were moved to speak the Word of God, and all the writers of the Holy Scriptures inspired to record infallibly the mind and will of God" (6.184; cf. 6.052). These words reflect the position of the Princeton school, but even here the confession makes it clear that the principal work of the Spirit is to set forth salvation in Jesus Christ: "[The Spirit] prepares the way for [the gospel], accompanies it with his persuasive power, and urges its message upon the reason and conscience of men" (6.184). Westminster's doctrine of Scripture cannot be separated from its understanding of Christ, the Spirit, and God's covenantal relationship with humanity. Similarly, the church today will not settle matters of faith once and for all by demanding that people simply accept the Scriptures as God's Word. Rather, the nature of biblical authority and interpretation asks us to enter a wider theological conversation about God's will and work.

Inward Illumination

For Westminster, as for Reformed theology more generally, the work of the Holy Spirit has less to do with guaranteeing the infallibility and inerrancy of every jot and tittle of Scripture than with opening our ears, eyes, and minds to receive God's living Word in the Bible. At times, the church has tried to establish the authority of Scripture by making arguments for its historical veracity, its literary power, or its continuing moral influence. But, as the Confession of Faith notes, such external proofs are insufficient. Ultimately, "the inward illumination of the Spirit of God [is] necessary for the saving understanding of such things as are revealed in the Word" (6.006). Without the work of the Holy

Spirit, people may find in Scripture interesting information about ancient cultures or stories of enduring literary value, but the Bible will be a dead letter, not God's living Word. If Scripture is to change us, if it is to call us into relationship with the God who loves us and forgives us, God himself must open us to its words.

The Reformed tradition has sometimes given liturgical expression to this insight by including a prayer for illumination in Lord's Day worship. Even today, Presbyterians pray, "Lord, open our hearts and minds by the power of your Holy Spirit, that as the scriptures are read and your Word is proclaimed, we may hear with joy what you say to us today."[11] Similarly, the Westminster Directory of Worship directed the pastor to pray "that the Lord . . . would graciously please to poure out the Spirit of Grace . . . and that the Lord would circumcise the cares and hearts of the Hearers, to heare, love, and receive with meeknesse the ingrafted Word."[12] As the Larger Catechism notes, it is only the Spirit of God that "maketh the reading, [and] especially the preaching of the Word, an effectual means of [salvation]" (7.265).

Both Westminster catechisms elaborate on the work of the Spirit. According to the Larger Catechism, "the Holy Scriptures are to be read with an high and reverent esteem of them" (7.267). We should receive them not only in Lord's Day worship but also by ourselves "and with [our] families" (7.266). The Shorter Catechism adds that we must attend to God's living Word with "diligence, preparation, and prayer; receive it with faith and love; lay it up in our hearts; and practice it in our lives" (7.090). The Spirit leads us into regular, disciplined reading and interpretation of the Bible in order to build us up "in holiness and comfort, through faith unto salvation" (7.089). We can be in conversation with the Scriptures only if we spend time with them and believe that they have a Word for us. Of course we bring questions to the text, but when the Spirit illumines us, the Scriptures also question and redirect us. The authority of the Bible is most clear when the lives of its readers and hearers are shaped by the way of Jesus Christ and the fruit of the Spirit.

Humanity's Chief End

Westminster's position on biblical authority and interpretation stirred debate in the twentieth century. One argument for composing the Confession of 1967 was that Westminster was no longer adequate in light of developments in biblical scholarship. Westminster points us to God's authoritative revelation in Scripture while C67, in contrast, argues that "the one sufficient revelation of God is Jesus Christ, . . . to whom the Holy Spirit bears unique and authoritative witness through the Holy Scriptures" (9.27). Westminster emphasizes divine inspiration, but C67 reminds us that the Scriptures "are nevertheless the words of men [and] reflect views of life, history, and the cosmos which were then current" (9.29).

Nevertheless, C67 is less an alternative to Westminster than a conversation with it. Both Westminster and C67 relate biblical authority and interpretation to life in Christ; both insist that the Bible is the church's book, not a private devotional manual; and both acknowledge our dependence on the Holy Spirit when we read Scripture (see 9.30). They do not treat these matters in identical ways, yet they are inseparable conversation partners. Conferring with both helps us to hear God's Word to us today.

Every conversation has to start somewhere, if only because no one can say everything at once. The Westminster divines wanted to be true to their Reformation heritage by placing their discussion of Scripture at the beginning of the Confession, believing that all their work rested on biblical foundations. Only reluctantly did they accede to Parliament's request that they add explicit scriptural proofs to the Confession and the catechisms, because they were certain that the biblical quality of the documents was clear enough! For Westminster, the point of beginning with Scripture is not to quote it, but to open us to the living God.

Westminster's insight becomes clearer if we consider all three documents together. Only the Confession of Faith places an article on Scripture at the beginning. The catechisms have a prior concern, namely, in the well-known question and answer of the Shorter Catechism: "What is the chief end of man? Man's chief end is to glorify God, and to enjoy him forever" (7.001; cf. 7.111). Only then does the catechism ask, "What rule hath God given to direct us how we may glorify and enjoy him?" answering, "The Word of God which is contained in the Scriptures of the Old and New Testaments is the only rule to direct us how we may glorify and enjoy him" (7.002; cf. 7.112, 7.115). A church that listens to Westminster's internal conversation will refuse to argue about biblical authority and interpretation in the abstract. We will not use the Bible simply to score points for one church agenda or another, nor will we try to end debate with the words, "But the Bible says . . ." Rather, we will ask again and again how God is calling us in Scripture to glorify and enjoy him forever; we will let the Bible move us to worship and adoration.

SANCTIFICATION

Where Will the Conversation Take Us?

Even a free and wide-ranging conversation tends to address certain concerns more than others. My conversations with my mother revolve around our everyday lives, while my conversations with students focus on course requirements or preparation for ministry. Certain colleagues and I talk only about our fields of expertise, but with friends I also share personal joys and concerns. My wife and I talk about many things, but each conversation focuses on something particular that we want or need to talk about.

No confession of faith can say everything. Each reacts to a particular crisis in the church, or speaks to a particular need. The Nicene Creed developed in the context of the christological controversies of the early church. The Apostles' Creed was used in baptismal instruction. The Reformation confessions clarified the freedom of the gospel over against the medieval church. The Theological Declaration of Barmen emphasized Christ's lordship in opposition to the claims of a totalitarian state. The Confession of 1967 and A Brief Statement of Faith lifted up issues of reconciliation and social justice distinctive to American society in the late twentieth century.

Although the Westminster Standards offer a comprehensive vision of the Christian faith, they give special attention to the Christian life. How can we grow more fully into our chief end, to glorify and enjoy God forever? At the time of the Reformation, Martin Luther reclaimed the centrality of justification by faith alone. Only God's grace offered in Jesus Christ makes us right with God, Luther declared; all other efforts to prove ourselves in God's sight fall short and entangle us in prideful self-assertion. Calvin affirmed Luther's insight but added an emphasis on sanctification, the process of growth in faith and fuller appropriation of God's grace. The Westminster Standards build on these Reformation insights by carefully explicating the order of salvation (*ordo salutis*): effectual calling, justification, adoption, sanctification, saving faith, repentance unto life, good works, perseverance, and assurance of grace and salvation (6.064–.100; cf. 7.031–.036 and 7.177–.191). The two catechisms add rich material related especially to sanctification.

Baptism and Sanctification

In the Reformed tradition, baptism marks the beginning of a journey as we "enter into an open and professed engagement to be wholly and only the Lord's" (7.275). Baptism is neither a ticket to heaven nor a magic charm to keep us out of harm's way. Rather, we must work at sustaining the identity that baptism confers on us: We are sons and daughters of the triune God. The Larger Catechism speaks of "the needful but much neglected duty of improving our Baptism . . . *all our life long*" (7.277, my emphasis). Despite our baptism, we easily forget who we are. We are tempted to assume false identities, whether personally imposed or socially defined. We wear the label "Christian," yet resist the new life in Christ; we live by self-interest rather than love; we lose our temper when we don't get our way; we fail to trust that God will provide; and we seek the world's approbation rather than God's will.

According to an ancient image, the church is a pilgrim people. We gaze upon the promised land, but only from afar. The Christian life never takes a straight and direct path; we regularly falter, lose our way, and resist God's guidance. Yet God seeks us out again and again, calling us to repent and return to him. Calvin argued that we never achieve holiness in this life, that only Christ is holy. But he was certain that we could make progress, for God's Spirit stirs us to more faithful living.[13] The Westminster Shorter and Longer Catechisms speak in particular of Word, sacraments, and prayer as "outward and ordinary means whereby Christ communicateth to us the benefits of redemption" (7.088; cf. 7.264). Disciplined use of these means of grace helps us grow in the life of faith; in them, we draw strength "from the death and resurrection of Christ, . . . for the mortifying of sin, and quickening of grace" (7.277).

The Commandments and Sanctification

Word, sacraments, and prayer strengthen us for the journey. We also need a compass and a map that describes the route that God asks us to take. The Reformed tradition has looked especially to the Ten Commandments, not as a moral checklist that pronounces us faithful or faithless, but as a description of the way of life that God makes possible for us in Jesus Christ. By telling us who we really are by virtue of our baptism, the law points us in the right direction and stirs us to action.

The Heidelberg Catechism is instructive. It treats the Ten Commandments not in its first section ("Man's Misery") or in its second ("Man's Redemption") but in its third and concluding section, titled "Thankfulness." We do good works "so that with our whole life we may show ourselves grateful to God for his goodness and that he may be glorified through us" (4.086). Similarly, the Larger Catechism says that the law is of special use to the regenerate, "to provoke them to more thankfulness, and to express the same in their greater care to conform themselves thereunto as the rule of their obedience" (7.207). In promoting sanctification, the law fulfills what the Reformed tradition has called its third and principal use. Beyond its role in accusing us of sin (first or spiritual use) or restraining us from evil (second or civil use), the law is a good guide for the life of a redeemed people.

In line with the wider Christian tradition, Reformed theology has treated the Decalogue as a comprehensive summary of the new life (characterized by love of God and love of neighbor) into which our baptism calls us. Among the rules for interpreting the law, the Larger Catechism lists three that are of particular interest. First, each commandment is a broad category, not just a narrowly focused behavior. Second, each commandment reaches into "the under-standing, will, affections, and all other powers of the soul; as well as words, works, and gestures," that is to say, it aims at shaping us in our inner attitudes as much as our external behaviors. Third, "where a duty is commanded, the contrary sin is forbidden; and where a sin is forbidden, the contrary duty is commanded" (7.209). By broadening and deepening each commandment, the Westminster catechisms identify a comprehensive set of practices and disci-plines of faith at which we must work over a lifetime.

Take the sixth commandment: "You shall not murder." First, as a broad cat-egory, the commandment forbids whatever would harm our neighbor, includ-ing "provoking words; oppression, quarreling, striking, wounding, and whatsoever else tends to the destruction of the life of any." Next, reaching into our inner attitudes, it forbids "sinful anger, hatred, envy, [and] desire of revenge." Finally, as a negative—"Do not kill"—it also implies a positive, to do everything that you can to preserve life (7.245–.246; cf. 7.068–.069). The Larger Catechism further emphasizes the sanctifying use of the law by listing the positive duties of the commandment *prior* to the sins forbidden; in other words, it first identifies the good at which we must and can work over a life-time, before it warns us of the evils to avoid.

In interpreting the commandments, the Larger Catechism gives us more than a wooden list of dos and don'ts. Rather, it points us to what Barmen would later call "God's mighty claim upon our whole life . . . for a free, grateful ser-vice to his creatures" (8.14). The commandment to honor father and mother asks us to have regard for "the dignity and worth of [every individual], in giv-ing honor to go one before another, and to rejoice in each other's gifts and advancement" (7.241). The eighth commandment, "Do not steal," has social justice implications: "truth, faithfulness, and justice in contracts and com-merce between man and man; rendering to everyone his due . . . and an endeavor by all just and lawful means to procure, preserve, and further the wealth and outward estate of others" (7.251). The catechism thus yields rich suggestions for the Christian life that we should explore today.

Predestination and Sanctification

Sanctification assumes human effort, yet Westminster asserts that God has ordained everything. If God has already taken care of our salvation, are we lit-tle more than puppets? Can we really *grow* in faith? The Confession of Faith warns that the "high mystery of predestination is to be handled with special prudence and care" (6.021), and the 1903 amendments reflect a nagging con-cern that belief in predestination can result in fatalism and complacency. Nev-ertheless, the Confession sees no contradiction between predestination and sanctification. On the contrary, growth in the Christian life is evidence that God has elected us, and "so shall this doctrine afford matter of praise, reverence, and admiration of God; and of humility, diligence, and abundant consolation to all that sincerely obey the gospel" (6.021).

Westminster sets forth the doctrine of predestination as a source of comfort: If I faithfully use the outward means of grace and do the good that God commands, I will come to deeper assurance of my salvation. This self-confident, activist spirit continues to characterize Reformed churches today. Reformed Christians do not always agree on the specifics of what God wills, but they do not doubt that God calls us to what the *Book of Order* calls the great ends of the church: "the proclamation of the gospel for the salvation of humankind; the shelter, nurture, and spiritual fellowship of the children of God; the maintenance of divine worship; the preservation of the truth; the promotion of social righteousness; and the exhibition of the Kingdom of Heaven to the world."[14] Nevertheless, at times in Reformed history the doctrine of predestination has also fueled anxious introspection and self-righteous zealotry.[15] This is a point at which the church's conversation must continue.

THE ETERNAL DESTINY OF THE SELF

Parting Words

Sometimes the last words matter the most. As two dear friends take leave, they promise to see each other again soon. A father drives a daughter to college, and his last words to her are filled with hope and anticipation, sorrow and pride. A minister retiring after many years of faithful service expresses her gratitude for the privilege of Christian service. Every conversation in this life comes to an end, but the end can be filled with the anticipation of new beginnings. It need not be only an ending but can also be a look into the future.

Every confession also comes to an end. The church has said everything that it knows to say in a particular situation. But the ending is as important as the beginning. The final words of a confession can speak to Christians' deepest hopes, even as the confessional conversation draws to a close. The ancient creeds point us to the resurrection of the body and the life everlasting. The Scots Confession anticipates God's coming day of judgment and calls on him even now to confound his enemies and to give his servants "strength to speak thy Word with boldness" (3.25). Heidelberg explicates the "Amen" that concludes the Lord's Prayer and its ascription of praise, "For thine is the kingdom and the power and the glory forever" (4.129). All of these concluding statements touch on eschatology, the church's teachings about the end of time and the fulfillment of God's ultimate purposes.

The Second Helvetic Confession is an exception, for its final article is devoted to civil magistracy. An eschatological note is present even here, however, for human government is seen as a faint yet faithful reflection of the kingdom of justice and peace that God will someday establish. Each of the twentieth-century documents also points us to God's coming kingdom and the work that God has given us to do as we wait. Barmen speaks of the church's commission to proclaim "the message of the free grace of God to all people," for "lo, I am with you always, to the close of the age" (8.25–.26). C67 declares, "Already God's reign is present as a ferment in the world . . . [and] with an urgency born of this hope, the church applies itself to present tasks and strives for a better world" (9.54–.55). A Brief Statement of Faith also calls on us to serve God "even as we watch for God's new heaven and new earth" (10.4).

The two Westminster catechisms, like Heidelberg, conclude with an explication of the closing words of the Lord's Prayer. Prior to the 1903 amendments, the final article of the Confession of Faith addressed the final judgment and ended with the words, "Because [we] know not at what hour the Lord will come . . . may [we] be ever prepared to say, 'Come, Lord Jesus, come quickly.' Amen" (6.182). At the end of time, we will no longer see in a glass darkly, but face to face. Knowing God, even as God knows us, we will finally achieve our life purpose perfectly and completely: "to glorify God, and to enjoy him forever." The end thus sends us back to the beginning. God created us to glorify and enjoy him forever, the Scriptures call us back to this way of life, and our daily pilgrimage into ever greater holiness deepens our capacity for it. Yet only at the end, as the confessional conversation finally falls silent, is the veil completely lifted; the church militant will become the church triumphant, filled with sheer glory and joy.

To Glorify and Enjoy God Forever

As we look back over the Westminster Standards, we can see that glorifying and enjoying God has three distinct stages, with growing intensification.

First, our baptism calls us to live in the way that will be ours for eternity. The Larger Catechism tells us that even here and now we receive "the first fruits of glory with Christ . . . [and] enjoy . . . God's love, peace of conscience, joy in the Holy Ghost, and hope of glory" (7.193). The traditional words of the church's eucharistic prayers, still used today, also make this point: In gathering to praise God, we join "with choirs of angels, with prophets, apostles, and martyrs, and with the faithful of every time and place, who forever sing to the glory of [God's] name."[16]

Second, because we always live with the certainty of death, we may doubt that we can really trust God in life and in death. Westminster calls us to see life's conclusion differently. For the believer, death is a deepening of our capacity to glorify and enjoy God. Upon death, soul and body separate. As the body returns to dust, the souls of the righteous return to God and are received into heaven, where they "behold the face of God in light and glory" (6.177; cf. 7.037, 7.196).

Third, this taste of eternal life is incomplete until the end of time and the day of judgment, when the body will be resurrected and reunited to the soul—the "self-same" body, yet "with different qualities" (6.178; cf. 7.197). The bodies of the just will be made spiritual, incorruptible, and "like to [Christ's] glorious body" (7.197). When the final judgment takes place, the righteous will again be "received into heaven, where they shall be fully and forever freed from all sin and misery; filled with inconceivable joy; [and] made perfectly holy and happy both in body and soul" (7.200).

Westminster thus identifies two stages of life after death. We are first a soul without a body, and then a soul and a body together. But if the soul already glorifies and enjoys God immediately after death, what is gained by later receiving a resurrection body? Perhaps simply this: God did not create humans as disembodied souls, but as soul *and* body. Moreover, Christ has redeemed both soul and body, so we are destined to glorify and enjoy God with both.[17] The way of life that believers practice on earth comes to fulfillment only at the end of time, as body and soul are reunited, and as all God's people are gathered in praise and adoration. The delights of heaven that the soul enjoys after the body's death can be deepened; only in the body does the soul finally receive "the immediate vision and fruition of God the Father, of our Lord Jesus Christ, and of the Holy Spirit, to all eternity" (7.200). The resurrection body completes our life before God.

Westminster also applies this threefold schema to those who fail to glorify and enjoy God: First, "The sense of God's revenging wrath, horror of conscience, and a fearful expectation of judgment, are to the wicked the beginning of the torment which they shall endure after death" (7.193). Second, after death, the souls of the wicked already experience "torments and utter darkness" (6.177). Third, when the world ends, "the bodies of the wicked shall be raised up in dishonor" (7.197; cf. 6.179), and the reprobate will again be "cast out from the favorable presence of God . . . into hell, to be punished with unspeakable torments both of body and soul" (7.199–.200; cf. 6.181). The life that we have to eternity is already foreshadowed here and now.

Amen and Amen

The notion that God has elected some to salvation but foreordained others (most?) to damnation deeply disturbs many Christians today. Here again the church may find itself arguing vigorously with the Westminster Standards. No confession, including Westminster, should have the last word. Only God has the final word, and we seek God's living Word as we attend again to the witness of the Scriptures. Nevertheless, as every Presbyterian minister, elder, and deacon has promised at ordination, our reading of Scripture should be "continually guided by our confessions," which are "authentic and reliable expositions of what Scripture leads us to believe and do."[18] To be a Christian is to be a theologian, one who thinks about the faith with the help of the wider church, past and present, in order to live the faith more deeply. Theology thrives on discussion and debate, including pointed conversation with the confessions and reflection on their differences with our insights.

In the end, theology should also lead us to worship, and confession of faith should lead us to praise and petition. Anticipation of the last things belongs to the life of prayer, in which we rehearse even now our eternal purpose to glorify and enjoy God forever:

> [We] join praises, ascribing to God alone eternal sovereignty, omnipotency, and glorious excellency; in regard whereof, as he is able and willing to help us, so we by faith are emboldened to plead with him that he would, and quietly to rely upon him that he will, fulfill our requests. And to testify our desires and assurance, we say, "Amen." (7.306)

NOTES

1. Some of the reforming groups came to be known as Puritans because of their efforts to purify the church.
2. See, for example, Luther's catechisms from the early sixteenth century, Calvin's Geneva Catechism, the Heidelberg Catechism, and the Roman Catechism of the Catholic Church, composed at the end of that century for the Council of Trent.
3. *The Constitution of the Presbyterian Church (U.S.A.)*, Part II, *Book of Order* (Louisville, KY: Office of the General Assembly, 2004), G-1.0304.
4. As one historian notes, "The Adopting Act required all ministers to accept the Westminster Confession and the Larger and Shorter Catechisms, but not categorically and verbally." Lefferts A. Loetscher, *The Broadening Church* (Philadelphia: University of Pennsylvania Press, 1954), 2.
5. See Edward A. Dowey, Jr., *A Commentary on the Confession of 1967 and an Introduction to "The Book of Confessions"* (Philadelphia: Westminster Press, 1968), 216.
6. The northern church also appended a "Declaratory Statement" (6.191ff.) to the Confession to clarify the meaning of God's eternal decrees in the Confession's third chapter.
7. Dowey, *Commentary on the Confession of 1967*, 216–17.
8. See, for example, Holmes Rolston, III, *John Calvin versus the Westminster Confession* (Richmond, VA: John Knox Press, 1972).

9. See "Confessional Nature of the Church Report," added as a preface to *The Book of Confessions* by the 209th General Assembly (1997).

10. Nevertheless, even defenders of infallibility recognize that some portions of Scripture should be understood as poetry. Not all have interpreted Genesis as scientific fact, for example.

11. *Book of Common Worship* (Louisville, KY: Westminster/John Knox Press, 1993), 60.

12. "A Directory for the Publique Worship of God, 1644," in *Liturgies of the Western Church*, ed. Bard Thompson (Philadelphia: Fortress Press, 1961), 362.

13. See John Calvin, *Institutes of the Christian Religion*, ed. John T. McNeill, trans. Ford Lewis Battles (Philadelphia: Westminster Press, 1960), 4.1.17 (LCC 2:1031). "The church is holy, then, in the sense that it is daily advancing and is not yet perfect: it makes progress from day to day, but has not reached its goal of holiness."

14. *Book of Order*, G-1.0200.

15. See, for example, Brian Gerrish, *Grace and Gratitude: The Eucharistic Theology of John Calvin* (Minneapolis: Fortress Press, 1993), 170–71.

16. *Book of Common Worship*, 70.

17. The Larger Catechism confidently asserts that "even in death [bodies] continue [to be] united to Christ" (7.196).

18. *Book of Order*, G-14.0405b.

5

A Conversation with Twentieth-Century Confessions

Margit Ernst-Habib

COBBLESTONES AND SUNRAYS

A friend of mine is pastor of a congregation in northern Germany. The church building is two hundred years old, but there is really nothing unique or extraordinary about it. Yet one thing makes the church special in my eyes. There is a wide square in front of the church that was a marketplace in former times. The square is laid out with cobblestones, some darker and others lighter, which of itself is nothing extraordinary. But when you stand in the middle of the square, you notice something unexpected. The light brown cobblestones form a pattern on the background of the darker cobblestones. Starting at the church door, the lighter stones spread out into the square like sunrays. Walking from the middle of the square toward the entrance into the church, you feel as if you are being guided by the sunrays made from stone. Inside the church, the pattern continues, leading to the center of the church: the pulpit and the table of the Lord's Supper. After the service, when you walk out of the church, the same cobblestones that led you into the church now lead you out of the church into the market square. Those two-hundred-year-old, worn-out cobblestones that have gathered the congregation around Word and sacrament now send the people out into the world.

If somebody were to ask me what use confessions of faith may have for a contemporary Christian community, I would begin my answer by using this church in northern Germany and its sunrays made from cobblestones as a metaphor. "Cobblestones and sunrays" may help us draw closer to declarations of faith that sometimes seem only to be historical documents to be examined and studied rather than confessions of faith that touch the heart of Christian faith and conviction today. Those cobblestones in northern Germany, laid out in a pattern of sunrays by generations long before us, have taught me something about our conversation with the Theological Declaration of Barmen (1934), the Confession of 1967 (C67), and A Brief Statement of Faith (1991). In order to find the purpose these confessions still serve in the formation of faith and faithfulness, I want to look at them and some of the patterns they form. How and where do they guide us, like the sunrays in the market square, into the heart of the church's faith and life? But we must also ask how and where they may be "stumbling blocks" for us today rather than a smooth stone path.

CONFESSIONS WITHIN THE REFORMED TRADITION

I want to begin by discussing briefly the Reformed tradition's understanding of confessions as it is expressed within the more recent confessions. We begin with the Reformed understanding not only because it is unique within the broader family of Christian churches, but also because it is decisive for our understanding of our confessions and the ways we relate to them today. We cannot begin a good conversation with them if we do not know and understand how those documents would like to be read and confessed.

The Reformed Tradition as a "Confessing Movement"

Cobblestones are durable, but they are not made for eternity. If they no longer fulfill their purpose, they may be rearranged, added to, removed, or paved over. Cobblestones are meant to be useful, to fulfill a certain purpose—not to be looked at and admired from afar. Similarly, confessions within the Reformed tradition are meant to be used, not to be admired, and certainly not to be taken for granted or buried. Reformed attention to confessions and confession making is unique within the family of Christian denominations. Reformed churches never stopped writing new confessions for new times and places, as The Book of Confessions demonstrates.[1] They do so because of the famous principle "Reformed but always being reformed according to the Word of God," which means that God's Word is the reason, ground, and principle for the ongoing confession of faith that shapes the ongoing reformation of the church. As the preface to A Brief Statement of Faith explains:

> No confession of faith looks merely to the past; every confession seeks to cast the light of a priceless heritage on the needs of the present moment, and so to shape the future. Reformed confessions, in particular, when necessary even reform the tradition itself in the light of the Word of God.

There is a sense in which we could call the Reformed tradition a "continually confessing movement." We are reminded of the old designation for different church traditions as "confessions" (with a focus on the act and content of what is confessed) rather than "denominations" (which simply refers to the name of a tradition). A church of the Reformed tradition is per se a confessing church—just as any Christian community that confesses "Jesus Christ is Lord!"[2] It has always been a hallmark of the Reformed tradition that it expects the Holy Spirit to guide churches in every place and every time, leading them to confess anew what it means to confess the lordship of Christ in this time and this place. The Reformed imperative to confess the faith is made explicit in two twentieth-century confessions:

> Here [at the Confessional Synod of Barmen] representatives from all the German Confessional Churches met with one accord in a confession of the one Lord of the one, holy, apostolic Church. (Theological Declaration of Barmen, 8.01)

> The church confesses its faith when it bears a present witness to God's grace in Jesus Christ. In every age, the church has expressed its witness in words and deeds as the need of the time required. . . . Obedience to Jesus Christ alone identifies the one universal church and supplies the continuity of its tradition. This obedience is the ground of the church's duty and freedom to reform itself in life and doctrine as new occasions, in God's providence, may demand. (Confession of 1967, 9.01–.03)

Reformed churches have tried to remain faithful to this basic conviction by making new confessional statements when they were convinced that that is what God was asking them to do at a particular point in time.

Confessions as Subordinate Standards

As a confessing movement, the Reformed tradition puts believers in a difficult position, however. Confessions place us in the middle of a tension between *authority* and *freedom*, a tension we have to endure but that we try to get rid of all too often. As Reformed Christians, we are not free agents; our confessions claim authority over us. Their authority is not absolute, however, but rather provisional, temporary, and relative.[3] The Theological Declaration of Barmen tries to explain this tension:

> Try the spirits whether they are of God! Prove also the words of the Confessional Synod of the German Evangelical Church to see whether they agree with Holy Scripture and with the Confessions of the Fathers. If you find that we are speaking contrary to Scripture, then do not listen to us! But if you find that we are taking our stand

upon Scripture, then let no fear or temptation keep you from treading with us the path of faith and obedience to the Word of God, in
order that God's people be of one mind upon earth. (8.04)

As with the Confession of 1967, Barmen makes explicit reference to obedience to the Word of God, which limits the authority of all confessions. Before
we can discuss the authority confessions have over us, we have to understand
the authority confessions themselves are subject to. The Reformed tradition
has always maintained that no confession can take the place of God's Word and
claim authority that is rightly only God's. Confessions are not the Word of God;
they lead us to the Word of God, just as the cobblestones lead the people into
the church, toward pulpit and table, and then out of the church again. A confession is not an end in itself. As the preface to the Confession of 1967 declares:

> Confessions and declarations are subordinate standards in the church,
> subject to the authority of Jesus Christ, the Word of God, as the Scrip-
> tures bear witness to him. No one type of confession is exclusively
> valid, no one statement is irreformable. (9.03)

It is important to note that C67 calls confessions *subordinate* standards, but
it is equally important to note that they are called *standards*. They are subordinate because they are always subject to the one Word of God: Jesus Christ,
as he is attested for us in Holy Scripture (Barmen, 8.11). One might ask, then,
why we need confessions at all. Is the Bible not enough? Can't we simply read
Scripture and follow its guidelines? There is a sense in which this question
would have to be answered "Yes." Together with other Protestant churches,
Reformed churches affirm the Reformation axiom *sola scriptura*—Scripture
alone. Yet confessions perform a particular service; they could be understood
as "go-betweens, intermediate between the Scripture and contemporary life
and language."[4] Confessions are not substitutes for Scripture, but rather a primary commentary on Scripture. While the confessions do not do away with
our responsibility to Scripture, we enter into Scripture by a way that is "con-
fessionally determined."[5] Although Scripture is the primary background and
source against which we have to test any confession, it is not the only one. The
Holy Spirit has spoken to the Christian church many times before, and the
Christian church has answered prior to today. Therefore, we also have to test
any one confession against other confessional statements.

Confessions understand themselves as *subordinate* standards, but it is equally
important to note that they nevertheless claim to be *standards*. They claim that
they have found themselves in a situation where the Holy Spirit is asking the
church to speak a new word, or to interpret an ancient one for a new time and
place. They claim that this new word is not just any word, but the word that
leads us the right way, the word that leads us to the one Word. Reformed con-

fessions claim to stand upon Scripture and other confessional standards. If we find this claim to be reliable, then we are urged to "let no fear or temptation keep [us] from treading . . . the path of faith and obedience to the Word of God" (8.04). If these conditions are fulfilled, then the confessions hold authority over us. Then we are called to trust them to teach and guide us in both our communal and individual life of faith.

Between Freedom and Authority

The individual believer and the community of believers are placed in a difficult position. On the one hand, our confessions claim authority over our whole life. On the other hand, we have to make sure that they do not stand against God, the Scripture, and other confessions, and we have the duty to decide over and over again whether we are now called to say a new word.[6] Because this is not an easy position for the church and the individual believer to be in, people who cannot stand the tension between freedom and authority try to find a way out of it either by giving all authority to the confessions (or rather, their favorite parts of selected confessions), or by simply ignoring the confessions' existence if they do not suit their purposes. Actually, there are times we all pick and choose what we like in the confessions, and times we all claim vague authority for what we are doing as the "true Reformed way." Yet both ways of dealing with the confessions are not really Reformed, for they try to escape the confessional tension between authority and freedom.

All three twentieth-century confessions explicitly refer to this understanding. The Theological Declaration of Barmen, the Confession of 1967, and A Brief Statement of Faith are clear that they are only cobblestones that act as sunrays that lead us to the center of the faith, and that they themselves are *not* the center of the faith. And yet the three confessional statements are also convinced that they do their very best to lead believers to the center of faith, and that, at least at this time, other ways are misleading. Barmen explicitly names those misleading ways, and with the harsh and resolute tone of the Reformation rejects the false doctrines that oppose its positive statement about the gospel. The other two confessions are not as explicit about what they reject, although C67 does become pointed in its section on "Reconciliation in Society" (9.43–.47). Within the positive faith claims they make, however, it is easy to detect the negative, idolatrous claims they reject.

It is important here to note that all three twentieth-century confessions in *The Book of Confessions* include accompanying messages or prefaces. Within these introductions the confessions explain how they want to be read, understood, and confessed. Each one places itself in the midst of the situation in which it was written—and yet they do not want to be limited to only one time and place. They want to speak to all people in all times, because they want to proclaim Christian faith as they understand it then and there.[7]

A CONVERSATION WITH THE THEOLOGICAL DECLARATION OF BARMEN

"In every age, the church has expressed its witness in words and deeds as the need of the time required" (C67, 9.02). This may be easily said, but it expresses one of the most difficult responsibilities of every Christian community and every Christian believer. What does obedience to Jesus Christ demand from us today? What do we have to do and confess? There are particular times when the church needs to say a new word, or say an old word in a different way, when a confessional document seems to be the required answer to God's call. Of course, it has always been a difficult task to find out whether a church is in a situation where it is "forced" to confess in order to obey Christ (what theologians call a *status confessionis*).[8] A confession may be easily written and issued, yet there are many dangers to consider. Are we sure that we are not opening a door for a heresy, a wrong teaching that would lead the church in a wrong direction? Are we ready to tell those who do not adhere to our conviction that they are heretics, that they have turned away from Christ? Are we willing to accept the consequences of a step that might divide the church? And once again, is this God's call, or are we misled by our own hidden desires and ambitions?

Though our three confessions were issued in very different times, they share a common condition:

> In each time and place, there are particular problems and crises through which God calls the church to act. The church, guided by the Spirit, humbled by its own complicity and instructed by all attainable knowledge, seeks to discern the will of God and learn how to obey in these concrete situations. (C67, 9.43)

The historical situation of the Theological Declaration of Barmen is used frequently as a clear and easily understandable example of a *status confessionis*.[9] Indeed, we can learn a lot from Barmen about the issue at hand, but we also need to be careful and look closely at the situation before we can carry on a conversation with this confession of faith. More often than not, when asked about the background of Barmen, people assume that it was directed against Hitler and his brutal and murderous government, that the church came together to reject this idolatrous regime and proclaim the real truth. Yet the actual story is different. During the first years of the Nazi regime in Germany

(1933–1934), the majority in the Protestant churches stood behind Hitler and celebrated him not only as the führer in the political area, but also as their führer in the church. The so-called German Christians introduced to the church a crude mixture of pagan and pseudo-Christian elements, trying to prove that the Aryan race was superior, created by God to rule the world. They rejected everything "Jewish"—whether it was the Old Testament, huge parts of Paul's theology, or Christian pastors with Jewish ancestors. The latter issue was one of the immediate motivations for the Theological Declaration of Barmen. The church government, a majority of whose members belonged to the German Christians' church party, decided to apply the so-called Aryan paragraph in the civil service regulations (that no one could be employed who had Jewish ancestry) to the church. This not only meant the exclusion of a number of pastors from their office, it also made "race" the decisive criterion for church membership.[10] Finally, it meant that the churches were subjecting themselves to an outside power. A confessional synod met in the town of Barmen from May 29 to May 31, 1934, with representatives from all "Confessional Churches" (Reformed, Lutheran, and Union), churches that were not governed by the German Christians or that had split off from the German Christians. Following a long period of discussion, the synod accepted the text that had been prepared by Swiss theologian Karl Barth.

The Center and Source of Our Faith: Jesus Christ

It may have been the Barmen Declaration's first thesis that made me think of the cobblestones in northern Germany as a metaphor for the confessions. It definitely leads us right to the center of our faith: Jesus Christ. In 1934, the churches in Germany had to hear and confess the word of Christ again, because they were being led astray to trust and obey other "words." However, twenty-first-century Christians also have to hear and confess the one Word of God. Barmen defines who we are as Christians, not by naming first what separates believers from those who deny the good news, but by stating the good news in an almost classical formulation:

> Jesus Christ, as he is attested for us in Holy Scripture, is the one Word of God which we have to hear and which we have to trust and obey in life and in death. (8.11)

If we follow Barmen's lead, we will not identify ourselves primarily by what separates us from others, whether within our own church or within the broader Christian family. We will not first concentrate on what makes us "unique," drawing the borders of our community in order to make sure that we are "in" while those who differ from us are "out." We are not living in a

situation comparable to that of the German churches in the 1930s, yet we live
in a church fighting over many issues and living under the threat of a church
split, so we too need the call to direct our attention to the center rather than
to the borders. The first thesis of Barmen urges us to look first at the center,
to "trust and obey" this one Word of God. Turning from the borders to the
center is being obedient, but it is also trusting our God, who is more powerful in holding us together than we are in separating from each other. These
confessional cobblestones bring us together, gathering us as one community
around the foundation of our faith. They are not stones meant to build walls
between us.

But, of course, there is also a rejection within the first thesis. It is easy to
identify what the Synod of Barmen had in mind when it spoke about the "other
events and powers, figures and truths" that were acknowledged as a source of
the proclamation of the church besides the Word of God. It is more difficult to
identify the events, powers, figures, and truths that *we* substitute for the Word
of God. Barmen reminds us that the old fight against idolatry, which is a key
issue in the Reformed tradition, is not over and will not be over any time soon.
Barmen also reminds us that idols claiming our loyalty are not only found outside the church, but may be found in the middle of the church's life and proclamation. Urged by the sixth thesis, we have to examine continually whether the
church "in human arrogance" places "the Word and work of the Lord in the
service of any arbitrarily chosen desires, purposes, and plans" (8.27).

We live in a religiously plural society, not in an homogenous Christian context. Does this mean that if we want to live peacefully with other faith communities we should refrain from putting Jesus Christ in the center of our
proclamation? Is the third thesis of Barmen a stumbling stone?

> As the church of pardoned sinners, it has to testify in the midst of a
> sinful world, with its faith as with its obedience, with its message as
> with its order, that it is solely [Christ's] property. (8.17)

What does this mean for interreligious dialogue? Do other religions and faith
traditions belong to the "sinful world" and the "godless fetters of this world"
(8.14), while Christians are the chosen ones? A careful reading makes it clear
that Barmen nowhere suggests excluding or condemning those who are not
Christians. Rather, the second thesis puts *us* into the middle of the sinful world:
We are sinners, forgiven sinners to be sure, but still sinners just like the rest of
the world. Our "joyful deliverance" is not an end in itself; rather, we are delivered "for a free, grateful service" to God's whole creation (8.14). Barmen was
not meant primarily as a judgment of the world outside the church, but rather
as a judgment of a church that had gone astray, and a call to return to the center and to go from the center in service to the world. Confessing today to be

Christ's possession, then, is primarily about us and not about others. Perhaps Barmen's theses can provide a starting point for an interreligious dialogue, helping the other partner to know who we are and how we identify ourselves.

The Double Grace: God's Gift and Task for Us

Barmen's second thesis encapsulates another typically Reformed emphasis that had to be brought back to the consciousness of the German churches in the 1930s, namely, what Calvin had called the "double grace" of God:

> As Jesus Christ is God's assurance of the forgiveness of all our sins, so in the same way and with the same seriousness is he also God's mighty claim upon our whole life. (8.14)

In the German original, this twofold grace is expressed even by a careful choice of words. "Assurance" in the German text is *Zuspruch*—God speaks to us in Christ and declares our pardon. "Claim" in the German text is *Anspruch*—God speaks to us in Christ and claims our whole life. The roots of the words are the same. Thus, what Barmen tries to express is that God's one Word must be heard in a twofold way. The Christian life, according to the Reformed tradition, is marked by double grace: We are to know and trust that all our sins are forgiven in Christ; at the same time, we are called to live a life in which Christ alone is the Lord. There are no "areas of our life in which we would not belong to Jesus Christ, but to other lords" (8.15).

How can we understand Christ's lordship as double grace? We confess that Jesus Christ is Lord, but what this means for us often remains somewhere in the shadows. We continually say, "Lord, Lord," yet many of us are hard pressed to explain to ourselves and others what consequences Christ's lordship has for us. Moreover, for some Christians the designation "Lord" describes an omnipotent male ruler who would subject them and turns them into passive, obedient persons. Discomfort with the term "Lord" has led many faithful Christians to look for alternatives. Perhaps we can learn something from Barmen that will contribute to this discussion. Barmen describes Jesus Christ as the Lord, the one we have to obey, the one who has a claim upon our life. But this very same Jesus (and this is the twofold grace) is the one who is our "righteousness and sanctification and redemption" (1 Cor. 1:30). This Lord is the one who became a slave for our sake, and that can mean only one thing for us: Not one single person can claim our ultimate loyalty, not one single person can claim any form of lordship over us and turn us into "slaves." Christ's lordship means freedom for us, for there are no other lords in any areas of our life. This is a revolutionary claim. With its understanding of the lordship of grace, Barmen has given us the freedom to criticize every destructive lordship, revealing it as an idol.

The grace-filled lordship that Barmen speaks about is costly, not cheap, but it is grace nevertheless—a grace on which the ministry of the church is grounded:

> The church's commission, upon which its freedom is founded, consists in delivering the message of the *free grace* of God to all people in Christ's stead, and therefore in the ministry of his own Word and work through sermon and Sacrament. (8.26, emphasis mine)

Stumbling Stones

Curiously, it is not something in the Barmen Declaration that makes me stumble, but rather some "missing stones" that cause me to trip. First, a clear reference to the Jewishness of Jesus is missing. While people did not know in 1934 what we know now about the Holocaust, they did know about the Nazi attitude and action toward Jewish people. Furthermore, the Barmen Declaration was written in part against the so-called Aryan paragraph, which prohibited everyone with Jewish ancestors from holding office in the church (which would have meant that neither Jesus nor Paul nor Peter could have been a pastor). It would have been important to recognize explicitly that this Jesus Christ, who is the center and source of our faith, was a "Palestinian Jew," as C67 puts it (9.08), and that "God expressed love for all humankind through Israel, whom God chose to be a covenant people" (9.18). Moreover, it would have been important to confess that the Hebrew Scriptures are the written Word of God in the face of a group within the church who wanted to omit them completely because of their "Jewish character."

My second stumbling stone is Barmen's reaction against the attempt to make "race" a condition for church membership by declaring that a church cannot abandon the form of its order "to its own pleasure or to changes in prevailing ideological and political convictions" (8.18). Yet it never explicitly affirms that there are no conditions for church membership other than faith in Jesus Christ. The Dutch Reformed Mission Church in South Africa, a church of so-called colored people, considered Barmen a direct source for its own Belhar Confession (1982).[11] Belhar was dealing with a similar issue— church membership was restricted because of categories such as "race"—and it names what Barmen failed to confess:

> We believe in one holy, universal Christian Church, the communion of the saints called from the entire human family. We believe . . . that true faith in Jesus Christ is the only condition for membership of this Church.[12]

Although official segregation has ended in our churches, a glance into most sanctuaries on any Sunday morning will show that we still have to go a long way until we can claim that membership in our local congregations has as its only condition true faith in Jesus Christ, and not race, socioeconomic class, or political convictions.[13]

A CONVERSATION WITH THE CONFESSION OF 1967

The context of the Barmen Declaration was quite dramatic. In contrast, the Confession of 1967 appears to be the rather formal result of the 1958 union of the United Presbyterian Church of North America and the Presbyterian Church in the U.S.A. to form the United Presbyterian Church in the United States of America.[14] Actually, discussions about confessional changes had started long before. The Westminster Confession and Catechisms had been the confessional standards of American Presbyterian churches for centuries, yet it became obvious by the end of the nineteenth century that there were questions about their adequacy. New theological insights and questions concerning such issues as the authority of Scripture challenged believers, and the Westminster documents did not seem to provide satisfactory answers. A special committee was established in 1958, chaired by Prof. Edward A. Dowey of Princeton Theological Seminary, to work on a "brief contemporary statement of faith." Drawing heavily upon the dialectical theology of Karl Barth, it made reconciliation the central theme of the confession:

> God's reconciling work in Jesus Christ and the mission of reconcilia-
> tion to which he has called his church are the heart of the gospel in any
> age. Our generation stands in peculiar need of reconciliation in Christ.
> Accordingly, this Confession of 1967 is built upon that theme. (9.06)

After years of intensive and often quite hostile discussion within the church, the confession was adopted in 1967. It is structured in three parts: God's Work of Reconciliation, The Ministry of Reconciliation, and The Fulfillment of Reconciliation. The first part follows the trinitarian pattern of the apostolic benediction in 2 Corinthians 13:13, while the second part discusses mission and equipment of the church, and the last part concludes the confession with a biblical and eschatological vision of reconciliation.

God's Work of Reconciliation and Human Sin

C67 claims that everything we confess is based upon the reconciling work of our God, whom we know as the reconciler and redeemer. With this statement, C67 displays a theological concern of great importance for us today. Theologians have always wondered where to put the discussion of sin. Should we discuss sin before or after we have discussed God's redeeming work in Christ? Do we follow the order of creation-fall-redemption, identifying God as the Creator, Redeemer, and Sanctifier, or is the grace of our Lord Jesus Christ the adequate starting point? It may sound like a purely theoretical discussion, but at its core it is a deep pastoral concern that has consequences for preaching, pastoral care, and catechesis. For instance, how do we preach about sin (if we preach about it at all and do not ignore it because it makes people uncomfortable)?[15] Do we begin our sermons by describing how sinful human beings are, so as to bring to light how gracious our God and how wonderful God's salvific work is? Some preachers follow this order, reveling in descriptions of how mean, bad, and evil we all are. Those preachers seem to think that the smaller and meaner they make human beings, the greater is God's work. C67 does not follow this movement, but abides by a different, more Reformed development. C67 places the discussion of human sin *after* the discussion of Christ's redemptive work, because only against this background can we recognize ourselves as sinners. "The reconciling act of God in Jesus Christ exposes the evil in people as sin in the sight of God" (9.12).[16] Why does C67 use this order? The answer lies in a small paragraph that provides the good news in a nutshell:

> This work of God, the Father, Son, and Holy Spirit [i.e., the reconciling work], is the foundation of all confessional statements about God, humanity, and the world. (9.07)

We know ourselves as sinners only when we know ourselves as already reconciled to God! Our God meets us as the sinful people we are, yet God's first and last word to us is a Yes and not a No. The one who is our judge is the same one who "won the victory over sin and death for all" (9.08); this judge is our redeemer (9.11). This movement is not one C67 invented; following Calvin, many Presbyterian churches use it every Sunday morning when the assurance of pardon precedes the confession of sin. To proclaim the assurance of God's pardon before confessing our sins expresses a very deep theological and pastoral meaning: We do not earn God's forgiveness by confessing our sins or living "good" lives; rather, we can confess our sin and try to live good lives because we have already been forgiven and reconciled to God. This is good news for people who are torn by self-doubt and feelings of unworthiness. We are certainly reconciled to one another, but it is equally important to know that we also are reconciled to ourselves. We can love ourselves because we are loved by God.

It would misinterpret C67, and the Reformed tradition generally, if we were to understand this as some form of therapeutic "feel good" theology. To know ourselves as forgiven sinners is not an end in itself but the work of the Holy Spirit, who fulfills the work of reconciliation:

> The Holy Spirit creates and renews the church as the community in which people are reconciled to God and to one another. The Spirit enables people to receive forgiveness as they forgive one another and to enjoy the peace of God as they make peace among themselves. In spite of their sin, the Spirit gives people power to become representatives of Jesus Christ and his gospel of reconciliation to all. (9.20)

The Spirit is the active agent who brings God's forgiveness and who gives us power to become messengers of reconciliation in word and deed. We often think of our sins as individual, private acts, ignoring the pervasive communal character of sin and the sinful structures we are a part of. C67 not only describes sinful people as those who turn against God, but also as those who turn against fellow men and women, becoming "exploiters and despoilers of the world" (9.12). In the 1960s, the United Presbyterian Church perceived urgent structural problems and crises arising from the sin of human beings, such as racial discrimination (9.44), the Cold War and threat of nuclear warfare (9.45), enslaving poverty (9.46), and the relationship between men and women (9.47). Unfortunately, none of these problems has been resolved in the past forty years. The Confession of 1967 is—as even its title suggests—a document that places itself in a certain time; yet it still describes our life. We have to ask ourselves what it means for our lives, individually and communally, that a confession of our church claims reconciliation in society to be a part of the ministry of the church. What does it mean for us today to confess that being reconciled to God has concrete national and international consequences, as C67 claims?

> The church, in its own life, is called to practice the forgiveness of enemies and to commend to the nations as practical politics the search for cooperation and peace. This search requires that the nations pursue fresh and responsible relations across every line of conflict, *even at risk to national security*, to reduce areas of strife and to broaden international understanding. (9.45, emphasis mine)

This paragraph was one of the most hotly debated ones during the process of formulating the confession, and it has lost nothing of its searing relevance. Can we—should we—confess with C67 that the church cannot accept the elevation of national security to a primary aim of governmental politics if this elevation causes other nations or groups of people to suffer, if it is a turning against God rather than a carrying out of its mission as an ambassador of reconciliation?

I would like to add that reconciliation *in church* is also a part of our ministry. What would happen if we were to take the call to be reconciled to God and with one another seriously? What would it mean if, for example, those who support the ordination of gay, lesbian, bisexual, and transgender persons would understand themselves as being reconciled with those who do not, and vice versa? Over and over again, C67 urges us to discover in our time and context what it means to confess that "to be reconciled to God is to be sent into the world [and church] as God's reconciling community" (9.31) and that "each member is the church in the world, endowed by the Spirit with some gift of ministry and is responsible for the integrity of his or her witness in each particular situation" (9.38).

Courageous Hope in Action

Have you ever noticed how reading a book for a second time changes the way you see the development of the story and the characters? If you know how the story ends, everything that happens before appears in a new and different light. This is similar to how Christians are called to live our lives. We know the end, or rather, we know the one who is Alpha and Omega, the beginning and the end. This is why we who have been reconciled to God and to one another have a hope that is rooted in God's reconciling work in Christ. But what are we hoping for? What does the fulfillment of reconciliation look like? C67 turns to the Bible for an answer:

> Biblical visions and images of the rule of Christ, such as a heavenly city, the household of God, a new heaven and earth, a marriage feast, and an unending day culminate in the image of the kingdom. The kingdom represents the triumph of God over all that resists the divine will and disrupts God's creation. (9.54)

God's "kingdom" is at the center of the New Testament's message, but it may sound strange in our ears today. What kind of king can we, who live in a democracy, imagine, and can we see Christ as this king? By turning to the Bible, C67 suggests that our questions have to be turned around. God's kingdom must be defined by who God is and what God has done, not by an abstract understanding of the term:

> Human thought ascribes to God superlatives of power, wisdom, and goodness. But God reveals divine love in Jesus Christ by showing power in the form of a servant, wisdom in the folly of the cross, and goodness in receiving sinful men and women. (9.15)

The "kingdom" we hope for should not be confused with any earthly kingdom or reign, for it is *God's* reign. This reign of God is not something that will happen sometime in the future, for the future is already coming toward us and meeting us here and now: "Already God's reign is present as a ferment in the world, stirring hope in all people and preparing the world to receive its ultimate judgment and redemption" (9.54).

We are even given a concrete opportunity to experience physically the reign of God at the Lord's Table, where we "rejoice in the foretaste of the kingdom" and where we celebrate our reconciliation (9.52). The reconciled community gathers around the table to partake in Christ, to receive the benefits of Christ's death and resurrection. These benefits that include hope now are not like a present we receive and then keep for ourselves. True Christian hope is never a passive and purely individual hope, but because it is the hope in the promised coming of Christ the Reconciler, it is always and everywhere "hope in action." Action may take a variety of forms, including things that do not seem very active, such as prayer. Yet all share an urgency with which they are acted out:

> With an urgency born of this hope, the church applies itself to present tasks and strives for a better world. It does not identify limited progress with the kingdom of God on earth, nor does it despair in the face of disappointment and defeat. In steadfast hope, the church looks beyond all partial achievement to the final triumph of God. (9.55)

> In the power of the risen Christ and the hope of his coming, the church sees the promise of God's renewal of human life in society and of God's victory over all wrong. (9.32)

Yet those who strive to serve God in both church and society often despair "in the face of disappointment and defeat" and lose hope. How can we remain hopeful if we look with open eyes and hearts at the world around us? It is not easy; hope in action needs courage. But we will not find the courage we need within ourselves. Hope's courage is a gift we receive from God, centered in the communal event of the Lord's Supper. We go out from the Lord's Table with the hope and courage that equip us for the service for which God has called us (see 9.52). The strength we need grows from "confidence that God's purpose rather than human schemes will finally prevail" (9.25). Does that sound foolish to us who have seen "human schemes" prevailing over and over again? Judged by the wisdom of the world, it certainly seems foolish; yet we are called to judge by the wisdom of the cross. The wisdom of cross and resurrection reveals the "sure achievement of God's reconciling work" (9.09), and that is the foundation of courageous hope in which we look "to the final triumph of God" (9.55). Because we already know the end of the story of God's covenant with creation, we have reason for our hope. With these cobblestones, C67 helps us to walk on sure ground toward the future, because our God is coming toward us to meet us.

Stumbling Stones

A feature of C67 that has caused some to stumble—its exclusively male language—has been addressed by an inclusive language version, which was prepared by the PC(USA) Office of Theology and Worship in 2002. Even so, issues remain that may be stumbling stones for various groups in the church. One of these is C67's understanding of the authority of Scripture. The section on the Bible (9.27–.30) represents a "careful political compromise,"[17] which may be the reason for its problematic character. In short, C67 tries to combine two different understandings of the "Word of God." One understanding follows the Barmen Declaration in confessing Christ as "the Word of God incarnate"; the second one understands the Bible as "the word of God written" (9.27). What seems to be just another technicality, a purely theoretical discussion about the use of a capital *W* and a lowercase *w*, still troubles the church. How do we understand the Bible? What kind of authority does the Bible have? How do we deal with the historical and human character of the biblical text?

An illustration of these questions can be found in the current debate about the Bible's guidance on the issue of the ordination of gay, lesbian, bisexual, and transgender persons. Both sides in this discussion claim to possess the biblical truth, but both sides are working with very different understandings of the authority of Scripture. C67 does not help to solve this problem. In fact, it does not lead us anywhere, and may even add to the confusion. In the words of one theologian, it represents a "hodgepodge which attempts to combine the viewpoints of 1967 and 1647." This combination sought to keep the unity within the church, to avoid a division "at the cost of an unstable theological compromise."[18] Has the formulation C67 chose, the "unstable compromise," served the church well in the ensuing years? The church did not split in 1967, but because the underlying problem remains unresolved, the threat of a split continues to hover over almost every General Assembly. It is impossible to say what should have been confessed in 1967, and it is a worthy cause to preserve the unity of the church, but we have to wonder whether compromise in a confession of faith can prove more harmful than helpful. Yet the compromise of C67 impels us to find our own stance with respect to the authority of Scripture.

A CONVERSATION WITH A BRIEF STATEMENT OF FAITH

At first glance, the context of A Brief Statement of Faith seems to be similar to that of C67.[19] Here too, the union of two churches provided the occasion for a new confession. In 1983, the United Presbyterian Church U.S.A. and the Presbyterian Church U.S. reunited after a separation of 124 years. Reunion was the result of a fourteen-year-long process, yet the process demanded more than an ecclesiastical act. A new confession, in addition to the confessional documents of the two previous denominations, seemed to be needed as common theological ground to provide support for creating and building the identity of the new denomination. In typical Presbyterian manner, the whole church was included in the process of writing this new confession. A special committee worked for five years to produce a draft document. The 201st General Assembly (1989) then installed a second committee to review the statement and to produce a revised draft. This draft then was sent to the presbyteries by the 202nd General Assembly (1990), where it was approved and sent to the presbyteries. Finally, after long years of tedious work, diligent study, and often passionate debates, A Brief Statement of Faith was added to *The Book of Confessions* in 1991.

Some Presbyterians were not in favor of issuing a new confessional statement. In their view, reunion provided "the *occasion* for a new statement of faith, but it was not obvious that it offered an adequate *reason*." Although there were no specific and dramatic crises, nevertheless the committees were convinced that a *status confessionis* existed, marked by current problems in the "ongoing life of the church."[20] Among the issues in the ongoing life of the church, A Brief Statement of Faith addressed cultural and theological diversity and pluralism, the problem of individualism, the ecological crisis, and gender-inclusive language.[21] Yet another urgent issue came out of the life of the congregations: the need for a basic introduction into the Christian faith and how the Reformed tradition interprets it. A Brief Statement tries to address this need in a document that is useful for teaching and study, and appropriate for use in worship.

God's Sovereign Love and Our Trust

"In life and in death we belong to God" (10.1). This opening sentence of the Brief Statement, quoted from the first question of the Heidelberg Catechism,[22] determines the tone of the whole document. The Heidelberg Catechism offered comfort to believers by summarizing the good news in the confession that we belong to God. A Brief Statement serves the same purpose. It is comforting to know that we belong to God, because we know that God is not a neutral and uncaring God, but the God of sovereign love. The sovereignty of God has often been understood as a typically Reformed emphasis, yet sovereignty has often been abstracted from God's love. Even today, many Christians understand God's sovereignty and God's love as opposing attributes. Sovereignty seems to indicate power, while love seems to suggest weakness. Once again, we are misled if we characterize God by starting with human understandings of power and love. Instead, we are to define God's sovereignty and love by God's revelation in Christ. Here we discover that we cannot divide sovereignty and love when we talk about God. A Brief Statement of Faith makes this insight explicit when it speaks about creation—"In sovereign love

God created the world good" (10.3)—but the whole document reflects this understanding. The power of God is not neutral or abstract power, but the loving power with which "God raised Jesus from the dead, . . . delivering us from death to life eternal" (10.2), the power with which "God acts with justice and mercy to redeem creation" (10.3), and the power with which we are justified "by grace through faith" (10.4).

The sovereign love or loving sovereignty that God has made known to us is the ground and assurance of our trust in the one triune God. Each of the main sections of the confession dealing with the persons of the triune God begins, "We trust," and this signifies an important change. A Brief Statement is not meant as a summary of all doctrines (as some Reformation confessions claimed); it is not first of all about theological systems, but about our trust in God. Basically, the Brief Statement reminds us that to confess faith means to trust God. Barmen indirectly claims the same thing: Because we trust Christ as our Lord, we may and must confess that no others lords can claim our loyalty. C67 also claims that, in all areas of life, we can trust that God has reconciled us to God and one another. However, all three confessions also stress that our trusting faith has content, truth that we can know and proclaim. It would be a serious misunderstanding to think of "trust" as simply a warm feeling. Question 21 of the Heidelberg Catechism defines true faith by combining "wholehearted trust" with "certain knowledge"; both are created in us by the Holy Spirit. This knowledge involves "the whole person, the emotions no less than the intellect, the senses no less than thoughts, devotions no less than deduction."[23] A Brief Statement of Faith calls us to examine our own understanding of faith as well as the content of our faith, offering guidelines for our exploration.

Living as Disciples: The Imitation of Christ

Christians of all times and places have tried to discover what it means to follow Christ. Yet, surprisingly, there is not much about Christ's life and ministry in the classical confessions. For instance, all we find in the Apostles' Creed about Christ's life between birth and passion is a comma—not much to imitate! A Brief Statement of Faith fills this void with biblical material from the Gospel narratives. The opening sentence of the paragraph about Jesus Christ provides the central statement about his life and ministry: "Jesus proclaimed the reign of God" (10.2). In all he said and did, in all that he was, Jesus proclaimed that in him the reign of God had drawn near. If we want to imitate Christ, then we are called to do the same, to proclaim the reign of God in all we do and say. This is the central commission of Christian discipleship, for the church as well as for the individual believer. Following this summary, A Brief Statement gives a list of Jesus' activities in proclaiming the reign of God:

preaching good news to the poor
   and release to the captives,
teaching by word and deed
   and blessing the children,
healing the sick
   and binding up the brokenhearted,
eating with outcasts,
forgiving sinners,
and calling all to repent and believe the gospel. (10.2)

    This list is not meant to provide eight activities we can copy from Christ's life and ministry and implement in our lives. Our "imitation" of Christ poses questions to us: What good news are we to preach to the poor? What kind of release for what captives are we talking about? How do we bless children or bind up the brokenhearted? For all of this we need gifts of imagination and courage—the gifts of the Holy Spirit (10.4). We live in "a fearful and broken world," and yet "we strive to serve Christ in our daily tasks and to live holy and joyful lives." To imitate Christ is to rely not on our own power but on the work of the Holy Spirit, who is "everywhere the giver and renewer of life." "Everywhere" means exactly that: *Wherever* we find renewal of life—whether in church, society, politics, science, the arts, etc.—we can be sure that it is the work of the Holy Spirit. We Christians do not have to solve all problems of the world by ourselves. The Spirit gives us courage "to work with others for justice, freedom, and peace" (and, I would like to add, for the integrity of creation). This helps us avoid the trap of overestimating our power and ability in working for change. Christians are not the only ones who care about the world's problems and who are actively engaged in finding and implementing solutions for these problems. Living as Christ's disciples means cooperating with those who do not confess Christ as Lord, yet whose work is inspired by the Holy Spirit. In imitating Christ, we are engaged in trying to fulfill what we have been created for:

In sovereign love God created the world good
   and makes everyone equally in God's image,
      male and female, of every race and people,
   to live as one community. (10.3)

Christ's life and ministry show us what it means to be created in God's image, disclosing the substance of full humanity. At the same time, it discloses our sin:

But we rebel against God; we hide from our Creator.
   Ignoring God's commandments,
   we violate the image of God in others and ourselves,
   accept lies as truth,

exploit neighbor and nature,
and threaten death to the planet entrusted to our care. (10.3)

We ignore God's commandments, but Jesus' life and ministry display, as Calvin
puts it, "the whole course of his obedience."[24] In Christ we learn that Christian obedience does not mean blindly following orders, but living out God's
love for ourselves and others in an imaginative and courageous way; in short,
to proclaim the reign of God.

Stumbling Stones

The ecological crisis remains one of the most pressing issues before us.
Although its urgency has seemed to vanish from public discussion, it remains
an undisputable fact that we cannot continue treating the world as we do without risking the survival of the whole creation. A Brief Statement addresses this
issue concretely in its second paragraph:

> In sovereign love God created the world good.
> . . . .
> But we . . . exploit neighbor and nature,
>   and threaten death to the planet entrusted to our care.
>   We deserve God's condemnation.
> Yet God acts with justice and mercy to redeem creation. (10.3)

While these formulations have lost nothing of their contemporaneity and
value, something in A Brief Statement makes me stumble a bit. Although the
creation is mentioned several times in the confession, it is limited to the second paragraph only, the paragraph on God the Creator. The nonhuman creation is not mentioned in the paragraph on Jesus Christ or in the paragraph
on the Holy Spirit. This gives the impression that A Brief Statement remains
an anthropocentric document. In this confession, the whole life and ministry,
death and resurrection of Jesus have no obvious benefit for the nonhuman creation. Scripture acknowledges the longing of the whole creation to "obtain the
freedom of the glory of the children of God" (Rom. 8:21). A Brief Statement
does mention that God acts to redeem creation, but this line remains somewhat shallow since it is nowhere related to the work of Christ. In addition, A
Brief Statement misses the opportunity to relate the work of the Holy Spirit
directly to the nonhuman creation. It is possible to interpret the second line—
"everywhere the giver and renewer of life"—with respect to the nonhuman
creation, yet the rest of the paragraph deals with humanity only. A Brief Statement even misses out on a chance to include conservation of God's creation
with working together with others for justice, freedom, and peace. Again, it is

possible to interpret "justice" as including eco-justice, but explicit naming would have avoided the impression that the confession cares chiefly about humanity, and the rest of God's creation only incidentally. What we need now is the development of a new relationship between the human and the nonhuman creation, a new understanding of our place in God's creation. Are human beings the center of creation? Has the rest of creation been created exclusively for our sake? A Brief Statement does not really help us in finding new answers for these questions.

GLORY BE TO GOD!

It is my hope that this chapter may give a hint of how enriching and challenging a conversation with the confessions of the twentieth century can be. The Barmen, C67, and Brief Statement cobblestones can indeed guide us in our Christian faith and life. The conversation is not always easy, but there is much to gain for us as individuals and as a community. Not least, these confessions give us a chance to meet the Holy Spirit working through documents of faith. We are given a chance to meet our God, who is our gracious Lord, the Reconciler of all, and the One in whom we can trust. We are given a chance to learn who we are as ones created in God's image, called to follow Christ. And we are led to give thanks and praise to God. The appropriate conclusion of any conversation with the confessions is found in joining our voices to A Brief Statement of Faith:

> With believers in every time and place,
>   we rejoice that nothing in life or in death
>   can separate us from the love of God in Christ Jesus our Lord.
> Glory be to the Father, and to the Son, and to the Holy Spirit. Amen.
> (10.5–.6)

NOTES

1. For confessions of Reformed churches worldwide, see Lukas Vischer, ed., *Reformed Witness Today: A Collection of Confessions and Statements of Faith by Reformed Churches* (Bern: Evangelische Arbeitsstelle Oekumene Schweiz, 1982); and *Confessions and Confessing in the Reformed Tradition*, Studies from the World Alliance of Reformed Churches 2 (Geneva: WARC, 1982).
2. I am aware that it is our responsibility to interpret very carefully what kind of lordship Jesus Christ executes and how this differs from worldly lordships of our time and all times.
3. See "Confessional Nature of the Church Report," in *The Book of Confessions*, xviii, xix.

4. Edward A. Dowey, Jr., *A Commentary on the Confession of 1967 and an Introduction to "The Book of Confessions"* (Philadelphia: Westminster Press, 1968), 30.
5. See Karl Barth, *Church Dogmatics*, I/2, ed. G. W. Bromiley and T. F. Torrance; trans. G. T. Thompson and Harold Knight (Edinburgh: T. & T. Clark, 1956), 650.
6. For a more detailed explanation of Reformed understanding of confessions, see "Confessional Nature of the Church," xvi–xviii.
7. The assignment for the writing of A Brief Statement of Faith was to produce a "brief statement of the Reformed faith," yet the committee came to share the Reformers' opinion that the purpose of confessing is to confess the "'biblical' faith or the 'catholic' (that is, universal) faith of Christians." William C. Placher and David Willis-Watkins, *Belonging to God: A Commentary on A Brief Statement of Faith* (Louisville, KY: Westminster/John Knox Press, 1992), 9.
8. See, for example, the discussion with respect to A Brief Statement of Faith in Eugene TeSelle, "How Do We Recognize a *Status Confessionis?*" *Theology Today* 45, no. 1 (1988): 71–78.
9. For brief introductions into the historical background, see Jack Rogers, *Presbyterian Creeds: A Guide to "The Book of Confessions"* (Louisville, KY: Westminster/John Knox Press, 1991), 175–91; and *The Book of Confessions: Study Edition* (Louisville, KY: Geneva Press, 1996), 303–8.
10. "Race" can only be used with great care here, since it was a term the Nazis used in a pseudoscientific way in order to designate the superiority of the "Aryan race" and the inferiority of the "Jewish race" (and other "races"). These theories were later proven to be unscientific and purely arbitrary. To continue speaking uncritically in this context about "race," as if it were a given reality, means to accept the Nazis' race theories.
11. For the text and a discussion of the Belhar Confession, see G. D. Cloete and D. J. Smit, eds., *A Moment of Truth: The Confession of the Dutch Reformed Mission Church 1982* (Grand Rapids: Eerdmans, 1984).
12. Ibid., 1, 2.
13. Belhar can prove to be a call for repentance for *our* churches too: "We reject any doctrine which absolutises either natural diversity or the sinful separation of people in such a way that this absolutisation hinders or breaks the visible and active unity of the church, or even leads to the establishment of a separate church formation; which professes that this spiritual unity is truly being maintained in the bond of peace whilst believers of the same confession are in effect alienated from one another for the sake of diversity and in despair of reconciliation; which denies that a refusal earnestly to pursue this visible unity as a priceless gift is sin; which explicitly or implicitly maintains that descent or any other human or social factor should be a consideration in determining membership of the Church."
14. For brief introductions into C67's historical background, see Rogers, *Presbyterian Creeds*, 202–19; and *The Book of Confessions: Study Edition*, 315–20.
15. In 1990, James D. Brown reported that a number of Presbyterian churches no longer used prayers of confession "because they are a 'downer' and make people feel discouraged." Brown, "Confessions in the Life of the Church," in *To Confess the Faith Today*, ed. Jack L. Stotts and Jane Dempsey Douglass (Louisville, KY: Westminster/John Knox Press, 1990), 99.
16. Here and in the following quotations, I use *The Confession of 1967: Inclusive Language Text* (Louisville, KY: Office of Theology and Worship, 2002).

17. Rogers, *Presbyterian Creeds*, 216.

18. George Hendry, quoted in Rogers, *Presbyterian Creeds*, 216.

19. For brief introductions into the historical background of A Brief Statement, see Rogers, *Presbyterian Creeds*, 231–60; and *The Book of Confessions: Study Edition*, 333–38.

20. Placher and Willis-Watkins, *Belonging to God*, 12.

21. See, for example, George H. Kehm, "The Contemporaneity of the Brief Statement of Faith," and Clarice J. Martin, "Inclusive Language and the Brief Statement of Faith: Widening the Margins in Our Common Confession," in Stotts and Douglass, *To Confess the Faith Today*, 107–29.

22. I always found it intriguing that the English translation speaks about "life and death," whereas the German original speaks about "life and dying." From a pastoral perspective, there seems to be a considerable difference between these two terms.

23. Placher and Willis-Watkins, *Belonging to God*, 44.

24. John Calvin, *Institutes of the Christian Religion*, ed. John T. McNeill, trans. Ford Lewis Battles (Philadelphia: Westminster Press, 1960), 2.16.5 (LCC 1:507).

6

Who Is God?

Laura Smit

Knowing God is the great goal of the Christian life. With the psalmist, we can say:

> One thing I asked of the LORD,
>   that will I seek after:
> to live in the house of the LORD
>   all the days of my life,
> to behold the beauty of the LORD,
>   and to inquire in his temple.
> . . . .
> "Come," my heart says, "seek his face!"
>   Your face, LORD, do I seek.
> Do not hide your face from me.
>   (Ps. 27:4, 8–9)

What is it to behold the beauty of the Lord and to seek his face? This beholding is not a matter of invention or of imagination, but of encounter and reception. True knowledge of God must come from God's self-revelation, as the Westminster Confession tells us:

> The distance between God and the creature is so great, that although reasonable creatures do owe obedience unto him as their Creator, yet they could never have any fruition of him, as their blessedness and reward, but by some voluntary condescension on God's part, which he hath been pleased to express by way of covenant. (6.037)

When we encounter God's self-revelation, our own small ideas about what God might be like are revealed as inadequate. C. S. Lewis puts it well when he writes, "Images of the Holy easily become holy images—sacrosanct. My idea of God is not a divine idea. It has to be shattered time after time. He shatters it Himself. He is the great iconoclast. Could we not almost say that this shattering is one of the marks of His presence?"[1] I believe that in our Presbyterian confessions, we encounter truths and realities about God's nature that will shatter many of our inadequate, imaginary ideas about God.

Augustine, to whom our tradition owes a great debt, made clear that the process of encountering God is not an individual matter. Augustine began his intellectual quest with an act of intellectual submission to the community of faith, through which he affirmed the orthodox Christian faith and took it as his starting point: "This is also my faith inasmuch as it is the catholic faith."[2] Such submission is profoundly foreign to most of us, living as we do in a culture that values individualism and independent thinking. I have belonged to several different presbyteries in the course of my ministry, and in all of them I have heard frequent appeals to the right of private judgment,[3] but almost none to the need for intellectual submission to the church's teaching.[4]

Augustine taught that the community of the church and the faith taught by the church provide a "wholesome regimen" that "makes the ailing mind well for the perception of unchanging truth."[5] Those who think themselves above such guidance and who want to find truth by reason alone meet with Augustine's scorn: "The reader of these reflections of mine on the Trinity should bear in mind that my pen is on the watch against the sophistries of those who scorn the starting-point of faith, and allow themselves to be deceived through an unseasonable and misguided love of reason."[6] Although Augustine is himself a master of reasoned argument and uses it to good effect, he does not think that reason alone is capable of bringing him to understanding. It is necessary to begin the search for understanding from within a commitment to a communal tradition that is bigger than one's local church, bigger than one's contemporaries, extending back through history and around the globe to encompass the great cloud of witnesses who make up the church triumphant. For those of us in the Presbyterian Church, that communal tradition is condensed in *The Book of Confessions*. In dialogue with the confessions and with brothers and sisters in Christ through history, faith is received or grasped, not constructed or attained.

For the Reformed tradition, all theology begins with the doctrine of God. Not all traditions begin here. Some traditions begin with the personal experience of salvation and move from there to deduce what God must be like. Many Presbyterians do this as well, beginning with their own experience of faith and constructing a doctrine that conforms to their experience, but this is not the Reformed way. It is a central understanding of our tradition that God is free and sovereign, and that we undervalue that freedom and sovereignty when we understand God primarily in terms of our own salvation or in terms of the ways in which God's work benefits us. First we must understand who God is; only then can we understand who we are and how God works in our lives. All other Christian doctrines are controlled by our doctrine of God.

However, when we enter into conversation with Presbyterian and Reformed confessions about the doctrine of God, we find that the matter is not covered with the same depth we find when looking at other topics, such as justification or the sacraments. Although Reformed confessions typically begin their theological exploration with the doctrine of God, the confessions give it less aggressive development than many other doctrines because the doctrine of God was not a divisive issue for early Reformers. Actually, there is little difference between Roman Catholic and Reformed teaching about the doctrine of God. These two traditions have employed distinct methods, exegeses, and emphases, but in the main they have agreed in their conclusions about God's nature and attributes. In fact, there has been a remarkable ecumenical and historical consensus around this doctrine, extending from Augustine until the twentieth century, a period of more than 1,500 years.

In the sixty years since World War II, however, that consensus has been under attack from all sides and from within almost all Christian traditions, including the PC(USA). Almost twenty years ago, Ronald Goetz observed in the *Christian Century*, "The ancient theopaschite heresy that God suffers has ... become the new orthodoxy."[7] Theologians such as Jürgen Moltmann assert that in the light of the Holocaust we must understand God in a new way, as one who shares our vulnerability and pain. This assertion has been so widely accepted that few of the undergraduates at the Christian college where I teach have ever heard a sermon or a Sunday school lesson in which the classic confessional understanding of God's nature is articulated, let alone defended. My experience as a visiting preacher in numerous congregations suggests that this is also true of many Presbyterians. Fifteen hundred years of ecumenical consensus is collapsing, and few people care enough to register concern. In many cases, abandonment of the classically confessional doctrine of God has been unexamined and largely unconscious.

Every officer in the Presbyterian Church has taken vows to be instructed, led, and guided by our confessions. While guidance is not synonymous with prescription, I believe that the ordination vows obligate those of us who have made them to listen carefully to our confessional tradition, especially when it is under widespread attack, and to acknowledge that the burden of proof is ours when we disagree with that tradition. In other words, we need solid biblical and theological reasons to disagree with the confessions, and in the absence of such reasons we are bound to agree with them. This is what it means to "exercise freedom of conscience within certain bounds,"[8] as ministers, elders, and deacons have promised. It is my conviction that contemporary theologians who have discarded the confessional doctrine of God have failed to meet this burden of proof. Unless that burden is met, faithful officers in the Presbyterian Church (U.S.A.) are bound to the confessional understanding of who God is.

LANGUAGE FOR GOD

From very early in the church's teaching, Christians have recognized that the language we use to speak of God is limited. After all, God is not like us. God is the Creator, the source of everything that is. The Reformed tradition has always insisted on remembering the distinction between the Creator and creatures in everything that we say about God. Our Directory for Worship observes, "When people respond to God and communicate to each other their experiences of God, they must use symbolic means, for God transcends creation and cannot be reduced to anything within it."[9] Given this principle, we might reasonably expect that language will not apply to God and to human beings in quite the same way. When I say that my sister loves me, and I also say that God loves me, does the word "love" mean the same thing in those two statements? Most Christians would say, not quite. There is a relationship of meaning between the two uses of "love," since all experiences of love can somehow be traced back to God. However, the love I experience from my sister and the love I experience from God are also fundamentally different. The difference is not just one of scale (that God loves me *more* than my sister could) but also one of quality (God's love is in some way a *different* sort of action from my sister's love). This is one reason why my everyday experience is not a trustworthy starting point for my beliefs about God's nature.

Language that is related but not identical is analogical language. All language for God is on some level analogical. Analogies can go one of two ways. When I say that God is the rock of my salvation, then I am taking a term that applies most properly and originally to created reality and applying it to God. When I say that my sister loves me, then I am taking a term that applies most properly and originally to God and applying it to my sister.

Gendered language for God clearly fits into the first category. God is beyond male and female, so when we use either male or female language for God, we are speaking analogically, using language that applies properly and originally to human experience and applying it to God. Some people argue that instead of using gendered language, we should avoid the use of either male or female language when speaking of God, simply repeating the word "God" in place of using pronouns such as "he" or "himself." I once used such God-language for about a year, avoiding pronouns when speaking of God by always substituting the noun "God." By the end of the year I noticed something rather disturbing: My idea of God had become impersonal. Since our human experience of personal interaction is always gendered, ungendered language suggests a lack of personal presence, and I had come to think of God as an impersonal force rather than a personal being. This is a significant problem, since being personal, like being loving, is a quality that belongs properly and originally to God and is applied to human beings only analogically. Language that makes us think of God as *less* personal than humans should be avoided, just as we should shun any language that makes us think of God as less loving than we are. Insofar as ungendered language is an effort to speak more literally (or univocally) about God without using analogical language, it is doomed to failure, since human language is simply not up to the task. But we should note that ungendered language also fails to function analogically, since we have no analogous experience of relating to an ungendered person that might illuminate such language when applied to God.

Some people have assured me that they can avoid gendered language for God without having "God" become an impersonal concept. While this may be true for them, it is not true for me, and so I could not risk using such language for very long. I had to use either male or female language, or some combination of the two. Thus, I spent another year of my life using male language for the Father and the Son, while using female language for the Holy Spirit. As my understanding of the unity of God deepened, however, I came to realize that such language suggests that the three persons have different natures. In fact, it leads toward tritheism, as if the Trinity is made up of three separate gods rather than three persons who share in one nature.

As we will see again and again in what follows, no human language is adequate to God's nature, and so we must settle for language that is the least misleading. Not every Christian will make the same decisions about language use, and I believe that we should be gracious to one another in such matters. For me, it seems wise to be guided by both Scripture and Christian tradition and to use male-gendered language for God, always with the understanding that this language—like all our language for God—is analogical at best. The new Presbyterian *Study Catechism* makes this clear by specifying that masculine God-language in no way means that God is male, nor does such language legitimate male authority over women.[10] Nonetheless, the catechism concludes that we should call God "Father" for three reasons: "First, because God is identified in the New Testament as the Father of our Lord Jesus Christ. Second, because Jesus Christ is the eternal Son of this Father. Third, because when we are joined to Christ through faith, we are adopted as sons and daughters into the relationship he enjoys with his Father."[11]

John Calvin used "accommodation" instead of "analogical," a term that is also used in our Directory for Worship.[12] Calvin believed that throughout

God's self-revelation in Scripture, God translates his ineffable and inexpressible nature into language that we can understand. For instance, God is always accommodating himself to our limited understanding by speaking of himself as existing within time. Since our everyday experience is relentlessly temporal, and since we can only sustain the idea of an eternal Being who transcends time for a few seconds before our heads begin to swim, God speaks of himself in temporal language throughout Scripture. Similarly, since all our experiences of personal beings are also experiences of gendered beings, God speaks of himself in gendered language throughout Scripture. But such language must not be taken literally. It is God's way of stooping to our weakness, accommodating himself to our small understandings.

We make similar accommodations in our language all the time. When we speak about the earth's daily orbit around the sun, we don't speak in literal terms at all. Instead, we speak from within our own experience of "sunset" and "sunrise," of the sun "crossing the sky." We know quite well that the sun is not actually setting, or rising, or moving in any way. These figures of speech come naturally to us because they are rooted in our own experiences of the sun. However, when we speak or write about the nature of the sun itself, we abandon such language very quickly and begin speaking instead about the orbit of the earth around the sun. In the same way, our everyday speech about God as changing his mind, or being saddened by our behavior, or repenting of a particular action does not present a problem. When we move into the realm of theology, however, we must examine such language and recognize it for the figurative, accommodated language that it is. Most problems in our understanding of God's nature come from underestimating the difference between ourselves and God, so that we expect words to mean exactly the same thing when applied to God as when applied to us. We expect God to be tame and predictable, familiar and like ourselves. These domesticated, comfortable ideas about God are shattered by an encounter with his presence.

GOD'S EXISTENCE

Throughout the history of Christian theology, a great deal of effort has been invested in the project of proving God's existence. Given the limits of our present discussion, we cannot investigate such proofs in any depth, but even the most confident proof would not claim to establish the existence of the God we know in the Bible. Proofs for God's existence may help us to believe that there is a higher power of some sort, but they do little or nothing to tell us what sort of power that might be. Proofs may be helpful to our faith by reassuring us that belief in God is not irrational, but ultimately we are dependent on God's self-revelation in order to know him truly and fully.

In our tradition, we confess that knowledge of God is drawn from God's self-disclosure in creation and in his providential care for his people through-out history. However, because of human sinfulness, such sources are "not sufficient to give that knowledge of God, and of his will, which is necessary unto salvation," which is why God has further revealed himself in Scripture (6.001). God's ultimate self-revelation is found in Jesus Christ, in whom the fullness of God is revealed in a human being. Of course, reason does play a role in our understanding of God. Much of our theology is derived from Scripture by using our reason rather than simply quoting what Scripture has to say. This is especially true with a doctrine such as the Trinity. However, our confessional tradition reminds us that reasoning about Scripture is always a corporate act, and that in discerning the truths of Scripture, we are to trust the wisdom of the confessions more than our individual ideas. Reason alone will not get us very far when it comes to having a relationship with God. As the Westminster Larger Catechism says, "The very light of nature in man, and the works of God, declare plainly that there is a God; but his Word and Spirit only, do sufficiently and effectually reveal him unto men for their salvation" (7.112).

A key affirmation of Christians is that God's existence is necessary. As the Westminster Confession puts it, "Nothing is to him contingent or uncertain" (6.012). I could imagine a world in which I do not exist, or in which human beings do not exist, or even in which our cosmos does not exist. But God *must* exist. In fact, God may be "defined" as the One who exists necessarily. Everything else is contingent, that is, everything else could have *not* existed. God's very nature is *to be*. God revealed his nature to Moses at the burning bush by naming himself "I AM."[13] Everything within creation might have remained mere ideas in the mind of God, ideas that never came into existence. But that is not possible with God, because, unlike anything or anyone else, God is self-caused. This is true only of God and is one more way in which God's existence is not like ours. As Psalm 14:1 tells us, only a fool would think that there is no God, because God is the necessary being who makes all nonnecessary beings possible.

This is one way in which God is *simple*, that is, not composite, or, as the Westminster Confession puts it, "without body, parts, or passions" (6.011). I am composite in many ways: There is an idea of me that exists in God's mind, and there is my existence; I am both a body and a soul; I have an identity as a member of the human species and an identity as an individual. There is the part of me that is actualized at any given moment, and there is my potential, most of which will never be actualized; and there is my own nature and my participation in God, without whom I couldn't exist. God is not composite in any of those ways. Since God exists necessarily, there is no idea or nature of God that comes into existence after being thought; rather, God's nature and God's existence are one and the same. God does not have parts that are not themselves fully God but that come together to make God. God is not part of a species called "god," an individual instance of some bigger category. There is nothing imaginary in God, for God is the source of all reality and the one ultimate Reality against which everything else is measured. God has no potential, because everything that God could be he actually is right now. God is already infinitely and dynamically loving, good, merciful, great, and joyful. God can't get better, because God is already unimaginably the best. All of God's intrinsic properties are essential and always "in play," so there is nothing static or passive about God. God's nature is not arbitrary, so there is no sense in which God could have been unjust, or cruel, or evil. None of that is who God is. God does not depend on anyone or any force beyond himself to maintain his existence. In all these ways, God is unlike everything he has made. Such a God is very hard for us to think about clearly because many of the categories of our own experience fail to apply. No wonder people since the beginning of time have been tempted to remake God in our own image, to reduce him to something we can understand.

In saying that God is simple, I am not saying that there are no distinctions to be made in God. Every theologian who has affirmed divine simplicity has also affirmed the Trinity. Rather, I am saying that God is not composite in the ways that we humans are composite. And yet there are distinctions to be made within the Godhead, both distinctions among the three persons in the doctrine of the Trinity and distinctions among different attributes in the doctrine of God's nature.

The doctrine of God's simplicity is important because it helps us solve some big theological problems. For instance, it might seem that when we talk about God being good there are only two alternatives, with neither of them satisfying. First, it is possible to say that goodness is whatever God declares it to be. The problem with this idea is that it makes morality seem arbitrary: "Goodness" is merely a designation that God has created, and he could have created some other standard and labeled that as goodness. Second, it is possible to say that goodness exists as a standard independent of God and that he chooses to conform to that standard. The problem with this idea is that it makes God dependent on something that exists independently, to which he is then accountable.

The doctrine of God's simplicity offers a third option. Since God is identical with his nature, God does not possess goodness; rather, God *is* goodness. This same identification of essence with morality is seen—in a far less complete way—in people of genuine character or honor. Such people do not lie or cheat, not because that would violate a rule to which they are bound, but because it would violate their character, contradict who they are. It should be the goal of all Christians to internalize God's will in this way, to write it on our hearts so that it becomes one with our character. Why then should it surprise us to think that this is perfectly true of God's own nature? It is perfectly true not just of God's goodness but also of God's truth, justice, mercy, joy, love, and every other perfection. Living according to God's will is thus not a matter of obeying a set of arbitrary rules, but rather of being in harmony with God's character.

Some people have argued that the doctrine of God's simplicity collapses all of God's properties into one, as if we must now say that there is no difference between God's justice, God's mercy, God's grace, and God's holiness. If God is identical with his goodness, he is also identical with his justice, mercy, and every other attribute. This suggests to some that God's attributes are indistinguishable from one another. But this is a misunderstanding. While the reference of all these attributes is the same in that they all refer to the fullness of God's nature, the *sense* of the attributes is different. In much the same way, we may speak of the "evening star" and the "morning star"—both of which refer to the planet Venus—without confusing morning with evening, or we may speak of 2×2 and 2^2—both of which equal 4—without conflating two different mathematical functions.[14]

What is important for us to remember about God's identification with his attributes, however, is that, while they are distinguishable, they are not in conflict. Since God is identical with each attribute, we may not think of God as having two "sides" to his nature. Some theologians in the Reformed tradition have forgotten this point when they have suggested that God's grace is exemplified in his treatment of the elect, whereas his justice is exemplified in his treatment of the nonelect.[15] But God is not two-faced. All of God's actions are consistent with his nature as love and goodness.

THE TRINITY

In thinking about the doctrine of God, there is a long debate about whether it is better to start with an understanding of God's oneness or to start with an understanding of God as Trinity. Since the Bible itself starts by telling us that God is one and only in the New Testament reveals fully that God is also three persons, most theologians throughout history have followed the same pattern. This was not because they thought that the Trinity was less important than God's essence, although that is how some contemporary theologians characterize the church's tradition. Rather, the pattern reflects the reality that God chose first to tell his people about his oneness. This can be seen in God's revelation to Moses of the divine name I AM, and in his command to the people of Israel that they should constantly remind each other, "The LORD is our God, the LORD alone" (Deut. 6:4). Only in the coming of Jesus Christ do we understand fully that there are three persons—Father, Son, and Holy Spirit—in the one God and that God's deepest name is not I AM, but "Love" (1 John 4:8, 16). "God is love" makes no sense apart from the Trinity, for only a community of persons can *be* love itself. Many Christian theologians have thought it wise to follow God's lead in deciding whether to begin with God's oneness or God's threeness, as have most of our Presbyterian confessions. The Second Helvetic Confession, for example, begins the chapter on God's nature with a paragraph entitled "God is One," followed by a paragraph entitled "God is Three."[16] Starting with God's oneness also makes some sense apologetically, since monotheism is often affirmed by those who do not accept the Christian gospel.

However, there is also a case to be made for thinking first about God as three persons. Given that we now know God to be triune, it may be inappropriate to go back, even hypothetically, to an understanding of God that does not involve the revelation of Jesus Christ. As the Barmen Declaration tells us, "Jesus Christ, as he is attested for us in Holy Scripture, is the one Word of God which we have to hear and which we have to trust and obey in life and in death" (8.11). For Christians, the Old Testament must also be read in light of Christ, who is the "one mediator between God and humankind" (1 Tim. 2:5).

There is only one God, and that God is triune. When the Old Testament speaks of God, it is the triune God who is spoken of, for there is no other. I often hear my students or parishioners speaking of God in the Old Testament as the Father, rather than as the Trinity. We must not make the mistake of assuming that only the Father is active in the Old Testament and that the Son and Spirit come on the scene in the New Testament. All three persons are present at creation, at the flood, at the exodus, and throughout salvation history.

We have to recognize that some Reformed confessions distinguish the work of the three persons in ways that suggest a division of God's acts between the three persons over history. For instance, the Heidelberg Catechism states that the Apostles' Creed is divided "into three parts: the first concerns God *the Father* and our *creation*; the second, God *the Son* and our *redemption*; and the third, God *the Holy Spirit* and our *sanctification*" (4.024). While there is some truth in this way of speaking, it is a misleading oversimplification. It is true that the Father is the Source of all that is, but the act of creation includes the Word who is spoken and the Spirit who enlivens. The Second Helvetic Confession teaches, "This good and almighty God created all things, both visible and invisible, by his co-eternal Word, and preserves them by his co-eternal Spirit" (5.032). The Scots Confession also ascribes the act of creation to the triune God:

> We confess and acknowledge one God alone, to whom alone we must cleave, whom alone we must serve, whom only we must worship, and in whom alone we put our trust. Who is eternal, infinite, immeasurable, incomprehensible, omnipotent, invisible; one in substance and yet distinct in three persons, the Father, the Son, and the Holy Ghost. By whom we confess and believe all things in heaven and earth, visible and invisible, to have been created, to be retained in their being, and to be ruled and guided by his inscrutable providence for such end as his eternal wisdom, goodness, and justice have appointed, and to the manifestation of his own glory. (3.01)

Similarly, the Westminster Confession ascribes creation to all three persons: "It pleased God the Father, Son, and Holy Ghost, for the manifestation of the glory of his eternal power, wisdom, and goodness, in the beginning, to create or make of nothing the world, and all things therein, whether visible or invisible, in the space of six days, and all very good" (6.022).

Christians have always had difficulty explaining the doctrine of the Trinity. How is it possible for God to be both one and three? Augustine said that if you think you have understood the doctrine of the Trinity, then you are not actually thinking about God. God's triune nature is another way in which God is radically unlike us. C. S. Lewis provides us with a helpful analogy. He says that a human being trying to understand God's triune nature is like a two-dimensional being trying to understand a three-dimensional being. What would a two-dimensional being think of the claim that a cube is a single object made of six squares? From a two-dimensional perspective, such a claim would be nonsensical.[17] Given the insights of contemporary physics about dimensionality (which I understand very imperfectly!), I like to think of God as infinitely dimensional. This helps me to understand why I cannot understand him better, while still allowing me to think of God as able to interact with our world without difficulty. Just as I have no difficulty interacting with a flat piece of paper, or drawing in two dimensions, even though I myself am three-dimensional, so an infinitely dimensional Being would have no difficulty interacting with me, even though I could not understand nor correctly perceive that Being.

In the twentieth century it became fashionable to claim that there is no difference between the "economic Trinity" and the "immanent Trinity." "Economic Trinity" refers to the Trinity as known in the economy, or ordering, of salvation, that is, the triune God in relation to and for us. "Immanent Trinity" refers to the relationship of the three persons within God's Being, without reference to his saving actions in the world. The equivalence of the economic and immanent Trinity was popularized by the Roman Catholic theologian Karl Rahner's formulation, "The economic trinity *is* the immanent trinity." Rahner thought that the way we encounter the three persons working to save us is the way God really is and all that God really is. We can see Rahner's influence in the Confession of 1967:

> God's sovereign love is a mystery beyond the reach of man's mind. Human thought ascribes to God superlatives of power, wisdom, and goodness. But God reveals his love in Jesus Christ by showing power in the form of a servant, wisdom in the folly of the cross, and goodness in receiving sinful men. The power of God's love in Christ to transform the world discloses that the Redeemer is the Lord and Creator who made all things to serve the purpose of his love. (9.15)

Many contemporary theologians have gone beyond Rahner to teach that God has chosen to enter into a mutually vulnerable relationship with us, that he has emptied himself for us—both in the act of creation and also in the act of salvation—and that he has even come to need us in some way because of his love for us. While God's self-revelation in Jesus Christ is reliable and truthful, showing us his very nature, we must also affirm that God is both sovereign and free. Who God is cannot be reduced to his relationship to us, even though it is a relationship of love and grace. Although the economic and immanent Trinities are not contradictory, it is misleading to say that they are identical.

Nowhere is this more obvious than in thinking about God's identity as Love. In the First Epistle of John, we read that God *is* Love. John does not say that God is loving, but that God is Love itself. On the face of it, this is a puzzling statement. Whether one thinks of love as an action or as a sentiment, it is hard to see how a personal being could be either. But remember our discussion of God's simple nature. Just as God *is* Goodness, so too God *is* Love. There is not a higher standard of Love to which God is accountable; rather, God's very character is that standard. Still, love requires an object, and it would seem that if God is Love then God would need to have someone around to be the object of his affections. In other words, it would seem that the creation might be necessary to God. Because God is Triune, however, this is not so. The Father, Son, and Holy Spirit love each other in a dynamic relationship of self-giving that is self-sufficient but that then graciously overflows into the acts of creation and redemption. The economic Trinity is the revelation of the triune God in that overflow, an overflow that truthfully expresses God's loving nature as the "fountain of all being" (6.012). But we should not assume that the love we receive from God is exhaustive of God's loving nature any more than a painting is exhaustive of the creative nature of its artist. God's love for creation and for his people is but the overflow. God would be Love even if we did not exist. Sometimes our discussions of God's plans for our lives suggest that the point of God's existence is to care for us and give our lives meaning and purpose. But God does not exist for our sake. Rather, we exist in order to give him glory:

> God hath all life, glory, goodness, blessedness, in and of himself; and
> is alone in and unto himself all-sufficient, not standing in need of any
> creatures which he hath made, nor deriving any glory from them, but
> only manifesting his own glory in, by, unto, and upon them. (6.012)

The great good news of the gospel is that through the high priestly ministry of Jesus Christ, we are brought into the inner life of the Trinity. Someday we will participate in the relationships between Father, Son, and Holy
Spirit, joining their dance of loving self-surrender. But even then, the relationships of love within the triune God will be beyond our comprehension.

The oneness of the three persons is another way in which God is not like
us, for none of the things that separate human people from each other separates the three persons of God's Being. We humans are separated from each
other by having different wills, different activities, different passions, different
gifts, and different loves. But none of these differences apply to God. In every
work of God in the world, the triune God is working; the distinction between
the persons is one of relation. Only the Father is the Origin, neither begotten
nor processing nor being originated: "The Father is of none, neither begotten nor proceeding" (6.013). Only the Son is eternally begotten of the Father
in an ongoing act without beginning. Only the Spirit eternally proceeds from
the Father and the Son. As the Second Helvetic Confession says:

> Thus there are not three gods, but three persons, consubstantial,
> coeternal, and coequal; distinct with respect to hypostases, and with
> respect to order, the one preceding the other yet without any inequal-
> ity. For according to the nature or essence they are so joined together
> that they are one God, and the divine nature is common to the Father,
> Son and Holy Spirit. (5.017)

Of course, the word "person" must be understood analogically and not in the
highly individualistic sense that we tend to use it in everyday discourse. Within
the doctrine of the Trinity, to say "person" is not to say "individual." Calvin
was so concerned about the potential misunderstanding of the word "person"
as too individualistic that he preferred to speak of the Father, Son, and Spirit
as three "subsistences," a literal translation of the Greek word *hypostases* used
in the Nicene Creed as well as in the quotation above.

On the other hand, we must not overemphasize the oneness of God, as can
easily happen if we use analogies from different functions within a single human
person. One of Augustine's favorite metaphors for the Trinity was memory,
understanding, and will—three functions of the human person that correspond
in some ways to the work of the three persons.[18] The danger with Augustine's
formulation is that we might undervalue the distinctions between the persons and fall into *modalism*, imagining that the one God simply appears to us in

different roles or modes of being, rather than as three distinguishable persons. Referring to God as the Creator, Sustainer, and Redeemer suggests such modalism, replacing personal titles with distinct activities. Modalistic language removes from view the creating work of the Spirit, the sanctifying work of the Son, the redemptive work of the Father, and the mediatorial work of Christ. We know the Father through Jesus Christ, and only through Jesus Christ. We receive the sustaining power of the Holy Spirit through Jesus Christ, and only through Jesus Christ. *The Study Catechism* concludes: "In the mystery of the one God, the three divine persons—Father, Son and Holy Spirit—live in, with and for one another eternally in perfect love and freedom."[19]

GOD'S NATURE

The Westminster Larger Catechism asks, "What is God?" and offers this answer:

> God is a Spirit, in and of himself infinite in being, glory, blessedness, and perfection; all-sufficient, eternal, unchangeable, incomprehensible, everywhere present, almighty; knowing all things, most wise, most holy, most just, most merciful and gracious, long-suffering, and abundant in goodness and truth. (7.117)

Clearly, this answer focuses on God's oneness, the divine Being that is shared by the three persons. These characteristics of God are commonly known as "attributes." It is important to note that many of God's attributes imply one another. So, for instance, the claim that God is eternal, not bound by time, suggests that God does not change as we do, since change is a temporal quality. This means that we cannot approach the catalog of God's attributes as if we are at a buffet, choosing to affirm God's eternality while simultaneously selecting the claim that he suffers with us. Some contemporary theologians have challenged various classical attributes, while wanting to hold on to others. Over time, this is being revealed as less and less coherent. The classical attributes of God are a package, and they must be accepted or rejected as a package. Recent developments in Christian theology, including the increasingly popular "Open Theism" movement, show that theologians are beginning to realize and accept the consequences of rejecting some of these attributes. Open Theists reject God's impassibility (freedom from suffering) and immutability (unchangeableness), but also freely admit the consequence of this rejection: God does not know the future and has limited power. A denial of God's unchangeableness, timelessness, or freedom from suffering must result in a denial of God's omnipotence and omniscience.

The Westminster Confession of Faith says of God's nature:

> There is but one only living and true God, who is infinite in being and
> perfection, a most pure spirit, invisible, without body, parts, or pas-
> sions, immutable, immense, eternal, incomprehensible, almighty;
> most wise, most holy, most free, most absolute, working all things
> according to the counsel of his own immutable and most righteous
> will, for his own glory; most loving, gracious, merciful, long-suffering,
> abundant in goodness and truth. (6.011)

In recent years, many theologians have come to question the claim that God
is "without passions" or "impassible," that is, that he cannot be hurt or changed
by external stimuli such as human behavior. Their argument is that a God
without passions is a static, unresponsive, distant deity who cannot truly love
us. The God whom we know through Scripture as Creator and Redeemer cannot be dismissed as static or inert. If God is changeless, it cannot be in the same
way that a rock is changeless. Once again, we come back to analogy and
remember that God is unlike humans. When a human being is unresponsive
or slow to change, it is seen as a deficiency, but changelessness is not a deficiency in God. God does not change, because, as we have noted, he is already
full and complete in his Being and his actions. The three persons of the Trinity offer themselves to one another in complete self-giving love, a love that
cannot increase because it is already God's entire nature. God pours out love
on us and on all his creatures constantly, a love that cannot increase because it
is already God's whole nature. The changelessness of a rock and the changelessness of God are infinitely different from one another. God does not change
because he is already maximally dynamic in his work of love, blessing, and joy.
That work cannot be diminished by anything that we do, but will always prevail in the face of all our little efforts to raise obstacles against it.

Reformed theologian Stephen Charnock lays the groundwork for God's
unchanging and impassible nature thus:

> The blessedness of God is hence evidenced. If God be Almighty, he
> can lack nothing; all lack speaks weakness. If he doth what he will, he
> cannot be miserable; all misery consists in those things which happen
> contrary to our will. There is nothing can hinder his happiness,
> because nothing can resist his power. Since he is omnipotent, nothing
> can hurt him, nothing can strip him of what he hath, of what he is. If
> he can do whatsoever he will, he cannot lack anything that he wills.
> He is as happy, as great, as glorious, as he will; for he hath a perfect
> liberty of will to will, and a perfect power to attain what he will; his
> will cannot be restrained, nor his power measured.[20]

God cannot suffer, because God is full love and joy in action. To suffer is to
lack something, and God can lack nothing.

Many contemporary Christians who find themselves in pain and suffering echo Dietrich Bonhoeffer in saying, "Only a suffering God can help." But, of course, human suffering is precisely the reason God was incarnate in Jesus Christ, the reason for Jesus to ascend as our heavenly high priest, fully human and fully divine for all of time. There would have been no need for such a mediator if God were already fully sharing in our suffering and pain. The confessions make clear that even in the incarnation, the two natures of Christ remain distinguishable. The Second Helvetic Confession teaches, "The divine nature of Christ is not passible, and the human nature is not everywhere. Therefore, we do not in anyway teach that the divine nature in Christ has suffered or that Christ according to his human nature is still in this world and thus is everywhere" (5.069). If God is changeable, suffering, and temporal, we have no need for a mediator, and the incarnation is valueless. It is only because God is eternal, immutable, and impassible that we marvel at his willingness to become a temporal, changeable, suffering human being.

Sin and its effects is the one place that we can hide from the overwhelming, glorious reality of God. Human suffering is a consequence of sin and evil, but God cannot be affected by these parasites that feed on goodness and replace truth with an illusion and a lie. God cannot participate in such a lie, but in taking on human nature, God in Jesus Christ enters into our illusions, letting loose the fullness of divine loving action and exploding the lie forever. The cross is the ultimate moment of human contact with the reality of God, resulting in the shattering of all illusions.

Our understanding of God's love in our pain and suffering is also analogical. When another human being loves us, that person suffers when we suffer. But it does not follow that suffering is constitutive of love. We draw this conclusion only if we believe that there is a *univocal* relationship between our experience of other people and our experience of God, that is, only if we believe that love is the same when we experience it from another human being or when we experience it from God. Suffering is part of creation, not part of the Creator, and to say that God suffers is to understand God in human terms, making human experience the definition of God. For many of us, it seems obvious that to be in relationship requires mutuality and the sharing of experiences. Indeed, God *does* share our experiences (this is the whole point of the incarnation), but our relationship with God will never be the reciprocal, mutual sort of relationship that we aspire to have with other human beings. What I need is not a God who feels my pain, but rather a God who is able to rescue me from my pain.

God is completely free, not accountable to any other principle or being. One of God's attributes is aseity, or self-sufficiency. All of God's extrinsic characteristics (i.e., all the ways in which God interacts with us) are free. *The Study*

Catechism asks the question, "Did God need the world in order to be God?" then answers, "No. God would still be God, eternally perfect and inexhaustibly rich, even if no creatures had ever been made. Yet without God, all created beings would simply fail to exist. Creatures can neither come into existence, nor continue, nor find fulfillment apart from God. God, however, is self-existent and self-sufficient."[21] This is a clear statement of God's self-sufficiency.[22] *The Study Catechism* then asks why God created the world, and gives the answer, "God's decision to create the world was an act of grace. In this decision God chose to grant existence to the world simply in order to bless it. God created the world to reveal God's glory, to share the love and freedom at the heart of God's triune being, and to give us eternal life in fellowship with God."[23] God's existence and nature is necessary, but God's dealings with us are free, not necessary at all.

Since God is free, none of his relations with his creatures is a necessary relationship. All of God's extrinsic properties—that is, his relations with creatures outside himself—are freely chosen; they could have been otherwise. Of course, once God has made a free choice, it becomes conditionally necessary. For instance, we know that God *has* created. Given that fact, his choice to create is now necessary. Since God is outside of time and since we know that he does make the free decision to create, then there is no point when he is not making that choice. Something that cannot "not be" is necessary. But with God, necessity is conditional on God's free choice.

God is both supremely transcendent and supremely immanent. We encounter God's transcendence in the narrative of the Israelites begging Moses to go up Mt. Sinai on their behalf. Our holy God is wholly other, unlike us in every way. On the other hand, we may also say that God is inescapably present to us. Not only in our redemption but already in our creation, we are bound to God by our complete dependence on him. There is no place that we can go to escape his presence, for he holds us in existence. As Paul says to the Athenians, "In him we live and move and have our being" (Acts 17:28).

Of all the good news that we receive in Jesus Christ, perhaps the best is this: that in Jesus Christ we see God, for Jesus is "the reflection of God's glory and the exact imprint of God's very being" (Heb. 1:3). The deep desire of our hearts is to seek God's face, and in Jesus Christ we are shown that face. For Jesus is our "helpmeet," divine help and presence come to us in one who is bone of our bones, flesh of our flesh, letting us know that we are not alone. Jesus wants to show us not only himself but also his Father, and to give us not only himself but also his Spirit, so that we may abide in union with the triune God. It is this triune God who is praised throughout our confessional tradition and throughout the history of Christianity. It is now our turn to join in giving him glory, honor, and praise.

To Thee, great One in Three,
The highest praises be,
Hence evermore!
Thy sovereign majesty
May we in glory see,
And to eternity
Love and adore.[24]

NOTES

1. C. S. Lewis, *A Grief Observed* (New York: Seabury Press, 1976), 76–77.
2. Augustine, *The Trinity*, trans. Edmund Hill (Brooklyn: New City Press, 1991), 1.2.7, p. 70.
3. See the *Constitution of the Presbyterian Church (U.S.A.)*, Part II, *Book of Order* (Louisville, KY: Office of the General Assembly, 2004), G-1.0301.
4. See the *Book of Order*, G-6.0108.
5. Augustine, *Trinity*, 1.1.4, p. 67.
6. Ibid., 1.1.1, p. 65.
7. Ronald Goetz, "The Suffering God: The Rise of a New Orthodoxy," *Christian Century*, April 16, 1986, 385. Accessed online at http://www.religion-online.org/showarticle.asp?title=1033 on May 3, 2005.
8. *Book of Order*, G-6.0108b.
9. *Book of Order*, W-1.2002.
10. *The Study Catechism* (Louisville, KY: Witherspoon Press, 1998), questions 11 and 13.
11. Ibid., question 12.
12. *Book of Order*, W-1.2002.
13. Or possibly "I WILL BE" (Exod. 3:14).
14. These examples were drawn from Michael Sudduth, "The Doctrine of Divine Simplicity," section 3, accessed online at http://www.homestead.com/philofreligion/files/Thomas3.html on June 1, 2004.
15. The Westminster Confession leans in this direction in 6.011.
16. Second Helvetic Confession, 5.015–.019. See also the Scots Confession, 3.01, and the Westminster Confession, 6.011–.013.
17. C. S. Lewis, *Mere Christianity* (New York: Macmillan, 1952), 126.
18. Augustine, *Trinity*, 10.11.18.
19. *Study Catechism*, question 17.
20. Stephen Charnock, *Discourses upon the Existence and Attributes of God*, vol. 2 (Grand Rapids: Baker Books, 1979), 86.
21. *Study Catechism*, question 25.
22. See also question 27, which refers to God as "self-sufficient."
23. *Study Catechism*, 26.
24. "Come Thou Almighty King," author unknown.

7

Who Are We?

Willie James Jennings

The Book of Confessions offers to teach us who we are. This is not an easy task because most people seem quite sure who they are. Yet the goal of *The Book of Confessions* is not to destroy our confident self-knowledge, but to guide it to maturity. The expression "immature confidence" would strike most people as a strange way to characterize human self-knowledge. Doesn't it make more sense to say that our confidence may be *pre*mature? Should we not say that our confidence must be guided by our degree of self-knowledge, so that as we grow in knowledge of ourselves our confidence will grow? But *The Book of Confessions* presents a different perspective on self-knowledge; the issue is not how much we know, but whether we are able to live with self-knowledge at all.

THE TROUBLE WITH BEGINNINGS

Dietrich Bonhoeffer summed up an ancient Christian insight by observing that from the beginning of our life to its end, self-knowledge is overwhelming. Reflecting on the creation of the world, Bonhoeffer said that knowledge of our beginning must be brought to us.[1] At one level he was simply saying that since no human being was present at the creation of the world, knowledge of that beginning must be brought to us by another. That knowledge of creation's beginning, Bonhoeffer suggested, is a gift given to us by God. At a different level, however, Bonhoeffer recognized another side of the gift: We cannot live with what we know about our world or about ourselves without God's help. What do we know? We know many things, but all that we learn and all that we know only circles around the center of our knowledge, and that center is the knowledge of our vulnerability. This relationship of knowledge to vulnerability is not self-evident. We are accustomed to believe that knowledge is power. Knowledge does give power, of course, yet knowledge also exposes the vulnerability and instability of life itself, particularly the vulnerability and instability of our own lives.

God created all there is, including us, out of nothing. *The Book of Confessions* eloquently articulates the implications of this Christian belief for understanding our human condition. "It pleased God the Father, Son, and Holy Ghost," says the Westminster Confession, "for the manifestation of the glory of his eternal power, wisdom, and goodness, in the beginning, to create or make of nothing the world, and all things therein, whether visible or invisible" (6.022). There is intense beauty as well as horror in knowing that our lives come out of nothing. The beauty finds expression in hearing the confessions speak of God's providential purpose in creating, caring for, and loving us. God, out of neither need nor compulsion, created us for love. God, out of neither need nor compulsion, intimately cares for us. The horror presents itself quietly in the thunderous joy of our creation; nothing has to exist, *we* do not have to exist. We have no inherent right to be, and our lives carry no inherent stability to shield us from chaos or death. All beginnings lack eternality. All beginnings carry inescapable fragility. All beginnings are troubled. All beginnings face death.

What lies between this beauty and horror is freedom. Our freedom echoes the freedom out of which God created the world, but it is only an echo. Our freedom requires God for its fulfillment. God must speak and we must hear in order to be truly free. But the story *The Book of Confessions* rehearses again and again is that we cannot handle knowledge of our freedom. A Brief Statement of Faith states the matter with stark simplicity: "We hide from our Creator. Ignoring God's commandments, we violate the image of God in others and ourselves, [and] accept lies as truth" (10.3). Our folly begins with the belief that we can handle the knowledge that nothing in the creation, including our bodies, is immutable or must be ordered in a particular way. All things may be adjusted, altered, or augmented, as well as manipulated or deformed. What greater folly than to look into the abyss of death and believe we can create personal arrangements, technological devices, and political systems that could negotiate a truce with death, even overcome it? Today we lack the humility of the Second Helvetic Confession, which reminds us that even "in the regenerate a weakness remains . . . [so] they do not easily accomplish in all things what they had planned" (5.049). The permanence of our mutability sets the stage for faith or folly. We often choose folly.

IN SEARCH OF GOD'S GARDEN

Who are we? We are creatures who desperately need to be taught to live with what we know. The history of the world could be written as episodes in the failure to live with knowledge. Such a history would turn on its head every story of human progress. The standard story of the world—told as the progression of human evolution, technological development, and the accumulation of knowledge—reflects our misguided quest. Knowing more has never been the crucial matter. Indeed, from the beginning God set us in a place where traversing the frontiers of discovery, knowledge, and understanding would characterize our journey. But the journey began badly with our banishment from God's garden, and with that banishment came the loss of deep communion with our Creator. "All mankind, by their fall, lost communion with God," says the Shorter Catechism, "and so [are] liable to all miseries of this life, to death itself" (7.019). The human quest for knowledge proceeds without the communion with God and others, and so, no matter how noble, the discovery of truth and the eradication of ignorance carry with them the impoverishment of loss.

"God has created human beings for a personal relation with himself that they may respond to the love of the Creator" (9.17).[2] Because God created us for communion, we require communion in order to live with knowledge. God created us as a home suitable for the divine presence which would embrace us, instruct us, and guide our feet along a path toward knowledge of our world and one another. Yet as *The Book of Confessions* powerfully registers, we have disrupted communion with God and one another. Acknowledgment of disrupted communion is not confined to older confessions. The Confession of 1967 voices the stark judgment that "in sin, people claim mastery of their own lives, turn against God and each other, and become exploiters and despoilers of the world. They lose their humanity in futile striving and are left in rebellion, despair, and isolation" (9.12). The disruption and corruption of original sin is a theological claim that requires us to look and listen carefully and patiently to understand its implications. This claim might seem counterintuitive: Don't we live in families, cultural collectives, social communities, tribes, and nations? Isn't community fundamental to our identity? Yet the implications of broken communion are all around us because we live without true communion, and its loss is our deepest deprivation.

In *Modern Social Imaginaries*, Charles Taylor suggests that our understanding of moral and social order is inextricably bound to the kind of social collective we imagine that we inhabit. Taylor argues that Western peoples, among others, are often unaware of the profound changes that have taken place in the way we imagine our social existence. So, for example, ideas such as individual human rights—which are part of a reconfigured social imaginary—now seem natural to a moral and social order. Taylor is not alone in articulating a social imaginary; other political philosophers have drawn similar conclusions.[3] Taylor and others have put their finger on something that may help us grasp the depth of our loss of communion, for how we imagine habitation reflects our damaged and damaging condition.

Our lives were meant to be lived in a garden with God. This is not a romantic fantasy that we abandon as we mature; it is the context from which we come to see our loss. It is from the garden that we see the world rightly, grasping the deep connections that create healthy habitation. Seeing rightly begins with the way we were intended to view one another as male and female in communion with God. The Confession of 1967 is explicit in its affirmation that "the relationship between man and woman exemplifies in a basic way God's ordering of the interpersonal life for which God created humankind" (9.47d). Our first loss is the loss of communion between men and women, for we live in a world where men and women live their lives in distorting isolation. Our sinful condition means that we live out a form of bad faith: We believe we do not need each other to know ourselves, understand ourselves, or see ourselves. Our relationships are shrouded by the isolation and distrust witnessed in our first parents. The Second Helvetic Confession captures this sense of loss:

> By sin we understand that innate corruption of man which has been derived or propagated in us all from our first parents, by which we, immersed in perverse desires and averse to all good, are inclined to all evil. Full of all wickedness, distrust, contempt and hatred of God, we are unable to do or even to think anything good of ourselves. Moreover, even as we grow older, so by wicked thoughts, words and deeds committed against God's law, we bring forth corrupt fruit worthy of an evil tree. (5.037)

We can appreciate the interpretive power of this assessment of our condition if we think first not of a lone individual (the great fiction of our times) but of the relationship between men and women in the world. Reading our relationship through this confessional statement touches the depth of difficult living we inherited from our first parents. Our relationship as men and women in the world is clearly "full of all wickedness, distrust, contempt and hatred of God," and we are indeed "unable to think anything good of ourselves." We struggle deeply to see each other beyond categories of either use-value or obstacle to our humanity, for we have not become "one flesh." We went from God's garden into God's world utterly ill-equipped to handle knowledge of one another. Men in the hands of women, women in the hands of men—like clay in the hands of novice potters, we constantly fail to shape what might be. Fumbling and bumbling without God's communion to guide us, we damage, distort, or destroy one another. Yet it is exactly at the point of relationships that our confidence in self-knowledge manifests not only immaturity but delusion. We are convinced that we understand love, navigating its currents and mapping out its ways. For us love has become a fetish that conceals that we are lost in the world. We need God to destroy our confidence in our love in order to free us to live. Human love searches for fulfillment, for its *telos*, its reason for being. We know this, but what do we do with such knowledge? We squander it.

THE ECOLOGY OF WEAKNESS

Our hands are filled with gifts that fall aimlessly to the ground. We carry into our relationship with the rest of creation the same novice status that marks our relationships as men and women. We handle dirt, but we have not learned how to handle the great lesson dirt teaches: We are one with the dirt. God brought us into being from the dirt, and to the dirt we shall return. Between that coming and going lies the exact nature of all life, human and nonhuman: Life is fragile and subject to chaos. A proper ecological sensibility begins with honoring our connection to all of creation. But to borrow from Taylor again, the Western social imaginary (among other social imaginaries) does not embrace such connectedness. Theologically speaking, something more damning is in play: All of creation suffers because of our aimlessness. In the words of A Brief Statement of Faith, we "exploit neighbor and nature, and threaten death to the planet entrusted to our care" (10.3). We do not know how to be with dirt and with God, and thus our immaturity blocks the creation from becoming what it is meant to be.

Our time is unique less for its comprehensive global abuse of the creation than for our illusion of mastery over it. While we shut our senses to the echo of God's word in the creation, we allow the creation to teach us only as it serves us. The lesson we learn (a false lesson to be sure) is that the land is mere private property, owned by someone or by some nation-state, ready to have its potential realized through sequestered cultivation or public development. Human communities have never been so disconnected from the land even as we claim to care for it. The land's fragility has become its transmutability; it can be used however we wish or become whatever we desire. As with land so with our bodies and the bodies of animals: They can be used however we wish or become whatever we desire. Yet our potential or realized irresponsibility with such power is not the point. The point is our inability to live into our connectedness with the creation. The ease with which creation may be manipulated mirrors the inherent instability of our lives. Creativity is bound to chaos, and only God can lead us to life.

We are inescapably subjected to chaos from the beginning to the end of life. God's presence to us was never meant to hide from us the weakness of our humanity. However, our sinful condition is not the equivalent of being human. As Ray Anderson says, our humanity appears on the field of our creatureliness.[4] To be human is to be subject to the winds, to be like grass. Broken bodies and minds—deformed, distorted, missing pieces, having too much or too little—find weakness where there should be strength, rigidity where there should be flexibility. All of this comes with being human. We might conclude that if we had not turned away from God at the beginning we would never have known our imperfections, but such speculation misses the point of our fragility. The Heidelberg Catechism captures this point:

> **Q. What is your only comfort, in life and in death?**
> A. That I belong—body and soul, in life and in death—not to myself but to my faithful Savior, Jesus Christ, who at the cost of his own blood has fully paid for all my sins and has completely freed me from the dominion of the devil; that he protects me so well that without the will of my Father in heaven not a hair can fall from my head; indeed, that everything must fit his purpose for my salvation. Therefore, by his Holy Spirit, he also assures me of eternal life, and makes me wholeheartedly willing and ready from now on to live for him. (4.001)

This statement richly presents the gospel story. Even more, it powerfully articulates the importance of belonging. If a sense of belonging to the triune God does not school us in the knowledge of our fragility, then fragility becomes a stumbling block. Fragility mishandled leads to creativity misused. A self-destructive artist whose work expresses our human fragility in ways that distort the soul is sister to a misguided scientist whose work damages the body while seeking to negotiate its weaknesses. Creativity and fragility were meant to live peaceably together, speaking to each other and helping us journey in a world of endless possibilities, but we constantly turn our creativity against our fragility. Such endless turnings witness the absence of God's presence.

God prepared us to live in weakness, not in sin and death. Sin and death turn weakness into our obsession. We search tirelessly for strength to cover weakness, for power that negates vulnerability. This is an honest search, but it need not be. God is the strength we need and the power our flesh longs to consume. Our hunger for power exposes our sinful condition's grotesque scars. That hunger turns human community into a series of failed and ever failing projects. Our failure to form life-giving community is a failure of imagination. Although we can imagine a worldwide community—"God has created the peoples of the earth to be one universal family" (9.43)—our imagination has been seduced and turned toward death.

The failure of community is the result of a seduced social imagination: "Our first parents, being seduced by the subtilty and temptation of Satan, sinned in eating the forbidden fruit. . . . By this sin they fell from their original righteousness and communion with God" (6.031–.032). The first children of the first parents further exemplify this seduction. Cain imagined Abel his competitor, the other who thwarted his thriving. Cain imagined Abel his enemy, not his brother. Thus, Cain shows us that violence is the fruit of a seduced social imagination. Our social imagination works isolation and violence. The first brothers typify the ways of nations and peoples. We wander the world with social imaginations distorted by sin, unable to enact what we know: that we are connected, of one family, of one flesh. Such an enactment would require that we live in an ecology of weakness, renouncing worldly power and offering ourselves to God to live in holy communion. But our failures ever haunt us, reducing this social imaginary to ridiculed fantasy.

THE MANY FOR THE ONE

For all our knowing and searching for knowledge, there is one thing that we do not know. We do not know that we need a savior. God is not the answer to the questions we pose; God is the question to the answers we offer up for the dilemmas we encounter in our wandering. In this regard, God is an unwanted question, a disruption to our mapped-out journey. Yet we are creatures in need of disruption, and God did just that by becoming flesh in Jesus of Nazareth. Despite their different origins over space and time, the confessions each find their way to this home, Jesus Christ. Jesus Christ presents to us the question of identity: Do you know who you are? The question is not a test of knowledge but an invitation to communion. In response to this question, we pose another question: How can this one man be decisive for us? Our question reveals that we in fact know our weakness. We know that no one can overcome the problems of our flesh: our failures in relating to one another, our fears of fragility, our warring madness, our captivity to death.

The Scots Confession addresses our problem directly: "Since . . . no flesh by itself could or might have attained unto God, it behooved the Son of God to descend unto us and take himself a body of our body, flesh of our flesh, and bone of our bone, and so become the Mediator between God and man" (3.08). From the Nicene Creed ("For us and for our salvation [the Son of God] came down from heaven" [1.2]) to A Brief Statement of Faith ("Loving us still, God makes us heirs with Christ of the covenant" [10.3]) the church's confessions proclaim Jesus Christ as the one in whom "true humanity was realized once for all" (9.08).

Jesus does not present us with more knowledge that would better enable us to master our weakness. Jesus offers us life with the one who has joined human weakness to divine strength. Jesus is the one who brings us to our new home with God, teaching us how to live with what we know. This is the journey of the many following the one: the great reversal of our distorted journey in which one follows the many.

The many and the one are bound together, never existing without the other. Perhaps the greatest achievement of Western modernity is that it helps us imagine with exquisite clarity the one over against the many—the individual's desires, hopes, dreams, and plans all detached from the many. The many become merely the stage on which the individual reaches self-realization. In this dream-become-reality, the one builds community by ever expanding her vision of possession: first a relationship, then a family, then a home, a community, a city, a nation—her life. The problem of individualism in our time is unrelenting, because this ideology is a compelling way of understanding the many. This ideology teaches us that we must safeguard our lives from the undue influence of the many. Indeed, the many is simply aggregated ones seeking to have power over others. Thus, the many must become a work-in-progress of the one. Slowly, by sheer choice, each one of us forms our own collective. Our claims for communal existence find their logic in the desire of the individual. Modern individualism distorts our vision. The love of people and the fear of people are so tightly woven together in us and in the formation of our communities that we really cannot distinguish the one from the other.

Jesus is the one who calls the many. The great reversal that Jesus establishes begins by becoming the only one that truly matters. He is the one who separates our fear of people from our desire to love by inviting us to love him as he loves us. Once accepted, this invitation ends the journey of the individual and begins the journey of the many. "Out of Israel, God in due time raised up Jesus. His faith and obedience were the response of the perfect child of God. He was the fulfillment of God's promise to Israel, the beginning of the new creation, and the pioneer of the new humanity" (9.19). The many are found together with Jesus. From the moment of that discovery we start the difficult and painful work of learning to love one another as he loves us. It is painful and difficult precisely because we indeed know one another. We know what evil we have done, continue to do, and are capable of doing.

But what becomes of the individual? The individual becomes a work-in-progress of the one true God revealed in Jesus Christ. The individual becomes a work-in-progress of communion. We find ourselves only as we enter this holy journey of discovery with our brothers and sisters. The individual does exist, yet slowly on this journey God unravels the patterned identity formed by our accumulated knowledge. This is a work of mercy and grace because there are many things we know about ourselves that we cannot handle alone. Only God working by the Holy Spirit through the many can cut a redemptive space between who I know I am and who God is calling me to be. Every confession reminds us that God is calling us to enter that space where the new creature emerges—never alone, always with others. The essentially communal character of this new creation is underscored by Westminster: "By the indwelling of the Holy Spirit all believers being vitally united to Christ, who is the Head, are thus united one to another" (6.054).

Jesus Christ invites us to learn who we are through a life of disciplined listening. Our time presents to us tremendous challenges to disciplined listening. Our bodies and minds are inundated with the noise of information. In every possible quiet space we attack silence, believing the lie that we might miss the revelation of new knowledge. Thus, for fear of missing the new, we allow into our souls a stream of technologically generated noise that thwarts disciplined listening. Our noise witnesses our chaos, no matter how much knowledge we receive from its currents. Disciplined listening requires not only a desire to know but a willingness to ask humbly for divine guidance.

Such guidance may be found in the imperfect witness of the many who have followed Jesus, trying to listen carefully to what the Spirit says to the churches. The witnesses offered within *The Book of Confessions* have power to instruct us precisely because they cut against the grain of our era's illusions.

NOTES

1. See Dietrich Bonhoeffer, *Creation and Fall: A Theological Exposition of Genesis 1–3* (Minneapolis: Fortress Press, 1997).
2. This and other quotations from C67 are from *The Confession of 1967: Inclusive Language Text* (Louisville, KY: Office of Theology and Worship, 2002).
3. See Charles Taylor, *Modern Social Imaginaries* (Durham, NC: Duke University Press, 2004); Susan Buck-Morss, *Dreamworld and Catastrophe: The Passing of Mass Utopia in East and West* (Cambridge, MA: MIT Press, 2000), 11–14; Cornelius Castoriadis, *The Imaginary Institution of Society* (Cambridge, MA: MIT Press, 1987); and Jean-Paul Sartre, *The Imaginary* (London: Routledge, 2004).
4. Ray S. Anderson, *On Being Human: Essays in Theological Anthropology* (Grand Rapids: Eerdmans, 1982), 21.

8

What Does God Have to Do with Us?

Cynthia L. Rigby

A certain sports T-shirt was quite popular a couple of years ago. On the front of the shirt was an image of a basketball, football, golf club, or fishing pole. Underneath the image were the words "Basketball is life" (or golf or fishing, etc.). On the back of the T-shirt in big bold lettering was the phrase "The rest is just details." Perhaps PC(USA) T-shirts could feature an open *Book of Confessions* with a single highlighted line: "In life and in death we belong to God." And, of course, on the back: "The rest is just details."

Clearly the confessions do not minimize the importance of details. As those who belong to God, we are called to obedience and good works (4.086). But too often we forget that everything else, however essential, is grounded in our identity as God's children. "What does God have to do with us?" The answer is simply stated, but hard to live into: God is the one to whom we belong. The confessions recognize through and through that it is precisely in knowing *whose* we are that we know *who* we are.

What does it mean to "belong to God"? In answering this question I first remember that our convictions about how God is related to us are shaped by our confessional inheritance. I then reflect, in conversation with the confessions, on how belonging to God brings *comfort*, and on how it poses *challenges*. Finally, I consider what it looks like to live as those whom God has claimed: What does it mean, exactly, to "wear" our belongingness to God?

OUR CONFESSIONAL CONTEXTS

Believers through the ages have wondered, "What does God have to do with us?" Looking at the divine handiwork displayed in the beauty of the night sky, the psalmist could not help but ask God "What are human beings that you are mindful of them?" (Ps. 8:4). And yet the psalmist, like the later writers of the confessions, recognized that, indeed, God is mindful of us. Hard as it is to believe, God has "crowned us with glory and honor," giving us authority and responsibility in relationship to the rest of creation (see Ps. 8:5–8).

The very existence of *The Book of Confessions* is premised on the conviction that God does have something to do with us. It is full not of lessons about God, but of testimonies to the character of God's involvement in our lives and in our world. The purpose of confessions is not primarily to disseminate theological information, then, but to bear witness to the "nonsensical" reality that we are known, loved, and embraced by the almighty creator of the universe.

As confessional people, we who bear witness to the reality of God's relationship to us continuously seek to understand the character of this relationship. Because we pray, believe, and testify in particular contexts, specific confessions have emerged that articulate how, in distinct historical moments, God has somehow been present. Consistent with our belief that God's Word meets us ever anew in each historical moment, *The Book of Confessions* encourages ongoing reflection on what God is saying to us both across time and today. In the context of sixteenth-century clericalism, for example, Luther's catechisms are framed by the revolutionary insight that God is related to us not by way of the church, nor by works, but by faith alone through Christ alone. In the face of Hitler's self-proclaimed messianism, the Theological Declaration of Barmen insists that what God has to do with us cannot be discerned by way of any lord other than Jesus Christ himself. The confessions remind us that to ask, "What does God have to do with us?" means asking, "What does God have to do with us at this moment, in this place?"

OUR ONLY COMFORT

While each confession in *The Book of Confessions* offers a salient example of how the people of God have understood God to speak a particular word in a particular moment, all share in developing some common theological insights. I will focus the remainder of this essay on the most fundamental of these: that incomprehensible mystery borne witness to by Paul's conviction that "neither death, nor life, . . . nor anything else in all creation, will be able to separate us from the love of God in Christ Jesus our Lord" (Rom. 8:38–39). The confessions insist that one can go no further in exploring what God has to do with us, if one has not first been overcome by this. It may be a surprise to some that the confessions are not trying to make sense of this love as much as urging us to stand in awe of it, as grateful participants.

Belonging to God brings us great *comfort*, according to the confessions. As the first question of the Heidelberg Catechism puts it, it is the fact that we belong "not to [ourselves]" but to our "faithful Savior, Jesus Christ" that is our "only comfort, in life and in death" (4.001).

What is so comforting about "belonging to God"? The answer to this question is not self-evident, particularly in twenty-first-century America. From where we stand, "belonging" to another is often understood to be far from ideal. It evokes in us painful memories of historical instances in which the belonging of one to another was abusive, not comforting. The nineteenth and twentieth centuries were times when consciousness rose regarding the ownership of slaves by masters, the absorption of wives' identities into those of their husbands, and the economic possession of some countries by others. In reaction to these oppressive power relationships, it is no wonder that we tend to value autonomy over interdependence. Even when we do recognize our investment in the lives of others we tend to articulate it in terms that emphasize mutuality. To speak the language of "belonging," by contrast, is to be suspected of codependency.

Related to this, we live in an age that is far more wary than the drafters of many of the confessions were about belonging to a God who is *sovereign*. The confession that the God to whom we belong "rules" and "guides" us by "his inscrutable providence for such end as his eternal wisdom, goodness, and justice have appointed" (3.01), for example, serves to highlight our lack of autonomy. But the confessional insistence that the God to whom we belong is in sovereign control of all things also raises the ante on theodicy, the question of God's justice in light of the pervasive presence of evil. The writers of the confessions were generally reassured by the idea that the God to whom we belong wills—and even sends—the harm that comes to us (see 4.001 and 4.026). Contemporary persons, by contrast, are often troubled by the notion that the God to whom we belong would in any sense will suffering or pain. In the popular book *When Bad Things Happen to Good People*, for example, Harold Kushner argues that we are more comforted in the face of suffering when we acknowledge that the God to whom we belong "can't do everything." Whatever sense of belonging is operative for Kushner, it is not belonging to a sovereign God. The writers of the Heidelberg Catechism would, no doubt, press Kushner on the matter of the degree to which he can be comforted by a God who is not, finally, in control. Surely, the authors of A Brief Statement of Faith might say that such a God cannot be counted on in death or in life.

Ironically, our very quest for autonomy has precipitated a deep yearning for belonging. Even as we have come to recognize how those who have been possessed have also been disempowered, we have also grown in our awareness of the vast scope of the cosmos. As those who are struggling to actualize their autonomy, this is, of course, disconcerting. William Placher and David Willis-Watkins suggest, in their commentary on A Brief Statement of Faith, that the realization that the cosmos is impersonal, as well as ever expanding, can add to our sense of malaise, our yearning to belong to one who knows us.[1] An old *Calvin and Hobbes* cartoon captures this sentiment. The little boy Calvin, staring up at the sky on a clear, starry night, lifts his hands in the air and cries, "I am significant! . . ." ". . . Screamed the dust speck," he adds—hands lowered—in the second frame. Notice that little Calvin's ruminations are very different from those of the psalmist in Psalm 8. The magnitude of creation in and of itself leads us to recognize our insignificance; the magnitude of creation, for those who know they are claimed by God, leads us to marvel at our own value and responsibility.

Coupled with our ambivalent relationship to the expanding universe is our growing commitment to pluralism, which can lead some to feel that they are "getting lost in the crowd."[2] I would guess that the basis of the success of recent television situation comedies such as *Cheers*, *Friends*, and *Seinfeld* is largely the reassurance they offer that there is a place "where everybody knows your name" and "they're always glad you came." People yearn for a place, and a community, to which to belong.

When I was a Master of Divinity student in the mid-1980s, one of my professors commented that he thought the fear of being alone far outranked the fear of death for most people. The professor went on to teach us that we, as future ministers, would have something to offer to those who are afraid of loneliness. In making his point, he quoted from the opening to the brand-new Brief Statement as well as from Paul Tillich's sermon "You Are Accepted." If we could only know that we belong to God, in life and in death! If we could only live into the realization that "we are accepted," our deepest fears would be lifted away. Everything, for us, would then be different.

But recognizing our belongingness is easier said than done. How does one go about knowing that one belongs? That one is accepted? How does a preacher go about convincing another that she belongs? That he is accepted? Near the end of his sermon, Tillich issues an imperative: "Do not seek for anything; do not perform anything; do not intend anything. *Simply accept the fact that you are accepted*," he says.[3] But how can I accept such a fact when I don't believe I really belong? Can one really recognize one's belonging, can one claim one's acceptance, by an act of sheer will?

The confessions acknowledge the problem. Apart from the grace of God, we are unable to know the grace of God. We cannot know we are accepted; we are ignorant of our belonging; we are stuck in the misery of our would-be autonomy, our utter loneliness. But God works, in and through the power of the Holy Spirit, to convince us of that which we cannot believe for ourselves.

According to the Westminster Confession of Faith, the Holy Spirit makes us "willing and able to believe" (6.039).

From the perspective of our contemporary tendency to glorify autonomy and free will, the idea that we are unable to come to knowledge of our belongingness apart from God's election of us only adds insult to injury. Not only do we belong to God rather than to ourselves, but we cannot even recognize our belongingness apart from God's help! On this point, the confessions clearly tend to reflect the view that human beings are "totally depraved." Contrary to popular belief, the controversial doctrine of total depravity is not meant to communicate how worthless we are. Rather, it names our incapacity to recognize how valuable we are, that we are valued by God.

How is it, then, that one comes to live in recognition of one's belongingness? I have suggested that coming to such recognition is not easy for at least two reasons. First, our cultural ethos in twenty-first-century America is in many ways resistant to "belonging" as an ideal. I mentioned that this is especially the case in relation to the notion that we belong to someone who is more powerful than us, a God who is sovereign. Second, as the confessions bear witness, coming to recognition of God's claim on us is impossible for us apart from the work of the Holy Spirit. In addition to being unable to recognize our acceptance, we are unwilling to recognize our incapacity to accept our acceptance, which adds to the quandary.

I suggest that there is a certain posture we can develop toward living in deeper recognition of the fact that "in life and in death we belong to God." I will describe two aspects of this posture as I see them reflected in the confessions. Neither of these, of course, circumvent the fact that knowing God's claim on us is God's work and not ours. But they do help position us to live in deeper recognition of the grace that has claimed us and will continue to reclaim us. As another of my teachers once put it, "You cannot find God. God finds you. But you can work on being enough of a person that God can find."

What, then, are the two aspects of this posture that the confessions themselves so well model? First, begin with our remembering that even the recognition of our belongingness is a divine work to which we contribute nothing. God's graceful work in, for, and through us is truly the impossible thing that God has made possible. Taking time to marvel at the character of God's amazing grace provokes renewed awareness of our corresponding wretchedness. As the Confession of 1967 puts it, "The reconciling act of God in Jesus Christ exposes the evil in people as sin in the sight of God" (9.12; see also 4.002).[4] There is nothing that provokes a sense of unworthiness faster than all-knowing, unconditional love, and nothing that better positions us to revel in the magnitude of grace than a profound recognition of our unworthiness.

Living in the dialectic of knowing we are claimed and knowing that there is nothing we can do to earn that claim frees us from the burden of trying to prove our value to God. It is precisely then that we *can* make a contribution as those who belong to God and are therefore fully included in the divine life and work. At their best, the confessions even bear witness to how our belongingness to this one on whom we are utterly dependent does not stymie us (as contemporary defenders of autonomy had feared), but frees us to be who we are called to be as God's children. Unlike the elder son in the parable of the prodigal (Luke 15), we no longer think in terms of earning and receiving our fair share. We know that salvation is not founded in a system of exchange, even a system that forgives debt in order to keep the mechanism running smoothly. As the father desires, we do recognize that we are always with God and that all that God has is ours (Luke 15:31).

The second aspect of a posture that is open to recognizing our belongingness, also modeled by the confessions, is attentiveness to the concrete manifestations of God's self-revelation as Father, Son, and Holy Spirit. God's acts do not make God's claim on us any more manageable, but they do give us who have been claimed by God a way of participating more deeply in the mystery of grace by reminding us that it is not an abstract principle. Rather, our belonging to God is known concretely, in and through the persons of the Father, the Son, and the Holy Spirit. Every one of the confessions evokes the Trinity, and in doing so simultaneously affirms God's claim on us by virtue of God's particular ways of being for us. To confess that God is triune is to recognize that the One who is unknowable has made God's very self known. It is to bear witness to the unfathomable reality that we have fellowship with the God who is all in all because this God has determined to have something to do with us. To say that God is Father, Son, and Spirit who creates, redeems, and sustains is already to say, specifically, what God *does* have to do with us. God the Creator guides us through salvation history, enlivening us to be ourselves creative, contributing to the shape of the coming kingdom. God the Son frees us from sin, reveals the loving character of the Father, and invites us to life abundant. God the Spirit intercedes for us when we cannot pray, testifies to the divinity of the Son, and fills us with courage to pray and to be prophetic "in a broken and fearful world" (10.4).

The confessions model for us, again, what it looks like to "posture ourselves" to be comforted, ever anew, by the fact of our belongingness to God. As those who recognize that we lack the capacity to conceive of God's claim on us, we look to the reminder of God's triune self-revelation. Revisiting, again, what God has to do with us in the persons of the Father, the Son, and the Holy Spirit, we witness God's acceptance in action and remember that it is God who has met us, so that we might be exalted to participation in the very life of God. We are baptized, and we eat the bread and drink the cup—even as the confessions instruct—not as those who always know that they are accepted, but as those who are accepted by virtue of the condescension and exaltation of God on our behalf.

NO OTHER LORDS

To belong to God brings challenge as well as comfort. As Karl Barth points out in his commentary on the first question of the Heidelberg Catechism, belonging uncompromisingly to Jesus Christ sets us up for a strange existence, from the perspective of this world. It means that we live "eccentrically." It means we are oriented not around our own selves (concentrically), but around "this Other" to whom we belong.[5] And to live as those whose center is Jesus Christ is to live as those who are comforted, rather than as those who are anxious. Insofar as "anxiety is the comprehensive expression for the existence of a comfortless man," explains Barth, "anxiety about myself is not my affair."[6] In a world where being in charge of one's own life, wallowing in one's own miseries, and taking credit for one's own successes is expected and encouraged, to live as one who belongs to God is to be nothing less than a misfit.

As the confessions reflect, God's uncompromising, identity-shaping claim on us is no more evident than in the first commandment of the Decalogue: "I am the LORD your God, who brought you out of the land of Egypt, out of the house of slavery; you shall have no other gods before me" (Exod. 20:2–3). According to the Heidelberg Catechism, adherence to this commandment entails that we "trust," "love," "fear," and "honor" God above all else. "I should rather turn my back on all creatures," it says, "than do the least thing against [God's] will" (4.094). The jealous God to whom we belong is intolerant not only of huge displays of disloyalty or unfaithfulness but also, it seems, of what we might mistakenly perceive as mere flirtations. Our belonging to God is so all-encompassing that it restricts us; the very limitations precipitated by God's radical claim on us frame a context in which we can fall more deeply in love with the one who has first loved us.[7]

The challenge for those of us who aspire to autonomy is, of course, that we do not like to be restricted. If we could somehow know that adhering to restrictions would lead to greater enjoyment of God *before* we actually embraced them, living the life of those who belong to God would be far less challenging. But one cannot know the "in life and death" comfort of God's protective arms until one has taken the leap that flees all idolatry, risks losing autonomy, and renounces ownership of one's very self. Apart from our awareness of God's embrace, any suspicion that "love so amazing, so divine" will demand "my soul, my life, my all" is liable to send us running away from the first commandment's demand for faithfulness, seeking those very idolatries that make us feel safe.[8]

This model also challenges those of us whose most pronounced sin is not our desire for autonomy but our resistance to recognizing ourselves as valuable individuals. Belonging to God and God alone restricts autonomy, and in that sense it offers a correction to the sin of pride. But it also upholds the value and irreplaceability of the one who is possessed, offering a correction to the sin of self-loathing. To know that one belongs to God so completely that the very hairs on one's head are numbered, that every day of one's life is known to God before one of them came to be, and that one has been called by name is challenging—to say the least—for those who do not believe they are worth knowing. The person who is guilty of self-deprecation and the person guilty of pride will both resist their belongingness to God, since knowing one's identity as God's child both affirms who we are and insists that we are not our own.

Another challenge related to our belonging to God is the level at which we are expected to contribute to this relationship. The confessions in no way try to minimize the demands of Christian discipleship. They could never be charged with propagating "cheap grace," as Bonhoeffer called it. They are clearly not in the business of marketing Christian life, particularly to a culture like ours, obsessed with finding quick fixes and low-maintenance solutions. On the contrary, an impossible number of "duties," required by the first commandment, are often indicated. As a manifestation of our absolute faithfulness, the Larger Catechism explains that the God to whom we belong desires for us to "worship and glorify" God by

> thinking, meditating, remembering, highly esteeming, honoring, adoring, choosing, loving, desiring, fearing of [God]; believing [God]; trusting, hoping, delighting, rejoicing in [God]; being zealous for [God]; calling upon [God], giving all praise and thanks, and yielding all obedience and submission to [God] . . . being careful in all things to please [God], and sorrowful when in anything [God] is offended; and walking humbly with [God]. (7.214)

As if this is not enough, the list of "sins forbidden" by the first commandment is twice as long (7.215)!

Clearly, adherence to all of the first commandment's "duties" and resistance to all of its sins is impossible. Most of us will be able to do (or not do) some of these things some of the time, but no one can be perfectly loyal to God. To focus on being so would itself be misplaced effort—an idolatrous way of life that has forgotten its identity in the God to whom it belongs, forsaking the relationship itself for the sake of keeping rules.

If the confessions aim to redirect us continuously toward our belongingness to God, why is there so much emphasis on our duties? Why is there such specificity about the sins we are to avoid? Perhaps the details themselves direct us to our belongingness. Were it possible to fulfill all of our duties, to circumvent all sins, our energy would be invested in working our way to perfection. But attending to these lengthy lists in the confessions cures us of any sentiment that we can "get it right," reminding us again that living fully into the fact of our belongingness is, in this world, impossible. Simultaneously, they remind us, therefore, of the depth of our belongingness—of the claim that God has made on us. As with Jesus' Sermon on the Mount, we either leave these conversations with the confessions in great frustration, or we hear in them the point that the call to perfection is a call to live ever in the recognition that we belong not because we have accomplished, but because we are loved.

Finally, according to the confessions, our belonging to God challenges the world as well as us. The Scots Confession, for example, closes with the prayer that not only the servants of God be given the "strength to speak thy Word with boldness," but also that "thine enemies be confounded." "Let them flee from thy presence that hate thy godly Name," the confession pleads (3.25).

Clearly, the idea that our identity as those who belong to God (and therefore are called to "speak boldly") should be directed against those we think do not (and therefore are destined to be "confounded") is ill-founded. Used throughout the centuries as a basis for supporting hatred and violence, any "we are right and they are wrong" mentality is clearly antithetical to the prophetic word of comfort we are called to share with the world. It is problematic to assume that to be Christian is to be right, since there is no necessary relationship between belonging and being correct. What is promised, by contrast, is that we belong even when we are wrong. What is challenging about the word we bring, as those who belong, is not that it battles against other words and emerges victorious (in the terms of this world), but that it brings comfort in a world full of anxiety, a world full of violence. This is the character of its victory, a victory won by One who is in noncompetitive relationship with us,[9] the One who shows us an entirely different way of existing.

What is challenging about the word we are called to speak as those who exist eccentrically is that consciousness of our belongingness changes everything, turning the world and its power plays inside-out by relativizing all in relationship to the One who has claimed us. Already I have discussed how everything we are as individuals—in our successes, failures, and anxieties—is seen differently when we are not our own. When we are living with another at the center, we are freed from the tyranny of being our own lords to be creatures in relation to the one Lord who has called us by name. It is this one Lord who also relativizes all other lords, insisting on shaping salvation history out of sinful historical existence, determined to convince the world of its belongingness.

The Barmen Declaration bears witness to this. Written in Germany in 1934, the document articulates the prophetic stance the Evangelical Church was compelled to take in response to the German Christian Church, which was supporting the lordship of Hitler.

> We reject the false doctrine, as though the church could and would have to acknowledge as a source of its proclamation, apart from and besides this one Word of God, still other events and powers, figures and truths, as God's revelation. (8.12)

Similarly, A Brief Statement reminds us that those who belong to God are given courage by the Spirit, "to witness among all peoples to Christ as Lord and Savior" and "to unmask idolatries in Church and culture" (10.4). In this global age, when we face the challenge of honoring and being in conversation with a diversity of perspectives, the confessions offer the important guidance that the lordship of Christ condemns would-be idols not only in the world at large but also in the church. The challenge of the community of faith who knows its belongingness to God is, then, to share the good news of comfort and challenge to the ends of the earth, while at the same time being itself subject to the One who comforts and challenges us, continuously decentering us in relationship to both our anxieties and our pride.

ECCENTRIC EXISTENCE

What does it look like to live in the world as those who "wear" their belongingness to God? To live an eccentric existence, with Christ at the center of our lives, is to have hope even in the face of seeming hopelessness. As those who cannot be separated from God in life or in death, we resist allowing our anxieties, our limitations, and our sin to define us. Correspondingly, we are continuously challenged to be who we really are in relationship to the One in whom our identity is formed and ever re-formed. To live as those who belong is, then, to live as those who are protected, loved, and believed in despite appearances to the contrary. It is to "strive . . . to live holy and joyful lives, even as we watch for God's new heaven and new earth" (10.4). As Barth puts it in commenting on the first question of the Heidelberg Catechism, living into our belongingness means that we who are "threatened by non-being" have reason "nevertheless to endure, nevertheless to take courage, nevertheless to be patient and joyful."[10] The confessions make clear that the hope we have "nevertheless" does not require a denial of our insecurities and sufferings. Naming these for what they are, hope nevertheless claims that a better reality has laid claim to us.

I have a friend who models this "nevertheless," who wears her belongingness in a way that offers comfort to others. Recently she was diagnosed with a painful and rapidly spreading form of cancer. Some time after this diagnosis, she and her husband, Ralph, came to our home for brunch along with another couple. Some of us worried that we had nothing to say that was hopeful, given that our friend had every reason to be discouraged, joyless, and fearful. Some also wondered if it would be better not to mention her impending death, for fear it would make her (and certainly us) feel uncomfortable.

As is often the case in such situations, it was my sick friend who ministered to the rest of us, rather than the other way around. Unlike us, Alice was not wary about talking about her death: "I told Ralph that, since I was going to be cremated, we should put the extra money we'd save—not buying a coffin, I mean, which is really expensive—into renting a cream-colored Cadillac. If I'm going to die, I figured I might as well go out in style." We looked out the window, and there, parked in the driveway, was the cream-colored Cadillac. We listened as Alice and Ralph told us stories of how they had spent a good chunk of their money flying thirty-one members of their extended family home for a three-day weekend to visit and to say goodbye. We heard about how they spent their forty-sixth wedding anniversary in one of the most luxurious bridal suites in the city of Austin. And we also heard about the difficult hospital visits, the struggles to find adequate pain medication, the impossibility of achieving closure with everyone in Alice's life.

Nevertheless was the operative word in Alice's discourse, even though it was not literally spoken. At the climax of her comments she made a simple statement that, by her own testimony, named and accounted for her eccentric existence: "When I discovered I was dying of cancer, I figured I had three choices," she said. "I could surrender to the cancer, to my own pain and sense of loss. But that didn't seem to be a very good idea. I could surrender to the medical establishment, but they didn't really seem to be able to do anything. Or I could surrender to God, who I figured *could* do something. So I decided to go with the third option."

I am not suggesting that all Christian believers can or should respond to terminal illness in exactly the way Alice has. I do see in Alice, however, an example of a person who is wearing her belongingness in relation to the real-world threats and anxieties all of us face, in one way or another. She reminds me that the comfort we know and the challenges we face as those who belong to God are not private possessions, but are meant to be shared. "We are in the world not to comfort ourselves, but to comfort others," Barth writes, along these same lines. Yet rarely do we actually wear our belongingness in this way, and Barth wants to know why:

> The one and only genuine comfort we may offer to [fellow human beings] is this reflection of heaven, of Jesus Christ, of God himself, as it appears on a radiant face. Why don't we do it? Why do we withhold from them the one comfort of mutual benefit? Why are the faces we

> show each other at best superior looking, serious, questioning, sor-
> rowful and reproachful faces, at worst even grimaces or lifeless masks,
> real Carnival masks? Why don't our faces shine?[11]

Could it be that the "reproachful faces," the "lifeless masks" that we wear,
reveal that we are indeed not living with a sense of our belongingness? That
we have refused eccentric existence for the sake of ordering our lives in a way
that "makes more sense" in light of our circumstances?

If so, we have not only missed out on the benefits that come with recognizing our identity in Christ (see 7.036). We have also abdicated our role in the
church's mission to spread the message of the gospel to the ends of the earth.
To live with the shining face of one who is comforted is to comfort others. This
shining face is not, again, the face of an inauthentic person trying to act the part
of a believer by denying the suffering of the world. Rather, it is the face of one
who exists eccentrically—who finds her identity not in relationship to herself
and her own life situation, but in relationship to Jesus Christ, to whom she
belongs. Reminiscent of the story of the Samaritan woman at the well, the shining face of an eccentric person leads others to come and meet Christ, where
they then experience the comfort he offers for themselves (see John 4:42).

The confessions shape our conviction, then, that the experience of belongingness, with its corresponding comforts and challenges, is indicative not
merely of our personal spirituality, appropriate to the private sphere. On the
contrary, virtually all of the confessions, regardless of the circumstances in
which they were written, are infused with the hopeful insistence that our experience of belongingness reveals what is true not only about God's relationship
to Alice, not only about God's relationship to Alice and her friends, but also
about God's relationship to the whole world. "God acts with justice and mercy
to redeem creation," A Brief Statement testifies, following Romans 8:21 (10.3).
"God's redeeming work in Jesus Christ embraces the whole of human life,"
insists the Confession of 1967, "social and cultural, economic and political, scientific and technological, individual and corporate" (9.53). Commenting on
the implications of this for the work of the church, C67 goes on to affirm:

> With an urgency born of this hope, the church applies itself to present
> tasks and strives for a better world. It does not identify limited progress
> with the kingdom of God on earth, nor does it despair in the face of
> disappointment and defeat. In steadfast hope, the church looks beyond
> all partial achievement to the final triumph of God. (9.55)

The hope that we have, as those for whom God dwells at the center, is also
hope turned outward. While it will not be realized until the kingdom of God
comes to earth as it is in heaven, it is neither squelched by failure nor enhanced
by progress. Our hope for the world is not grounded in the value of our

achievements, but in the unconditional love of our sovereign God, which never fails and is never less than complete.

What God has to do with us, in relation to all this, is unfathomably grace-full. For we belong to God not only as children belong to parents but also as comrades belong to a common endeavor. We are protected and we are loved; we are also included and counted on. In and through the person of Jesus Christ, we who claim eccentric existence are partners in the ministry of reconciliation (2 Cor. 5:17–20); we who were once servants are now identified as friends (John 15:15). Enlivened by the Holy Spirit, we who belong to God might even recognize—if only in glimpses—the depth of our inclusion, the vastness of our inheritance. "All that I have is yours," God reminds us (Luke 15:31). On this basis (and only on this basis), we who belong and hope are also empowered to be and to do, working "with others for justice, freedom, and peace" (10.4).

NOTES

1. William Placher and David Willis-Watkins, *Belonging to God: A Commentary on A Brief Statement of Faith* (Louisville, KY: Westminster/John Knox Press, 1992), 37.
2. Placher and Willis-Watkins, *Belonging to God*, 37.
3. Paul Tillich, "You Are Accepted," in *The Shaking of the Foundations* (New York: Charles Scribner's Sons, 1948), 162.
4. This and other quotations from C67 are from *The Confession of 1967: Inclusive Language Text* (Louisville, KY: Office of Theology and Worship, 2002).
5. Karl Barth, *Learning Jesus Christ through the Heidelberg Catechism*, trans. Shirley C. Guthrie, Jr. (Grand Rapids: Eerdmans, 1964), 30.
6. Ibid.
7. For more on how the limitations established by the commandments provide a context in which right relations (between God and us, and among ourselves) can flourish, see Paul Lehmann, *The Decalogue and a Human Future: The Meaning of the Commandments for Making and Keeping Human Life Human* (Grand Rapids: Eerdmans, 1995).
8. The quotations in this sentence are from the hymn "When I Survey the Wondrous Cross," by Isaac Watts, no. 100 in *The Presbyterian Hymnal: Hymns, Psalms, and Spiritual Songs* (Louisville, KY: Westminster/John Knox Press, 1990).
9. For more on the character of the "noncompetitive relationship" between God and us, see Kathryn Tanner, *Jesus, Humanity, and the Trinity* (Minneapolis: Fortress Press, 2001).
10. Barth, *Learning Jesus Christ*, 29.
11. Karl Barth, "Look Up to Him!" in *Deliverance to the Captives* (New York: Harper & Row, 1961), 48. This sermon was first preached in Basel prison in 1956.

9

What Do We Have to Do
with Each Other?

Kevin Park

Among the dizzying myriad of television programs, one show stands out that consistently provides profound commentary on American society and religion. The program, of course, is *The Simpsons*. One episode includes a scene in a Sunday school class where the teacher, Ms. Albright, introduces the topic of hell to the children. Young Bart Simpson is excited by the subject and exclaims, "All right! I sat through 'mercy' and I sat through 'forgiveness.' Finally we get to the good stuff!" After Ms. Albright explains what a terrible and frightening place hell is, the fascinated boy asks his teacher a couple of pertinent questions:

"Wouldn't you eventually get used to it, like a hot tub?"

"No."

"Are there pirates in hell?"

"Yes, thousands of them."

This answer delights Bart, and he responds, "Hoo hoo, baby!" Then Martin, a precocious student, asks the teacher, "So what you're saying is, there is a downside to the afterlife. How does one steer clear of this abode of the damned?" Ms. Albright answers, "By obeying the Ten Commandments. Ten simple rules that are easy to live by."[1]

Ms. Albright's understanding of the purpose of the Ten Commandments may not be too far from how most Americans think of them, whether churched or not. Perhaps she should have consulted the recent Presbyterian Church (U.S.A.) *Study Catechism*, which answers the question why one should obey the Ten Commandments:

> Not to avoid being punished, for then I would obey out of fear. With gladness in my heart I should obey God's law out of gratitude, for God has blessed me by it and given it for my well-being.[2]

135

The Reformed tradition's understanding of the Ten Commandments differs markedly from Ms. Albright's view. Although the Ten Commandments may not compete well with the topic of hell in generating excitement in Sunday school classes, the Reformed treatment of the Ten Commandments does give theologically illuminating insights as we seek to answer the question, "What do we have to do with each other?" In this chapter we will discuss how the three catechisms in *The Book of Confessions* treat the Ten Commandments, selectively focusing on those commandments that deal with our relationship to the "other." The Confession of 1967 with its overarching theme of reconciliation will be brought into the conversation in light of some current issues facing post-9/11 America.

"I AM THE LORD THY GOD"

Before we can begin to answer the question this chapter poses, we need to know what is meant by "we" and "other." The catechisms are clear. We cannot begin to know what we have to do with each other before we know who God is and who we are in relation to God. The catechisms emphasize the relational context of the Ten Commandments in the covenant between God and God's people. All three catechisms place the Ten Commandments in the dialectic of God's grace and the believers' response as thanksgiving to the grace already received.

Both the Shorter and Larger Catechisms include the question, "What is the preface to the Ten Commandments?" The Larger Catechism answers:

> The preface to the Ten Commandments is contained in these words: "I am the Lord thy God, which have brought thee out of the land of Egypt, out of the house of bondage." Wherein God manifesteth his sovereignty, as being Jehovah, the eternal, immutable, and almighty God; having his being in and of himself, and giving being to all his words and works; and that he is a God in covenant, as with Israel of old, so with all his people; who as he brought them out of their bondage in Egypt, so he delivered us from our spiritual thralldom; and that therefore we are bound to take him for our God alone, and to keep all his commandments. (7.211)

Thus, the commandments are placed squarely within the grace of God. The preface emphasizes the identity of the giver of these commandments as "the Lord thy God," immediately establishing an intimate relationship between God and God's people. This is the Lord God who has already initiated a personal relationship with the people whom God delivered from bondage in Egypt. The catechisms clearly teach that the commandments are not moral prerequisites to be fulfilled by the Israelites before God agrees to deliver them from slavery in Egypt. God has already delivered them from slavery; God has already delivered them from oppression; God has already given them a new identity as a beloved people.

This God is committed to these people. We are not speaking here of a mere philosophical or a cosmological impersonal deity. This is the Lord God who is radically involved in human lives and who has everything at stake before giving the law to the Israelites. Therefore, these commandments are not to be understood as moral obligations that will appease God, but as part of God's saving grace—as part of God's plan of salvation.

The catechisms declare that the purpose of the law is not to bind and oppress, but to guide and direct God's people in order to lead them toward a right relationship with God and with others. Exodus 3:7–8 echoes in the preface to the commandments:

> Then the LORD said, "I have observed the misery of my people who are in Egypt; I have heard their cry on account of their taskmasters. Indeed, I know their sufferings, and I have come down to deliver them from the Egyptians, and to bring them up out of that land to a good and broad land, a land flowing with milk and honey."

This is a compassionate God who hears the cry of captive people, who knows their sufferings intimately, who cares for them and draws near to them, who acts to rescue them from bondage, and who promises to deliver them to a destination that is good and abundant. This God is "God in covenant . . . with all his people." All of these characteristics of God are affirmed before the giving of the Ten Commandments. The catechisms emphasize this truth by affirming that the law is a function of God's grace.

The first four commandments establish who the Lord is and call the people to live in single-minded loyalty to their God. The last six commandments establish the kind of relationship God's people ought to have with others, given the relationship God has already established with them in the first four commandments. The catechisms emphasize that our relationship with God is inseparable from our relationships with each other. The Heidelberg Catechism answers the question, "How are these commandments divided?" as follows:

> Into two tables, the first of which teaches us in four commandments how we ought to live in relation to God; the other, in six commandments, what we owe to our neighbor. (4.093)

The Shorter Catechism sums up the meaning of the commandments with Jesus' words:

> The sum of the Ten Commandments is: to love the Lord our God with all our heart, with all our soul, with all our strength, and with all our mind; and our neighbor as ourselves. (7.042)

OUR IDENTITY

If God is the compassionate deliverer and the initiator of a gracious covenant, then we are people who have been called and claimed by God as God's own. Our identity comes from our relationship to God, a relationship that is initiated by God. This covenant relationship is infinitely more costly on God's side than ours, for God commits everything in delivering us from bondage to sin, paying for our redemption through the costly death and resurrection of Jesus Christ—all without a guarantee that we will receive that costly grace and respond with thanksgiving and obedience. This covenant relationship is not *quid pro quo* because the cost is skewed infinitely toward God, and the benefits are skewed infinitely toward us. That we are people who belong to God is exclaimed in the famous first question of the Heidelberg Catechism.

> Q. **What is your only comfort, in life and in death?**
> A. That I belong—body and soul, in life and in death—not to myself but to my faithful Savior, Jesus Christ, who at the cost of his own blood has fully paid for all my sins and has completely freed me from the dominion of the devil. (4.001)

We are the people of God's covenant who are called out from all kinds of bondage and who are now free to follow and obey this God who is unconditionally committed to us. We are the people who have received the grace of God in Jesus Christ through the Holy Spirit, and who gratefully respond with joyful obedience. So then, obeying the commandments is our free response of faith and obedience to God's grace to live as the Lord's people in the real world. Again, the Heidelberg Catechism puts it well:

> Q. **Since we are redeemed from our sin and its wretched consequences by grace through Christ without any merit of our own, why must we do good works?**
> A. Because just as Christ has redeemed us with his blood he also renews us through his Holy Spirit according to his own image, so that with our whole life we may show ourselves grateful to God for his goodness and that he may be glorified through us; and further, so that we ourselves may be assured of our faith by its fruits and by our reverent behavior may win our neighbors to Christ. (4.086)

The good works that we do through obeying the commandments are not our independent acts apart from God. Rather, obeying the commandments is our faithful response to God's grace of renewing "us through his Holy Spirit according to his own image." Obedience is our expression of thanksgiving to God, who has redeemed us for the glory of God. The catechisms teach the Reformed understanding of the law, that the commandments are given for the purpose of our sanctification. It is also noteworthy that the Heidelberg Catechism adds a missiological purpose to the commandments: that by obeying them, through our behaviors, we "may win our neighbors to Christ." The emphasis on obeying the commandments as our thankful response to God's grace is emphasized structurally in the Heidelberg Catechism, which places the Ten Commandments in part 3, "Thankfulness," after the brief part 1, "Of Man's Misery," and the whole of part 2, "Of Man's Redemption."[3] Because the Ten Commandments are given within the context of a covenant relationship with God, they cannot be reduced to a set of religious moralisms.

Having emphasized the covenantal foundation of the Ten Commandments, it is important for us to affirm that even after having been delivered from bondage and declared as people belonging to God, our obedience to the commandments does not become a matter of course. In fact, the catechisms emphasize the fact that even after having been delivered by God, we are still unable to keep God's law. The Heidelberg Catechism makes this point clear:

> **Q. But can those who are converted to God keep these commandments perfectly?**
> A. No, for even the holiest of them make only a small beginning in obedience in this life. Nevertheless, they begin with serious purpose to conform not only to some, but to all the commandments of God. (4.114)

The Larger Catechism agrees:

> No man is able, either of himself, or by any grace received in this life, perfectly to keep the Commandments of God; but doth daily break them in thought, word, and deed. (7.259)

Therefore, although the Reformed understanding of the law is mainly for the purpose of sanctification, the very understanding of sanctification must be clear. Sanctification through obedience to the law is not a linear progressive movement whereby we achieve holiness. Sanctification is the work of the Holy Spirit in and through us. Through the Holy Spirit the law of God exhorts, disciplines, guides, chastises, corrects, and reminds us that we are *sinners* redeemed by God. Thus, the commandments lead us to a constant and ever deeper awareness of the depth of our sinful condition, and yet at the same time lead us to an even deeper awareness of the infinitely greater grace of God.

THE FIRST AND THE THIRD USES OF THE LAW

At this point in our discussion it will be helpful to examine the classic "three uses" of God's law in the Reformed tradition. A succinct summary is found in the contemporary *Study Catechism*:

God's law has three uses. First, it shows me how grievously I fail to live according to God's will, driving me to pray for God's mercy. Second, it functions to restrain even the worst of sinners through the fear of punishment. Finally, it teaches me how to live a life which bears witness to the gospel, and spurs me on to do so.[4]

Pertinent to our discussion are the first and the third uses of the law.[5] The Reformed emphasis on the third, or "positive," use of the law must be understood in tension with the first, or "negative," use of the law, especially given our contemporary context in which the Reformed emphasis can easily be misunderstood as simple religious moralism. The first use of the law is associated with the Lutheran understanding. God's law functions here as a spiritual diagnosis declaring humans sinful, causing sinners to turn to Christ for salvation. Calvin expressed it this way: "The law shows the righteousness of God, and as a mirror discloses our sinfulness, leading us to implore divine help."[6] In the same vein, Calvin quotes Augustine: "The usefulness of the law lies in convicting man of his infirmity and moving him to call upon the remedy of grace which is in Christ."[7]

We need to be reminded at this point that the catechisms teach that the reason for our inability to obey God's law does not chiefly lie in the behavioral realm but lies in the heart. Behavior can be modified and controlled, but the root of our behavior, the heart, where actions are deliberated and willed, cannot itself be controlled at will. Therefore, it is not sufficient merely to refrain from sinful behavior; we are called to be transformed at the root of our behavior. The Heidelberg Catechism points this out with regard to the tenth commandment.

Q. What is required in the tenth commandment?
A. That there should never enter our heart even the least inclination or thought contrary to any commandment of God, but that we should always hate sin with our whole heart and find satisfaction and joy in all righteousness. (4.113)

The problem is that even after having received grace we are unable to live up to this. This very call for complete purity and joy reminds us that we are unable to comply, and thus we are guided back to Christ.

According to the first use of the law, then, the law is like an X-ray that gives a clear picture of a broken bone that will motivate the patient to seek treatment from a doctor. The purpose of an X-ray is strictly diagnostic—it is not the cure. The patient would be foolish to seek multiple X-rays hoping to get cured. Like an X-ray, the law exposes the broken human condition but cannot heal it. Paul said, "Through the law comes the knowledge of sin" (Rom. 3:20), and the law directs the sinner to Christ, who alone can cure. All three of our catechisms acknowledge the importance of this first use of the law. In fact, the catechisms understand the third use of the law as functioning in tandem with the first use of the law.

The Heidelberg Catechism is most clear in showing the relationship between the first and the third uses of the law. The first question in part 1 is, "Where do you learn of your sin and its wretched consequences?" to which the succinct answer is, "From the Law of God" (4.003). According to this catechism, it is only after the law does its work in making us realize that we need to be delivered from our sinful condition that we can understand the significance of Christ's costly redemption for us, and thus respond with thanksgiving and obedience.[8] That the Ten Commandments are placed in the thanksgiving section of the Heidelberg Catechism points to the Reformed emphasis of the third use of the law in Christian life. But this emphasis only makes sense as the law continues to expose our true condition. Without the true diagnosis, our patient may think that the injury is a mere sprain, hoping that the condition will improve on its own. Only after the X-ray reveals that the actual condition is a compound fracture will the patient be motivated with urgency to seek and receive proper treatment from a doctor, willingly and thankfully. In short, the third use of the law can only be appreciated in its proper relationship to the first use of the law.

The first use of the law has a theological parallel to the cross of Christ. The cross judges as well as saves. The cross exposes the complex web of human sin from individuals, religious communities, political institutions, and from followers and enemies of Christ alike—all of whom cooperate and converge together to crucify the God incarnate, the righteousness of God embodied. Jesus, on the cross, at the same time, absorbs all human sin into himself in order to redeem humanity. "Christ redeemed us from the curse of the law by becoming a curse for us" (Gal. 3:13). The law, by revealing the righteousness of God, judges us, exposing our sins, exposing our inability to measure up to God's requirements, and exposing our inability to obey the law on our own. We are most surprised and offended when the law exposes our sinfulness not only when we know that we are sinning but precisely when we think that we are doing our best morally and religiously. Having no power to redeem, the law rightly points to Christ so that sinners can turn to their only Redeemer, for "Christ is the end of the law so that there may be righteousness for everyone who believes" (Rom. 10:4). This critical use of the law is pertinent to our contemporary context because moralism has deeply infiltrated our churches. By "moralism" I mean reducing the Christian faith to dos and don'ts—understanding the Ten Commandments as "ten simple rules that are easy to live by," abstracted from the costly covenant relationship initiated by God. If we remove the Ten Commandments from the relational context between God who delivers from bondage and God's people who respond in thanksgiving, and simply understand them as rules that we need to follow apart from this relationship, then the whole thing degenerates into cheap moralism. Given the contemporary tendency toward the moralization of Christianity, the Reformed emphasis on the positive use of the law must be understood as functioning in tandem with the critical use of the law.

Calvin holds the tension between the two mutually complementary functions of the law: the law that exhorts and challenges and the law that liberates. He does this even when he explains the third use of the law:

> Now, the law has power to exhort believers. This is not a power to bind their consciences with a curse, but one to shake off their sluggishness, by repeatedly urging them, and to pinch them awake to their imperfection. Therefore, many persons, wishing to express such liberation from that curse, say that for believers the law—I am still speaking of the moral law—has been abrogated. Not that the law no longer enjoins believers to do what is right, but only that it is not for them what it formerly was: it may no longer condemn and destroy their consciences by frightening and confounding them.[9]

Adhering to the proper understanding of the purpose of the law, then, is to realize that even after we have been delivered from the bondage of sin and delivered into the covenant relationship with God, we are still unable to obey God's law on our own. We need the constant guidance and empowerment of the Holy Spirit. We continue to break all of God's commandments, and therefore we realize that we are utterly and constantly dependent on God's grace and redemption in Jesus Christ through the Holy Spirit. When we ask, "What do we have to do with each other?" we need to understand that we are *graced sinners* who are called to love God and others through the very grace that we have received. Therefore, by reclaiming the Reformed understanding of the law, we are constantly humbled by God's grace, and that proper humility needs to be expressed appropriately as we love others in Christ's name. The Heidelberg Catechism, again, emphasizes the dialectic between the first and third uses of the law:

> **Q. Why, then, does God have the ten commandments preached so strictly since no one can keep them in this life?**
> A. First, that all our life long we may become increasingly aware of our sinfulness, and therefore more eagerly seek forgiveness of sins and righteousness in Christ. Second, that we may constantly and diligently pray to God for the grace of the Holy Spirit, so that more and more we may be renewed in the image of God, until we attain the goal of full perfection after this life. (4.115)

The Reformed understanding of the role of the law of God affirms with Luther that we are saints and sinners at the same time. We are saints in that we belong to God and have been delivered from bondage, and yet at the same time we are sinners who constantly need to flee from sin and adhere to God's grace.

"OTHER"

"What do we have to do with each other?" The catechisms are broadly inclusive when identifying the "other" with whom we are commanded to have specific kinds of relationships. In its discussion of the last six commandments, the Heidelberg Catechism mentions relationships with parents (4.104), neighbor (4.105), enemies (4.107), and the poor (4.111), as well as covering sexual relationships in wedlock and in single life (4.108–.109), and wasting of gifts (4.110). The Larger Catechism adds relationships with our "superiors," "inferiors," and "equals" (7.235–.242), as well as with government (7.237), property, estate, and time (7.252), just to mention a few. It is striking that the catechisms expand the meaning of the "other" and our duties to others far beyond what is immediately mentioned in the commandments. The teaching of Jesus' Sermon on the Mount, in which he interprets and expands the meaning of the Ten Commandments, is implicit in the ways the catechisms interpret commandments five to ten.

The catechisms all point out the positive injunctions that are implied in the negatively stated commandments. The Larger Catechism, for example, has two questions for each of the "thou shalt not" commandments. The first question emphasizes the positive duties required for each of the commandments, and the second question emphasizes the sins forbidden for each of the commandments. Commandments five to ten, then, are presented as a call to live in proper relationship with others in a way that is consonant with our reconciled relationship with God. In the context of the ministry of reconciliation as articulated by the Confession of 1967 (C67), this call toward reconciliation becomes a missional imperative:

> To be reconciled to God is to be sent into the world as his reconciling community. This community, the church universal, is entrusted with God's message of reconciliation and shares his labor of healing the enmities which separate men from God and from each other. Christ has called the church to this mission and given it the gift of the Holy Spirit. The church maintains continuity with the apostles and with Israel by faithful obedience to his call. (9.31)

C67 emphasizes that the very integrity of being the church of Jesus Christ is tested by the quality of relationship its members have with others:

> The church disperses to serve God wherever its members are, at work or play, in private or in the life of society. Their prayer and Bible study are part of the church's worship and theological reflection. Their witness is the church's evangelism. Their daily action in the world is the church in mission to the world. The quality of their relation with other persons is the measure of the church's fidelity. (9.37)

This is certainly humbling. The church is called to be a missional body that engages life and touches people's lives outside the church. Faith in Jesus Christ must touch the world's reality. The "other" as defined by the confessions goes far beyond individuals we know in our religious and ethnic enclaves. In fact, this radically inclusive definition of the "other" is a judgment against our parochial cliques that are self-serving and often participate in various types of segregations. The "other" includes people who are different from us in religion, ethnicity, class, age, gender, political and national affiliation, as well as people whom we categorize in all kinds of classifications. In this context, the question "What do we have to do with each other?" becomes a far more challenging and overarching question than it seemed at first. Now the question challenges and expands our comfortable definition of the "other" to include people who are radically outside of our communal field of vision. Therefore, we cannot remain comfortable in our pews and hide behind our polity and continue to deal with only "our" kinds of people. C67 emphasizes each member's responsibility for witness in the world:

> Each member is the church in the world, endowed by the Spirit with some gift of ministry and is responsible for the integrity of his witness in his own particular situation. (9.38)

C67 continues to emphasize the missional imperative of each Christian to people of all religions:

> The Christian finds parallels between other religions and his own and must approach all religions with openness and respect. Repeatedly God has used the insight of non-Christians to challenge the church to renewal. But the reconciling word of the gospel is God's judgment upon all forms of religion, including the Christian. The gift of God in Christ is for all men. The church, therefore, is commissioned to carry the gospel to all men whatever their religion may be and even when they profess none. (9.42)

As we glean the catechisms' implications of the kind of relationship that we ought to have with each other, it will be important to keep in mind this missional imperative emphasized by C67, as well as the confessional affirmation that the "other" includes people who are strangers and even enemies.

CONTEMPORARY SIGNIFICANCE

The Heidelberg Catechism expands the scope of the fifth commandment, "Honor your father and mother," to include not only our biological parents but also all who have authority over us. However, the catechism also recognizes that all in authority are sinful humans who make mistakes and who need our patience with their failures (4.104). *The Study Catechism* goes even further and makes explicit the limits of our obligations in obeying them:

> No mere human being is God. Blind obedience is not required, for everything should be tested by loyalty and obedience to God. When it seems as though I should not obey, I should always be alert to possible self-deception on my part, and should pray that we may all walk in the truth of God's will.[10]

This call to resist blind obedience is especially significant for people such as Asian Americans who belong to cultures in which the wishes of the parents often compete with God's wishes. Catechisms are clear. Neither parents nor children nor families are allowed to become idols.

The Shorter and Larger Catechisms further expand the definition of "mother and father" by including our relationship with "inferiors," "superiors," and "equals" (7.064, 7.236) in "family, church, commonwealth" (7.234). The Larger Catechism even has a section for each of these relationships, thus emphasizing the importance of honoring others in all of the many nuanced layers in our relationships (7.237–.239), and emphasizing the importance of honoring the others' worth and dignity:

> The duties of equals are: to regard the dignity and worth of each other, in giving honor to go one before another, and to rejoice in each other's gifts and advancement as their own. (7.241)

The theme of honoring others is expanded in the sixth commandment, "You shall not kill," to include loving our neighbors as ourselves. The Heidelberg Catechism states:

> [God] requires us to love our neighbor as ourselves, to show patience, peace, gentleness, mercy, and friendliness toward him, to prevent injury to him as much as we can, also to do good to our enemies. (4.107)

The same catechism calls people to "lay aside all desire for revenge" (4.105). The Larger Catechism includes a call "to preserve the life of ourselves and others" as well as some injunctions that, at first reading, seem to have little resemblance to the original commandment: the importance of quietness of mind, sober use of meat, sleep, labor, recreation, as well as the readiness to be reconciled, protecting and defending the innocent, and many others (7.245).

Among the many duties listed in the catechisms' treatment of the sixth commandment, three stand out in the contemporary American context: doing good to our enemies, the readiness to be reconciled, and protecting and defending the innocent. These themes aptly come together in C67:

> The church, in its own life, is called to practice the forgiveness of enemies and to commend to the nations as practical politics the search for cooperation and peace. This search requires that the nations pursue fresh and responsible relations across every line of conflict, even at risk to national security, to reduce areas of strife and to broaden international understanding. Reconciliation among nations becomes peculiarly urgent as countries develop nuclear, chemical, and biological weapons, diverting their manpower and resources from constructive uses and risking the annihilation of mankind. Although nations may serve God's purposes in history, the church which identifies the sovereignty of any one nation or any one way of life with the cause of God denies the Lordship of Christ and betrays its calling. (9.45)

This is surprisingly contextual, even prophetic, given the situation facing post-9/11 America. Appropriately, national security has become the most urgent issue of our time. However, the issue of national security can easily become an idol, providing an excuse to disregard protection and defense of the innocent and the vulnerable. It can also become an excuse to abuse and oppress them. The catechisms and confessions are unambiguous: As people reconciled to God through God's costly self-giving grace in Jesus Christ, we are called to "pursue fresh and responsible relations across every line of conflict, even at risk to national security." These are hard words to hear at a time when we, as a nation, want to seek retribution and find scapegoats for the terrible tragedy that happened to America. But the catechisms, being faithful to God's Word, call us to "do good to our enemies" and to protect and defend the innocent.

Doing good to our enemies does not mean to suppress the truth and cater to the whims of those who do evil. The Larger Catechism forbids "calling evil good, and good evil" (7.255), a phrase which is reminiscent of the words of Martin Luther, who went on to say in his Heidelberg Disputation, "A theology of the cross calls the thing what it actually is."[11] Therefore, discerning and telling the hard truth to ourselves and to our enemies, and then standing up for that truth may be the most loving thing we can do as a people of God. However, we are called to speak the truth, not out of a spirit of revenge, but in the spirit of grace that unmasks falsehood in order to redeem.

The catechisms also remind us that although we may be tempted to blame whole ethnic or religious communities for crimes committed by a few, we are called to protect and defend the innocent and the vulnerable (7.245). In the present context, Arab Americans and other ethnic minority communities that are susceptible to becoming targets of xenophobia are vulnerable. As the people of God, we must stand with the "others" who are endangered or oppressed.

The preface to the Ten Commandments—"I am the LORD your God, who brought you out of the land of Egypt, out of the house of slavery"—reminds us why, as a people of God, we must love those who are treated as aliens:

> The alien who resides with you shall be to you as the citizen among you; you shall love the alien as yourself, for you were aliens in the land of Egypt: I am the LORD your God. (Lev. 19:34)

The problem with practicing this kind of hospitality is that the majority in America has no experience of what it is like to be an "alien." On the other hand, minority peoples in America have historically experienced the harsh reality of being treated as aliens by the dominant majority. African Americans, Native Americans, Hispanic Americans, Asian Americans, and many other minority communities have been treated as aliens in their own country. As a nation, the United States has been the preeminent world power for so long that the majority of Americans have no memory other than being the privileged people of the world. Our assumption of privilege has damaging consequences for the peoples and nations around us. Here, the catechisms' teaching on the ninth commandment, "You shall not bear false witness against your neighbor," becomes relevant.

In treating the ninth commandment, the catechisms repeat the theme of defending and promoting "my neighbor's good name" as well as forbidding prejudice that will injure our neighbor (4.112; 7.077). *The Study Catechism* explicitly raises the question of racism in relation to this commandment:

> Does this commandment forbid racism and other forms of negative stereotyping?

> Yes. In forbidding false witness against my neighbor, God forbids me to be prejudiced against people who belong to any vulnerable, different or disfavored social group. Jews, women, homosexuals, racial and ethnic minorities, and national enemies are among those who have suffered terribly from being subjected to the slurs of social prejudice. Negative stereotyping is a form of falsehood that invites actions of humiliation, abuse, and violence as forbidden by the commandment against murder.[12]

Thus, in various times and places, the catechisms articulate contemporaneous sins that we need to confront and confess, recognizing that an important function of the law is to uncover and name overt and covert sins.

One way of recognizing and confessing the sin of racism and negative stereotyping is "to hear the voices of peoples long silenced, and to work with others for justice, freedom, and peace" as written in A Brief Statement of Faith (10.4). It is notable that the very line "to hear the voices of peoples long silenced" was included in this document because of the voice of a Native American member of the committee.[13] Often the marginal peoples, the "peoples long silenced," have an epistemological vantage point from which to see and discern issues that the people at the center cannot see or refuse to see and discern. Therefore, it is not only important to hear voices from the margins, but it is also essential for marginal peoples to speak boldly so the majority can hear their voices and be challenged by them. Hearing and taking seriously the voices of the ignored minority peoples may be an important way to discern the will of God, because God often chooses those who have been silenced and oppressed as bearers of the divine message, as the Bible so often testifies.

The catechisms' interpretation of the law, then, provides a critique of our American situation. We are a society intoxicated with progress, technology, materialism, individualism, and all kinds of excess. The United States makes up less than 5 percent of the world's population, yet we consume more than 25 percent of the world's energy. We have become the world's most powerful nation, expecting economic, political, and military success in the international arena as if we have an inalienable right to be triumphant. When we do not experience success—corporately, individually, or even as a church—we often live in denial, suppressing our failures rather than confronting them. We are, in Douglas John Hall's words, an "officially optimistic society."[14] We are a society that thrives on producing artificial needs in order to enhance corporate profits. Even the church has bought into this worldview of relentless success, replacing the God of costly grace in Jesus Christ with a cheap god of civility, utility, and progress.

Through their teachings on the Ten Commandments, the catechisms tell us who we are in relation with God and, in turn, what we have to do with each other. They place before us a view of life that is radically different from the one that is all too familiar. The Ten Commandments are not "ten simple rules that are easy to live by" that will lead to a successful life. Rather, they tell us that we are to love God with all we possess and love our neighbors as ourselves even at the risk of our own security and well-being. The catechisms also tell us that our love for God and others is only possible because we have been chosen and loved by the One who risked all for us through the death and resurrection of Jesus Christ and who accompanies and empowers us through the Holy Spirit. What do we have to do with one another? The triune God, whose very being is divine community, desires to have communion with us and calls us to live in communion with others.

NOTES

1. *The Simpsons*, "Homer vs. Lisa and the 8th Commandment," episode #7F13, Twentieth-Century Fox Film Corporation, 1991.
2. *The Study Catechism: Full Version* (Louisville, KY: Geneva Press, 1998), question 91.
3. Although the gender exclusive language will be quoted from the catechisms and confessions as is, I will assume throughout the essay that male references refer to both male and female, unless the context says otherwise.
4. *Study Catechism*, question 92.
5. The second use is limited largely to the civil use of the law as a punitive measure to maintain order in society; therefore, it does not carry much theological significance.
6. John Calvin, *Institutes of the Christian Religion*, ed. John T. McNeill, trans. Ford Lewis Battles (Philadelphia: Westminster Press, 1960), 2.7.6 (LCC 1:354).
7. Ibid., 2.7.9 (LCC 1:357).
8. Given the historical context of the Heidelberg Catechism, it is arguably the most Lutheran-influenced document in *The Book of Confessions*; hence the emphasis of the first use of the law as well as the third use.
9. Calvin, *Institutes* 2.7.14. (LCC 1:362).
10. *Study Catechism*, question 106.
11. *Luther's Works*, vol. 31, ed. Harold J. Grimm (Philadelphia: Muhlenberg Press, 1957), 40.
12. *Study Catechism*, question 115.
13. Jack Rogers, *Presbyterian Creeds: A Guide to "The Book of Confessions"* (Louisville, KY: Westminster/John Knox Press, 1991), 270.
14. Douglas John Hall, *Lighten Our Darkness: Towards an Indigenous Theology of the Cross* (Philadelphia: Westminster Press, 1976), 43–59.

10

Why the Church?

Sheldon W. Sorge

One of the great treasures of the Reformed confessional tradition is its doctrine of the church. The confessions paint a rich vision of the covenantal life of God's people, rooted solely in the gracious election of God, who calls people who were nothing to become a community that enjoys the fellowship, reflects the nature, and embodies the mission of the triune God. Like the persons of the Trinity, the people of God are one, yet each member has personal identity and integrity that are never simply absorbed into the whole. Together, the three persons of the Trinity are always in mission: The Father sends the Son into the world to save the world, and together the Father and the Son send the Spirit to nurture the church's fellowship and empower the church's mission, until the work of Christ is fully accomplished, to the glory of God. It is God's very nature to be in perfect communion and persistent mission; it is exactly so for the church.

Why then are Reformed churches, with such a rich ecclesiological heritage, marked more by fractiousness than fellowship, more by membership loss than missional growth? The reasons are complex, but two factors stand out. First, the rich covenantal vision of the church rooted in the nature of God has been flattened into a model of church we blandly label "connectional." The terminology creates a world of ecclesial actuality that bears no inherent reference to God, no specifically *theological* identity. It is simply connection for connection's sake. The church becomes defined and eventually ruled by connectional polity rather than by the wisdom and power of its God-suffused confessional heritage.

A second reason for the current ecclesial crisis inevitably follows the first as the church comes to exist as an end in itself. It becomes so wrapped up in concern *that* it continue to exist that the question of *why* it exists is forgotten. Its chief mission becomes self-preservation. A church that defines itself more by polity than theology, and that is more focused on self-preservation than on mission, is sure to become exactly what it is trying to avoid: It will be increasingly fragmented and diffuse, until it eventually dissolves. If we wish meaningfully to address the question of "*Why* the church?" we must always be clear about *what* constitutes the living church of Jesus Christ. Just as the *why* and the *what* of the church cannot be separated if the church is to be true to its God-given nature and mission, theological reflection on the church must always keep both questions fully in view.

Ecclesiological questions were front and center in sixteenth-century Reformation struggles. The Reformers and their followers found themselves outside the bounds of the established church (either by force or by their own choice). In Rome's terms the church included only those who were in communion with a bishop who, in turn, was in communion with the pope. If the Reformers and their followers were to claim that theirs were "true" churches, they needed to demonstrate that Roman accounts of the true church inadequately represented authentic catholic teaching.

The critical ecclesial challenges facing the reformers launched three general trajectories of ecclesiological reflection. The first was the *ontological* question, the issue of identity: By which attributes can true churches be distinguished from pretenders? The second was a *practical* question: Which communal practices are essential for nourishing God's people? The third was the *teleological* question: Toward what ends does the church live and labor? These core questions may be cast in terms of a simple metaphor: If the church is construed as a living tree, what are its roots, what are its critical life processes, and what kind of fruit does it produce? Responses to these three lines of questions produce a distinctive gestalt of ecclesiological themes in the Reformed tradition.[1] These themes, relating to the church's core identity, practices, and purposes, are found in the church's confessions of faith.

The Book of Confessions of the Presbyterian Church (U.S.A.) is a broad catalog of ecclesial faith statements from Christianity's earliest centuries to the late twentieth century that together function as both source and manifestation of Reformed understandings of the essential marks and mission of the Christian church. This confessional corpus, in conversation especially with John Calvin, sets forth a distinctive (and, I believe, compelling) vision of the church's essential identity, practices, and purposes.

REFORMED ECCLESIOLOGY: THREE INTERWOVEN TRAJECTORIES

Ecclesiology is a Greek-based word meaning "words about the assembly"—in this case, about those whom God calls forth from the world to be formed into a holy people. In Christian theology, *ecclesiology* is the formal designation for discussion about the nature and purpose of this assembly, which we name *church*. It is typically the final and the longest movement in the overall symphony of theology. The first movement of theology focuses on "one God, the Father, the Almighty," including God's self-revelation in creation and divine providence. The second focuses on "one Lord, Jesus Christ, the only Son of God," tracing out his witness to God's reign and his gracious work of reconciliation on behalf of all humanity. The third movement considers "the Holy Spirit, the Lord, the giver of life" who makes available *to* us everything that Jesus Christ has provided *for* us. Finally, the mighty fourth movement brings it all to a climax by elucidating how God's nature, actions, and promises form a people that glorifies and fully enjoys God forever.

In the Reformed tradition, questions about the church's identity, practices, and purposes generate a web of ecclesiological trajectories that are each distinct, yet all interconnected and interdependent. The first trajectory of Reformed ecclesiology concerns the church's identity, the *ontological* question about the nature of the true church. The Nicene Creed, the ecumenical church's most ancient and broadly accepted faith statement, is foundational for both Reformed worship and theology, setting out the grammar of the church's core identity. In Reformed churches, the ancient creed (in either its Nicene or Apostles' form[2]) is often confessed in Lord's Day worship. The sequence of the creed shapes the successive movements of Calvin's paradigmatic theology and, together with the Ten Commandments and the Lord's Prayer, constitutes the core of Reformed catechesis.[3] PC(USA) catechisms—Heidelberg, Westminster, and *The Study Catechism*—work through the creed as the primary guide for teaching the nature of the triune God and the community of God's chosen people.

The Nicene Creed summons us to "believe in one holy catholic and apostolic Church." Calvin argues strenuously that this is not a call to "believe *in* the church," but rather simply to "believe the church."[4] The church is not an object of faith, but rather a (more or less) reliable guide to knowledge of the living God. Not all churches teach the same things about God, of course, so how can we know which church's account of God's nature and ways is trustworthy? Or to put it another way, what are the distinctive marks of a church whose testimony is dependably true to who God is and what God does? The Nicene Creed declares, and Reformed confessions confirm, that a "true" church in this sense is necessarily one, holy, catholic, and apostolic. The creed reflects the church's living encounter with the Holy One of Israel incarnated in Jesus Christ, and like all mirror images, creedal affirmations about the church reflect the life of the church inversely. The pattern of ecclesial life reflected in the creed does not move from unity to holiness to catholicity to apostolicity, but in precisely the reverse direction. We shall consider the significance of this reverse movement below.

The second trajectory of Reformed ecclesiology identifies specific *practices* that mark a congregation as an authentic Christian church. Sometimes these are termed the "notes" of the church (from the Latin *notae ecclesia*). The creed confessed by the first Reformed churches was the same as that confessed by the Roman church; they agreed, at least in terms of formal categories, on the essential *identity* of the church. But questions about essential *practices* of the true church set the Reformers apart from Rome. For Rome, maintenance of communion with a Catholic bishop was the key practice that guaranteed ecclesial authenticity. The Reformers, many of whom were expelled from the bishops' circles, understandably designated very different criteria for authentic church life.

John Calvin set the tone for Reformed churches by focusing the question of essential church practices not on maintenance of ecclesiastical relationships, but on the shape and substance of worship. In his account, the true church is marked not by who endorses it, but by what the church does when it assembles. It is not a matter of wearing accepted labels, but of promoting life-giving practices. For Calvin, the true church is actualized wherever the Word of God is purely preached and heard, and where the sacraments are administered according to Christ's institution.[5] Reformed confessions reiterate this double criterion of Word and sacrament, sometimes with the addition of a third: sound discipline in the church. Reformed ecclesiology is still of mixed opinion on whether the true church is instantiated by Word and sacrament alone, or by Word, sacrament, *and* discipline. Although Calvin acknowledges the indispensability of discipline in a vital church, he does not raise it to the level of Word and sacrament. But his heirs in the Reformed confessional heritage have often raised discipline to equivalent status. Current struggles over the enforcement of discipline in the PC(USA) demonstrate that this question remains unresolved. Another significant confessional departure from Calvin's double criterion is that often the first half is itself often only half present. In Calvin's formulation, the first mark is the preaching *and* hearing of God's Word, but subsequent confessional statements have often focused on preaching with virtually no commensurate attention to hearing God's Word. This exclusion eventually makes a significant difference, as we shall presently discover.

Finally, the Reformed ecclesiological tradition is always characterized by a third, *teleological* trajectory. This gets to the heart of this chapter's central focus. The first two trajectories are present in nearly all of our confessions, but no single confession addresses the full range of the church's purposes as understood by Reformed theology. Instead, each confession stresses distinct missional themes. Here, as much as anywhere, the PC(USA) benefits from the wisdom of including in its constitution a broad variety of confessions from various places and times. The confessional tradition not only offers us the wisdom of broad ecclesial consensus on significant matters, it also allows us to learn from particular insights of specific church communities as they faced unique historical and cultural challenges. For instance, the Barmen Declaration's insights regarding the church's relation to political powers appear nowhere else in the confessions.

All too easily the church becomes self-referential, absorbed with maintaining its own identity and viability (only the *What* matters). On the other hand, the church can become so committed to action-witness that it gives scant attention to its identity as church (only the *Why* matters), sapping the church of its distinctive voice, and thus of its special power. The confessional heritage is consistent: The church's identity, practices, and mission cannot be separated without the church losing its authenticity. Weaving the three trajectories together is more than theological artistry; it is a vital necessity for the church's faithfulness and fruitfulness.

The various teleological themes in Reformed confessional ecclesiology were gathered into a now classic formulation that was hammered out by the United Presbyterian Church in North America during the first decade of the twentieth century. "The Great Ends of the Church" remains a vital part of the PC(USA) constitution today. It is considered so important that it is set at the head of the *Book of Order*, second only to the paragraph on Jesus Christ as "The Head of the Church."

> The great ends of the church are the proclamation of the gospel for the salvation of humankind; the shelter, nurture, and spiritual fellowship of the children of God; the maintenance of divine worship; the preservation of the truth; the promotion of social righteousness; and the exhibition of the Kingdom of Heaven to the world.[6]

The church's great ends, significant as they may be, do not address the crucial issue of *what* church is called to strive toward these ends. Nor does it suggest a priority of these various purposes. Both matters must be addressed if the church is to be fully authentic in its identity, faithful in its practices, and fruitful in its mission. Many of the church's deepest and most protracted missional struggles result directly from failing to keep in view exactly *what* church and *which* priorities shape and effect vital ecclesial mission.

THE ONE, HOLY, CATHOLIC, AND APOSTOLIC CHURCH

Nothing matters more to the church's integrity and effectiveness than being true to its core identity, for all vital, faithful, and fruitful ministry draws from this deep well. In an era when mainline denominations are shrinking in membership, public significance, and missionary endeavor, we must face honestly the hard truth that the Western church today has lost the vitality, faithfulness, and fruitfulness that characterized Euro-American Reformed churches of earlier generations, and that are still abundantly evident in many non-Western Reformed churches.

Efforts to revitalize struggling denominations often focus on cosmetic appearance rather than core issues. Instead of asking whether the church is being truly apostolic, we tinker with worship styles, or improve our signage and parking. Rather than asking whether our church is being faithful to the one gospel that calls forth a new creation of one holy people joined to one Lord, we use market analysis and popular preferences to shape (or justify) our "product" in relation to a particular slice of the population that we want (or "feel called") to attract. We are more likely to shape our mission by the slogan "If you build it, they will come" than by Jesus' apostolic commission "Go therefore and make disciples of all nations" (Matt. 28:19).

The Nicene Creed has functioned for centuries as a succinct summary of Christian faith essentials. In its phrase on the church's identity, "We believe in one holy catholic and apostolic Church," the creed sets forth essentials, not ideals. And these ecclesial essentials function not as objects of faith but as conditions of the church's credibility: Which church can be believed? Only the church that is one, holy, catholic, and apostolic is a credible witness to the Christian gospel.

Two general characteristics of ecclesial identity need to be underscored before we consider its particular features. First, as we noted before, the creed is a reflection of actual Christian experience, and as such is an exact inverse of the lived faith it represents. The authentic church is first of all apostolic, and only as such is it catholic, which means "everywhere part of a single whole." The apostolic catholic church is holy—set apart from the self-serving, world-conforming ways of a people not yet liberated by the Christian gospel, all for the sake of those very people. In all this, the church is one, even as the God it worships is one, the Lord it follows is one, and his commission to his followers is one. The church will never be restored to authenticity and potency by rehabilitation efforts that focus first of all on its unity or holiness.

Second, these attributes of authenticity refer first and foremost to the inner identity of particular local congregations, and only subsequently to relationships among congregations or denominations. They are first of all intrachurch, rather than interchurch, descriptors. Unless particular congregations acknowledge and deepen their own character as the one, holy, catholic, and apostolic church, larger church bodies cannot demonstrate that identity. With these two points in mind, we turn to examine briefly each essential feature of the credible church.

First, the credible church is *apostolic*. As an apostolic body, the church is shaped first and foremost by the testimony of the apostles. It proclaims the same gospel proclaimed by Christ's apostles, as set forth in the Scriptures of the New Testament, which have their foundation and authentication in the Scriptures of the Old Testament. The apostolic church is a Scripture-shaped church. In the apostolic church, Scripture as apostolic witness to Jesus Christ authorizes the church, rather than vice versa. The Scots Confession puts it in earthy terms:

> We affirm, therefore, that those who say the Scriptures have no other authority save that which they have received from the Kirk are blasphemous against God and injurious to the true Kirk, which always hears and obeys the voice of her own Spouse and Pastor, but takes not upon her to be mistress over the same. (3.19)

As an apostolic body, the church is also intrinsically a missionary agency, a participant in the mission of God to reconcile all things through the life, death, and resurrection of Jesus Christ. The word *apostle* comes from the Greek word meaning "sent forth." Jesus extends his commission to the apostles, and through them to the whole church, "As the Father has sent me, so I send you" (John 20:21). The apostolic church is not a group that *does* mission; it *is* a missionary body. Without a missional identity, there is no credible church. It must be stressed that the church's mission is not self-selected. The church does not chart its mission in terms of familiar patterns, by what it is comfortable with, or by what it is good at. The church's mission is shaped solely by the mission of Jesus, passed on through his apostles, then through subsequent generations of faithful witnesses, and finally to us. If our mission is not an extension of *that* mission, then we are no longer a credible church.

A key ecclesiological motto of the Reformed tradition is *ecclesia reformata, semper reformanda*, that is, "the church reformed, always being reformed." The Reformed confessional tradition affirms that the apostolic church must always be open to new directions and tasks as the Spirit might lead, but this principle is easily susceptible to gross mischief when the full saying is abbreviated, or (as often happens) when it is mistranslated. The motto is set in its apostolic context when it is cited in its full form: "the church reformed and always being reformed *according to the Word of God and the call of the Spirit*." A believable church will always know and demonstrate that the Word of God is alive and active, never fixed and predictable and manageable (Heb. 4:12). But it also knows and demonstrates that this living Word is continuous with the apostolic witness preserved in Scripture. The church is reformed and being reformed, not according to the passions of reformists, but according to the Word of God in the power of the Spirit of Pentecost. The apostolic criterion stands front and center. Advocacy for change, whether from the right or the left, is not the same thing as being reformed under the Word of God. The apostolic witness powerfully reminds us that God's work always flows from God's Word; this inherent relation of authentic church life in all places and times to the apostolic witness must always be transparent.

The Latin phrase *ecclesia reformata semper reformanda* is frequently mistranslated, even in the PC(USA) *Book of Order*. The common mistranslation— "the church reformed and always reforming"—fails to recognize that *reformanda* is in the passive voice, so that the phrase should be translated "the church reformed, *always being reformed* [according to the Word of God]." The passive voice underscores that in the credible church, reform is effected not by internal debates, charismatic leaders, or cultural accommodations, but by divine agency. A church that promotes itself as a reforming church is skating on thin ice. Reform is God's work, not our own. Could it be that the current numerical decline and intractable political differences that exercise such an unyielding grip on mainline denominations are themselves signs of God at work to reform the church in ways none of us has yet imagined?

The credible church is *catholic*—a Greek-based word meaning literally "according to the whole." The church is credible only to the extent it identifies itself with the whole people of God. The authentic church identifies itself *with* rather than *against* or *alongside* the rest of God's people. The conservative church pitfall is to shape primary self-identity against other churches. For such churches, holiness precedes and qualifies catholicity. Holiness is important, of course, but it is distorted when it becomes a principle of exclusion rather than of election—which is what typically happens when it precedes catholicity. The liberal church pitfall is to adopt a self-identity alongside others; "live and let live" rules the day. In this case, catholicity devolves into nondiscriminatory tolerance of others. Nondiscriminatory tolerance is a good thing, of course, but raised to the level of an essential ecclesial characteristic it becomes an insulating avoidance of serious accountability to what the Spirit is saying to and through other churches.

The catholic church stands in solidarity with all who call upon the name of the Lord, relating to them as sisters and brothers whom we consider better than ourselves (Phil. 2:3). This grace must first be practiced within particular congregations, if it ever is to characterize interchurch relations. One of the Reformed confessional tradition's signal gifts to the larger church lies precisely at this point. It is exhibited in the confessions' insistence that "church" includes *all* the people of God, Jews and Gentiles alike, "from Adam to us" (Scots Confession 3.05, 3.16; Second Helvetic Confession 5.124–.129). In its catholic identity, the church identifies *with* rather than *against* or *alongside* God's chosen people before Christ. If, as our Reformed forebears insist, we count the Jews before Christ's coming within "our" church, how much more should we be in solidarity with, rather than against or alongside, Christian churches of all times and places.[7]

The catholic church is marked by *holiness*. It is set apart by God, for God's glory, to be a powerful apostolic presence in the very world from which God sets it apart. The classic paradigm for holiness is the identity of Israel at the time of the exodus. There God spoke to worldly power through the servant-prophet Moses: "Let my people go, so that they may worship me" (Exod. 8:1, 9:1, etc.). Right worship is impossible when the church is enmeshed in the power games of the marketplace. Only when we are freed from the seductions of socioeconomic idolatries can we embrace fully and truly the starting point for Christian identity, in which our chief end and purpose is to glorify and enjoy God forever (Westminster Shorter Catechism, question 1). Authentic worship always attends to God's majesty, rather than to what "works" in the marketplace.

The church's holiness is not rooted in how we differentiate ourselves from the world, but in God's sovereign election of a people who had been aliens and strangers, but now are made children of the Heavenly Father, joint heirs with Jesus the Son, by divine adoption through the midwifery of the Holy Spirit (Rom. 8:12–17). But the confessions speak of a holiness of the church that goes even deeper than that of adopted children. It is a conjugal holiness, replete with all the delight, intimacy, permanence, and exclusivity that such imagery entails. Not only are we made God's children, we are chosen to be the "body and spouse of Christ Jesus" (Scots Confession 3.16). Again, as God's holy people, we are chosen by God to be the "virgin and the Bride of Christ" (Second Helvetic Confession 5.130). In the passion of divine election, the church's members are, by God's grace, "joined to Christ as their head and husband" (Larger Catechism 7.176).

A church made credible by its holiness seeks God's pleasure and honor rather than self-preservation or self-promotion (Matt. 6:24–34). It resists conformity to the norms of a world ruled by the will of self-advancing marketers and promoters (Rom. 12:2). The holy church may be media illiterate, but it will always be God savvy. Tragically, the opposite is far too often the case in a church desperate to be "relevant" to its place and time, or in a church willing to lose its soul in order to stay intact.

The credible church is *one*. Another great gift the Reformed confessional tradition offers the larger church is its passion for ecclesial unity. It teaches that the unity of the church is rooted in apostolic practices that disclose the catholic identity of a people made holy by God's sovereign election. As a direct effect of this sturdy confessional commitment to church unity, Reformed churches have often been at the forefront of many ecumenical efforts, something we ought to celebrate. But when unity becomes the central focus and primary aim of our efforts to be authentically church, we set the cart ahead of the horse.

In Reformed confessional ecclesiology, church unity stands not as a goal of the church, but as its essential God-given identity. As the company of those united by the Holy Spirit to God in Christ, God's people are necessarily united to each other. The Westminster Confession puts it succinctly: "By the indwelling of the Holy Spirit all believers being vitally united to Christ, who is the Head, are thus united one to another in the Church, which is his body" (6.054). Similarly, the Confession of 1967 roots ecclesial unity not in our efforts to get along with each other but in our being reconciled to God: "The Holy Spirit creates and renews the church as the community in which men are reconciled to God and to one another" (9.20).

While the church's identity as one body is impossible for us to effect by even our best direct efforts, our body language toward each other bears immense consequence. Our failure to love one another always compromises the church's evangelical credibility. We cannot unite the church, but we can and must stop dividing it. The ongoing division of the church may be the greatest impediment to the effectiveness of its gospel witness. The world knows instinctively what the church itself so easily forgets: To be divided from our sisters and brothers is to repudiate our very identity as the church of Jesus Christ. The public mark of our authenticity as Christ's church is our love for one another (John 13:35).

A CHURCH OF WORD AND SACRAMENT

The second major trajectory of Reformed ecclesiology has to do with things more easily visible, with specific practices that mark a particular congregation as genuinely "church." If being rightly related to a bishop in communion with the pope could no longer be appealed to for ecclesial legitimacy, how could the Reformers and their followers claim to be truly the church? The Reformed tradition points not to relational connections but to worship practices.

Before discussing the core practices by which true churches authentically mediate divine salvation, we should note that the appeal to visible criteria for ecclesial legitimacy introduces an important theme in Reformed confessions, namely, the distinction between the "invisible" and the "visible" church. This distinction predates the Reformation, but Reformed ecclesiology raised it to new prominence. The "visible" church is the company of those who gather to worship God; the "invisible" church includes those from all times and places who truly belong to God. Reformed confessions assume that some persons are part of the visible but not of the invisible church (see, e.g., Second Helvetic 5.139). Such persons may have an external bearing of godliness, but are not regenerate within. All visible churches will include "some mixture" of the unregenerate among the true believers, according to Westminster. Some churches may even be comprised entirely of unregenerate persons! But no church is perfectly free from mixture (6.144). None of the confessions directly teach, conversely, that some may be members of the invisible church but not part of the visible church, but the seed of that notion is present in the idea that invisible and visible churches are not entirely commensurate. The Second Helvetic Confession may open up such a possibility when it states that "God can illuminate whom and when he will, even without the external ministry, for that is in his power" (5.007). If it is possible to obtain saving knowledge of the gospel apart from the external ministry, there is no compelling urgency to remain connected to the extant church. This may help explain why Reformed churches have proven particularly prone to schism.

The Reformed tradition has often wrestled with the tendency to speculate about who in the visible church is truly a member of the invisible elect, and who is not. Calvin repeatedly warns against such conjecture, and the Scots Confession concurs that the company of the elect is "invisible, known only to God" (3.16). Westminster teaches that the catholic church, the total company of the elect, the true body of Christ, is invisible. Yet it applies the same designations—catholic, elect, body of Christ—to the visible church (6.140–.141). Calvin protested against critics who accused him of fostering anxiety-ridden "who's in, who's out" speculation, but some of his heirs continue to wrestle with those questions nearly five hundred years later.

One of the reasons the Reformers stressed the impurity of visible churches was to encourage the faithful who were in congregations composed of or led by corrupt persons. Corruption among some in the church does not damn the whole church. Indeed, the confessions teach that God can and often does use corrupt ministers as instruments of divine grace. The Barmen Declaration points out that the church of Jesus Christ is "the church of pardoned sinners," not of immaculate saints (8.17). The visible church is very much a mixed multitude, whose only hope is the lavish generosity of God poured out in divine grace that transcends all our shortcomings.

In the Reformation era there was usually a single church in each community; membership in that one church constituted the only hope, yet never a sure guarantee, of salvation. In such circumstances, speaking of an invisible church was a salutary pastoral strategy to encourage gratitude for the privilege of being included in the company of the saints and to assure God's abiding presence whatever the conditions in the local congregation. In our place and time, the effect of stressing the difference between the invisible and the visible church can produce a very different yield. Sometimes this distinction is marshaled to justify schism in the visible church, since the "true" church is invisible anyway. The ease of schism in a mobile society in which available ecclesial alternatives abound renders the invisible/visible distinction a dangerous fire to play with.

Reformed confessions focus on the visible church as the primary theater of ecclesial concern; appeal to the invisible church is never an escape hatch from the struggles every visible church faces. Calvin fully accepts and even strengthens the church's historic teaching that the visible church is the mother of all believers, and that apart from her proclamation of the Word and administration of the sacraments there lies no hope of salvation.[8] Westminster generally follows Calvin by focusing on the visible church as the bosom of salvation and genuine felicity (6.141–.142; 7.173). In dealing with the visible church and its worship practices, we are dealing with the core of salvation itself. In Reformed ecclesiology, the visible church is God's agent of salvation for its members through two specific acts: the preaching and hearing of God's Word, and the administration of the sacraments.

As noted above, the confessions often add a third sign to these two: the administration of sound discipline. But while the presence of well-ordered discipline is a consistent characteristic of Reformed ecclesiology, it does not stand on equal footing with Word and sacrament; rather, it keeps space clear for God's grace to work regularly through Word and sacrament. If the church is laden with such disorder that free movement of divine grace through Word and sacrament is hindered, discipline is called for to clear such impediments away (see Second Helvetic, 5.132, 5.161).[9]

Preaching and hearing the Word are crucial to the church's viability as the womb of salvation. The Reformed emphasis on preaching arose against the backdrop of the medieval church's abandonment of proclamation in ways that the Word could be heard and engaged by the people of God. To the extent the Word was preached, it was usually in Latin, which most people could not understand. The reformers insisted that the church cannot be God's agent of salvation unless it preaches the Word in language people understand, since saving faith comes by hearing God's Word (Rom. 10:17).

Reformation-era confessions tend to lift up the importance of preaching without lifting up the corresponding importance of hearing, however (see, e.g., 3.18; 5.134). Westminster corrects that oversight (7.218), but a tendency to focus more on preaching than on hearing remains prevalent in many Reformed churches. Sixteenth-century reformers wisely insisted that churches use the vernacular in worship, but in many Reformed churches today, the language of both word and song is far removed from current usage, and so the church must honestly ask if people are really hearing what is being proclaimed.

Confessions routinely bind Word and sacraments together as the core ecclesial practices that participate in the mystery of God's grace being poured out upon those who are being saved. As means of divine grace, sacraments are always set on a liturgical level with Word—formally, at least. But for many reasons, while baptism and the Lord's Supper retain a place of formal liturgical equivalence with the Word in our confessions, actual Reformed church practices tell a very different story. Even in official PC(USA) worship resources, celebration of sacraments is optional for Lord's Day worship (the Directory for Worship requires only that the Lord's Supper be celebrated at least quarterly), while proclamation of the Word is always mandatory. Constitutionally, no PC(USA) congregation may have sacrament without Word, but most congregations regularly have Word without the sacraments. The practical disjunction of Word from sacraments in Reformed worship needs careful, critical attention. Like the Geneva city fathers of the sixteenth century, leaders in many of today's Reformed churches dismiss Calvin's insistence that Word and sacrament are bound together in the weekly worship rhythm of God's people. We would do well to give closer attention to Calvin's conviction that sacraments are as necessary as the proclaimed Word in making available all that Christ offers us.[10]

Over the past fifty years, the liturgical renewal movement has raised the consciousness of many Reformed churches to recognize that their received sacramental practices are, in fact, theologically un-Reformed. But long-worn ruts are even more difficult to escape than they are to identify. As they have come to appreciate more fully the deep disorder in the way Reformed churches typically marginalize the celebration of the Eucharist, a growing number of congregations in America are experimenting with a rhythm of worship life that lodges weekly Eucharist in an "alternative" worship service, whether on the Lord's Day or on a weekday. While such movements seem like progress for those who wish to see a more regular place for the Lord's Table in the church's worship life, we must ask whether such practices clarify or obscure the Reformed conviction that this table is the center of nourishment for the entire community of the baptized.[11] The church must also ask whether, in adopting such a strategy, it is underwriting a "buffet" rather than "table" identity for the church at worship, so that worship becomes an event where people pick and choose whatever their tastes demand rather than a place where the faithful gather to receive all that Christ offers.

Focusing on Word and sacrament as core ecclesial practices relating to salvation runs the risk of promoting clericalism in the church. This risk is already evident in the Second Helvetic Confession, where the church's *ministers*—not its *ministries* of Word and sacrament—are cast as means of divine grace (5.142). This stands in contrast to Calvin's insistence that elders share in governance of the church, thus exercising partnership with pastors in the church's ministry—although it must be admitted that seeds for a nascent clericalism are already present in some of Calvin's own work.[12] Post-Reformation Reformed confessional ecclesiology returns to Calvin's major emphasis, that pastors have no elevated privilege in the governance of the church (see, e.g., Barmen Declaration 8.20; Confession of 1967, 9.38–.40). Yet clerical control of the churches, governmentally as well as liturgically, remains alive and well in much Reformed church practice.

THE CHURCH AND GOD'S MISSION

With a solid grasp of essential ecclesial identity and practices, we are prepared to address directly the *why* question: Why the church? What is its raison d'être, its overarching mission? We must not forget that the church is not a body that, among other things, *does* mission; it *is* in mission in all it does. Salvation and mission are inseparable; the community of sinners saved by grace is unavoidably a missional community. In the words of the Confession of 1967, "To be reconciled to God is to be sent into the world as his reconciling community" (9.31). Apart from God's mission of reconciliation inaugurated in Jesus and continued through the apostolic community, there is no genuine church at all.

One of the significant benefits the Reformed confessional tradition can offer to the wider church today is the reminder that the purposes of Christian life can be fulfilled only corporately, by the church *as* church. By stating Christian aims in terms of "great ends of the church" rather than something like "God's plan for my life," the Reformed tradition emphasizes that God's purposes in Christ cannot be accomplished merely with the personal improvement of individual Christians, or even the robust growth of individual congregations. Without a view of the "great ends" that puts us in solidarity with the whole people of God toward those purposes, the church's vision falls short of what it must be.

The six great ends of the church may be fairly summarized by six words: evangelism, fellowship, worship, theology, justice, and embodiment.

> *Evangelism:* Proclamation of the gospel for the salvation of humankind.
> *Fellowship:* The shelter, nurture, and spiritual fellowship of the children of God.
> *Worship:* The maintenance of divine worship.
> *Theology:* The preservation of the truth.
> *Justice:* The promotion of social righteousness.
> *Embodiment:* The exhibition of the kingdom of heaven to the world.

Like the church's ontological attributes of apostolicity, catholicity, holiness, and unity, the great ends lay claim upon individual congregations as well as upon the whole church. While churches in different places and times may place particular stress on one of the great ends or another, the call to embrace *all* these missional aims—not just those a given church feels comfortable with—applies as fully and equally to each congregation as it does to the whole church. When a particular congregation or denomination shapes itself by some of the great ends while leaving others to the "church down the street," it becomes something less than the church of Jesus Christ.

The message of reconciliation lies at the heart of the salvation effected through the life, death, and resurrection of Jesus Christ: "In Christ God was reconciling the world to himself, not counting their trespasses against them, and entrusting the message of reconciliation to us" (2 Cor. 5:19). "For he is our peace; in his flesh he has made both groups into one and has broken down the dividing wall, that is, the hostility between us" (Eph. 2:14). "For in him all the fullness of God was pleased to dwell, and through him God was pleased to reconcile to himself all things, whether on earth or in heaven, by making peace through the blood of his cross" (Col. 1:19–20).

The first great end of the church is the proclamation of this good news of God-initiated reconciliation for the salvation of humankind. The final great end of the church is the embodiment of this gospel as the church exhibits "the kingdom of heaven" in its public life. These two constitute the bookends of the whole mission of God's people; the mission always begins with proclamation that is sealed with demonstration of the good news of what God has done in Christ to restore all that sin has ruined. The church is the place where this gospel is proclaimed and embodied through the power of the Holy Spirit. Apart from the church living publicly as a reconciled and reconciling community, gospel proclamation is only empty words. And without public proclamation of the faith by which it lives, the gospel remains the church's private secret. But when the message of reconciliation is both proclaimed and embodied in the public life of the church, it carries the sure ring of authenticity.

Why the church? To put it starkly: no church, no gospel. Only as the fruit of the gospel is publicly displayed in an inner life marked by reconciliation does the church's declaration of what God does in Christ through the Spirit carry real weight. Being reconciled to God in Christ necessarily reconciles us to one another, as powerfully witnessed in the Westminster Confession: "By the indwelling of the Holy Spirit all believers being vitally united to Christ, who is the Head, are thus united one to another in the Church, which is his body" (6.054).

If the proclamation and embodiment of the good news of what God has done for humankind in Jesus Christ are the bookends of church mission, worship of the living God is what binds the entire mission together. The church exists in order to ensure that right worship of the living God continues unabated. Such worship is the "chief end" for which all men and women live, according to the Westminster Catechism (7.001). The purpose for which God calls a holy people out from their slavery in Egypt is not primarily that they might be freed from oppression, but that they may worship God rightly. The other great ends of the church are all included in the call to worship. In Exodus, the call to worship is the first movement of the Israelites' call to *salvation* from bondage. The first act of worship is to commemorate God's mighty deliverance from Egypt with a festival that *nurtures* the whole community physically as well as spiritually. Gathered before the holy mountain in worship, God's exodus people are entrusted with holy law that becomes timeless *truth* for right living with God and neighbor. As the community takes shape with the tabernacle of God's presence at the center, Moses' role as worship leader in the center becomes indistinguishable from that of advocate and guarantor of *justice* for neighbor and stranger. With the ark of God at center, the people of Israel become a tangible *demonstration* of God's reign to the surrounding nations. Worship stands at the core of God's formation of a missional people. The truthfulness, fervor, and fullness of members' participation in the church's public worship both reflect and shape its authenticity qua church. Worship is the church's core practice.

Why the church? That God may be worshiped rightly. The primary features of this right worship are authentic preaching and hearing of God's Word, and faithful administration of the sacraments. Worship is more than current church practice; it is the church's ultimate telos, as the book of Revelation so vividly reveals. In worship we are always striving toward something unattained yet already present in the heavenly chorus of saints and angels, as the Eucharist's Great Prayer of Thanksgiving continually reminds us. This drive forward is always marked and sustained by persisting ecclesial dissatisfaction, by a clear sense of the penultimacy of everything status quo. Vital churches are always driven forward by an insatiable desire for a better country, for a heavenly city, and worship is the cutting edge of that drive. By pointing to the nature and glory of God, the church exists to testify that all is not yet as it should be, indeed, as it shall be.

Getting the form of worship right is not enough, of course. Both Heidelberg and the Confession of 1967 stress that the church's identity is not marked by external forms and rites, but by the truth and unity of the catholic faith that forms and reflects the content of our worship (5.141, 5.240; 9.34). While some forms lend themselves more adequately to authentic and appropriate worship than others, it is not the form but the content of worship that matters most. This is one reason why churches in the Reformed tradition usually eschew fixed liturgical templates in favor of flexible liturgical guides.

As the kinetic center of the church's forward thrust, worship in the Reformed tradition always spills into the rest of the church's ends. Sound worship practices constitute core internal correctives to subversions and seductions to which church mission is all too readily susceptible. *Evangelism* apart from central attention to glorifying God becomes institutional self-preservation and self-advancement strategy. *Fellowship* apart from central attention to glorifying God all too easily disintegrates into a thin veneer of quasi-hospitality on the one hand, or gets mired in enclaves of group therapy on the other. *Theology* apart from worship dissolves into ideology or hardens into dogmatism. *Justice* pursued apart from glorifying God is soon enslaved to one or another sociopolitical program. Finally, any account of *kingdom* that is sundered from catholic worship of the one true God in company with the whole people of God collapses into personality cults focused on particular charismatic leaders.

What keeps the church truly the church—apostolic, catholic, holy, and one—as it pursues its appointed ends? Nothing more, and nothing less, than continual, disciplined, corporate attention to God through faithful preaching and hearing of the Word and participation in the sacraments. Calvin reminds us that both the proclamation of the Word and the administration of the sacraments present us with the same thing, namely, with Christ himself.[13] The church is true to itself and to its mission only as it remains vitally connected to its head, Jesus Christ. This bond begins and ends in worship, with the Christian church's most ancient creed: Jesus is Lord!

The opening words of the *Book of Order* powerfully point to Christ as the foundation and goal for all the church is called to be and to do:

> All power in heaven and earth is given to Jesus Christ by Almighty God. . . . God has put all things under the Lordship of Jesus Christ and has made Christ Head of the Church, which is his body. . . . In affirming with the earliest Christians that Jesus is Lord, the Church confesses that he is its hope and that the Church, as Christ's body, is bound to his authority and thus free to live in the lively, joyous reality of the grace of God.[14]

Why the church? To glorify Jesus Christ by proclaiming and demonstrating in its way of life the message of reconciliation that he proclaimed and demonstrated in his own life—a proclamation and demonstration that is sustained and kept on track by faithful worship of the triune God.

Soli Deo Gloria.

NOTES

1. By "Reformed" I refer to the portion of the Reformation rooted in Switzerland, with primary branches extending to Eastern Europe, the Netherlands, and Scotland. The single most influential thinker in this tradition is John Calvin.

2. While the Nicene Creed is more ancient in its present wording and more widely ecumenical in appropriation, the Reformed churches have tended to prefer the more concise Apostles' Creed in worship. The Apostles' Creed in nascent form functioned as the Christian baptismal faith statement for Christians as far back as the second century, and is free of the elaborate, controversy-rooted christological nuances that encumber the Nicene Creed. The ecclesiological phrase of the Nicene Creed is more precisely focused than that of the Apostles' Creed, and its categories constitute the basis of much Reformed ecclesiological discussion of the church's identity. See especially book 4 of Calvin's *Institutes*, as well as the Heidelberg Catechism and the Study Catechism in *The Book of Catechisms* (Louisville, KY: Geneva Press, 2001).

3. *Catechesis* refers to the formal impartation of instructions to new church members—whether adults or younger confirmands—in the essentials of Christian life. *Catechisms* are sets of prescribed questions and answers that are designed to cover these essentials of Christian faith and practice.

4. John Calvin, *Institutes of the Christian Religion*, ed. John T. McNeill, trans. Ford Lewis Battles (Philadelphia: Westminster Press, 1960), 4.1.2 (LCC 2:1012–13). Calvin argues that ancient witnesses are divided on whether "in" should be included, but in any case only God is the proper object of faith. Karl Barth concurs and adds helpful commentary in *Church Dogmatics* IV.1, 686.

5. Calvin, *Institutes* 4.1.9 (LCC 2:1023).

6. *The Constitution of the Presbyterian Church (U.S.A.)*, Part II, *Book of Order* (Louisville, KY: Office of the General Assembly, 2004), G-1.0200.

7. In Romans 9–11, the apostle Paul struggles mightily with how the exclusive saving work of Jesus Christ and the irrevocability of God's election of the Jewish people who do not recognize Jesus as Savior can be reconciled. The Reformed churches have likewise struggled with this question, a struggle that becomes evident when the Confession of 1967 states that the church "began with the apostles" rather than with the covenant people of the Old Testament (9.10). The danger here is that we commit the "evangelical" error of making inclusion in the church overly dependent on human response to the gospel message, to the diminution of its antecedent dependence on the sovereign call of God that comes to us before we even know who God is, or what Jesus has done for us.

8. Calvin, *Institutes* 4.1.1–4 (LCC 2:1011–16).

9. A noteworthy instance of this is seen in the practice of "fencing the Table," by which the church's officers deny Communion as a form of discipline toward those who resist the claims of Christ on their lives—both for their own sake and for the sake of the rest (see Scots Confession 3.23; Heidelberg Catechism 4.082). While such an action is no longer practiced in most Reformed churches, the principle of using discipline to preserve the integrity of the church's encounter with divine grace in Word and sacrament is yet alive.

10. The sacraments are "necessary," according to Calvin, not because God's Word is incomplete in itself, but because our human frailty renders us incapable of receiving the benefits of Christ's grace except that God "condescends" to our limited spiritual-cognitive receptivity. Sacraments are necessary not because God needs them, but because we need them (*Institutes* 4.14.3 [LCC 2:1278]).

11. Various other incremental strategies for "rehabilitating" the church's celebration of Eucharist have found some currency. Most commonly, churches with a tradition of Communion once a quarter—a pattern particularly characteristic

of Presbyterians in the southern United States—have moved in the past fifty years to celebration of the Lord's Supper monthly or bimonthly. However, there is little evidence that this shift from rare to not-quite-so-rare Communion celebration either reflects or precipitates any substantive difference in the nature or understanding of the Communion celebration in the churches. The Lord's Supper is still experienced by most worshipers in such places as an appendix to worship, rather than as something "integral" to the church's worship, as the Directory for Worship rather wishfully describes it (*Book of Order* W-2.4009). The 215th General Assembly (2003) of the Presbyterian Church (U.S.A.) called upon each of the denomination's 173 presbyteries to adopt an initiative to ensure that the Lord's Supper is celebrated in at least one of its congregations each Lord's Day, so that at least presbyteries, if not particular congregations, can enact the ideal of weekly Eucharist. Whether presbyteries will in fact do this remains to be seen; in any case, the question remains whether such an incremental movement toward the full coinherence of Word and sacrament in worship is truly helpful toward that end.

12. Calvin, *Institutes* 4.1.6 (LCC 2:1020–21); 4.3.8 (LCC 2:1060–61). See also Calvin's attribution of the exercise of the keys entirely to the ministry of Word and sacrament (*Institutes* 4.1.22 [LCC 2:1035–36]).
13. Calvin, *Institutes* 4.14.12 (LCC 2:1287) and 4.14.16 (LCC 2:1291–92).
14. *Book of Order*, G-1.0100.

11

Why the Bible?

Thomas G. Long

Years ago, film actor Max von Sydow starred in a Hollywood costume drama about the Bible called *The Greatest Story Ever Told*. Today the title might have to be *The Greatest Story Rarely Told* or perhaps even *The Greatest Story Ever Forgotten*. It is widely recognized that knowledge of Scripture has been in dramatic decline over the last several generations in our society. When a prominent politician recently announced that Job was his favorite book in the New Testament and then went on to describe Job in ways that showed he was as confused about the contents as he was about the correct testament, it was hard to know whether to laugh or to cry.

Presbyterians, like many other Protestants, are in an ironic situation regarding the Bible. On the one hand, Presbyterians are as firm as ever about lifting up the Bible theologically as the Word of God, but, on the other hand, fewer and fewer actually lift up the Bible physically from the coffee table, bookshelf, or nightstand for serious reading and study. Psalm 1 describes the blessings that come to those who meditate on God's Word day and night, but many Presbyterians significantly engage the Scripture only episodically, mainly in sermons—clergy in preparing them and laity in listening to them. Only one Presbyterian in seven reports reading the Bible daily, and even those who do read the Bible regularly do so primarily in brief devotional bursts.[1]

Officially, Presbyterians know better. One of the Presbyterian confessional documents, the Westminster Larger Catechism, insists that the Bible should have a comprehensive influence on every aspect of life, pointing boldly to the Scriptures as "the only rule of faith and obedience" (7.113). However, in all honesty we must confess that, if that was ever true, it is certainly less so today. Rank-and-file Presbyterians figure out what to believe and how to live from many sources of influence and authority. The Bible is just one voice, and sometimes not even the main voice, calling the plays. Moreover, in a time of biblical amnesia, a time when fewer and fewer churchgoers know much about biblical content, preachers have learned, some of them the hard way, that scriptural allusions in sermons often produce blank stares and wrinkled brows. Our great-grandparents named their churches Carmel, Sharon, Bethsaida, and Sardis, but many Presbyterians today could not say why, perhaps not even recognizing these as biblical names. Our youth can often give us full biographies of the drummer, keyboardist, and lead guitar player in their favorite band, but would probably be hard pressed to identify Ruth, Samuel, Rachel, or Timothy.

This is a strange condition. We have a book we revere but rarely read, call holy but do not really know, claim to be authoritative but treat as a stranger. As a result, the Bible often functions for Presbyterians like some classified military weapon—powerful, hidden, full of secrets, understood only by experts, and brought out mainly when we do battle.

At first glance, this seems like a moral failure. It is tempting to say that we Presbyterians *should* be more knowledgeable about the Bible, that we *must* read and study the Bible more often, and that we *ought* to be ashamed at the hypocrisy of saying the Bible is God's Word and then often paying it little heed. But the problem is not primarily a moral one, but one of communication and interpretation. The Scriptures have power many Presbyterians do not know how to tap. If people truly understood the Bible and found it full of meaning and life, they would attend to it expectantly and study it faithfully, but the problem is the disconnect between what we profess about the Bible and people's actual experience of it. Most Christians desperately want to encounter the power of Scripture, but simply do not know how to do so. Sales of study Bibles are at an all-time high, a sign of the hunger to understand this book that we know is important but that we often find so remote, obscure, and difficult to understand. In some ways, the Bible is like a grandmother in an immigrant family. The children love their grandmother, they want to know her, and they are aware that she has much wisdom to offer, but she speaks only the language of the old world, a language they never learned.

Ours is not the first generation, of course, to struggle with the place and power of the Scripture. We bemoan biblical illiteracy, but the church has lived through periods when many Christians were illiterate, period. What is the role of the Bible when only the educated elite can read it? We fret because our youth cannot name the sixty-six biblical books, but the church has experienced seasons when there were strenuous disagreements about how many books belonged in the canon in the first place. We worry when church members seem more interested in the "spirituality" of some self-help guru on television than in the theology of Ephesians, but the church has wrestled with the tension between culture and Scripture many times before, sometimes when the stakes were life or death. Evidence of many of these struggles can be found in the church's confessional documents. The historic confessions, creeds, and catechisms of the Presbyterian Church are not antiseptic statements of abstract doctrine. They are, instead, the journals of hard-won truths wrought from trial, debate, and conflict. What insights, then, can we discover in these documents about the role of the Bible in our time?

THE STEAM IN THE ENGINE

Anyone who goes to *The Book of Confessions* seeking help on issues about the Bible is in for a surprise: the creeds, confessions, and catechisms have very little to say directly about the Bible. A major rallying cry of the Reformation was *sola scriptura*—"Scripture alone"—and the authority of Scripture is a major motif in Reformed theology, but *The Book of Confessions* is unexpectedly reticent about Scripture. The Apostles' Creed doesn't mention the Bible at all, the Nicene Creed has only the brief phrases "rose again in accordance with the Scriptures," and "[the Holy Spirit] has spoken through the prophets," while Scripture receives only three lines out of eighty in A Brief Statement of Faith. In the catechisms—Heidelberg and the Westminster Larger and Shorter—the Bible is the specific subject of a mere handful of questions out of hundreds, and even those documents that are the most loquacious about the doctrine of Scripture—the Scots Confession and the Westminster Confession—contain at most a few paragraphs about the character of the Bible. Why?

A careful reading of *The Book of Confessions* reveals the answer. The confessional documents rarely stop to speak explicitly about Scripture because scriptural language and ideas are woven into almost every sentence. There is little need for the Presbyterian creeds, confessions, and catechisms to expound the importance of the Scripture in one place because it is powerfully pervasive in every place. The confessions do not labor over the doctrine of Scripture for the same reason that judges do not labor over the nature of the law before trying a case or homeowners do not give dissertations on electricity before turning on the lights or flicking on the television. Scripture is the assumed context of, the intrinsic authority for, the implied power behind every word in the confessional heritage.

In his masterly book on art and culture, *The Voices of Silence*, Andre Malraux pondered what he called "the disappearance of Christ" in modern art. Why was it, he wondered, that modern artists so rarely painted the figure of Christ, especially since Christ had been portrayed so frequently and so compellingly in the great works of earlier periods? Malraux concluded that, in fact, Christ had not disappeared at all from modern art, but instead the power and inspiration that earlier artists had found in the face of Jesus had been absorbed into the modern artistic vision. Once Christ was the subject *of* much art, but now, claimed Malraux, Christ was the dynamic energy *in* the art.[2]

In a similar way, Scripture is the dynamic energy in every one of the Presbyterian creeds, catechisms, and confessions. The Bible is only here and there the subject; it is always and everywhere the source. It is the steam in the engine, the air in which the birds fly, the inspiration by which the poet sings. The documents display this in various ways, suited to their historical circumstances. The Westminster Confession of Faith carefully footnotes its statements with scriptural references. The language of Romans reverberates in every chamber of the Heidelberg Catechism. The Theological Declaration of Barmen, which was composed with Nazis banging on the doors of German churches and the claims of National Socialism menacing the peace in Europe, begins each of its major sections with a verse of Scripture and rouses the attention of the reader with a dare: "If you find that we are speaking contrary to Scripture, then do not listen to us! But if you find that we are taking our stand upon Scripture, then let no fear or temptation keep you from treading with us the path of faith and obedience to the Word of God" (8.04).

The pervasive presence of Scripture in the confessions is no accident. It mirrors the Reformed understanding of how the Bible operates in the Christian life. The objective of gaining knowledge of the Bible is not to master biblical facts or to score well in Bible Lotto but to be shaped continually by Scripture. Being a Christian, Presbyterian style, does not mean being able to prattle on incessantly *about* the Bible, but to allow the biblical story to influence all that we say and do. In the confessions, the Bible is less like an encyclopedia to be consulted from time to time and more like theme music, setting the rhythm for all of life and summoning the words to be sung every day. In his book *Experiments with Bible Study*, Hans-Reudi Weber tells a story from an East African village:

> A simple woman always walked around with a bulky Bible. Never would she part from it. Soon the villagers began to tease her: "Why always the Bible? There are so many books you could read!" Yet the woman kept on living with her Bible, neither disturbed nor angered by all the teasing. Finally, one day she knelt down in the midst of those who laughed at her. Holding the Bible high above her head, she said with a big smile: "Yes, of course there are many books which I could read. But there is only one book which reads me!"[3]

After telling this story, Weber goes on to describe how studying the Bible can cause a figure-ground reversal in which the book being read turns the tables:

People start out by listening to an old message, by analyzing ancient texts, by reading—naively or critically—the biblical documents of antiquity. They experience this exercise as dull or instructive, as something Christians ought to do or something they have been led to do by their own . . . interests. Yet a mysterious change of roles can then occur. Listening, analyzing, and reading, students of the Bible meet a living reality which begins to challenge them. . . . This divine presence starts to question, judge, and guide us. Perhaps gradually, perhaps quite suddenly, the book which was the object of our reading and study becomes a subject which reads us.[4]

WRITTEN WORD, LIVING PRESENCE

A staple joke in magazine cartoons is for someone to approach a clerk at an information counter and ask, "So, what's the meaning of life?" The gag, of course, is that no clerk could possibly answer such an impossible, imponderable question. Who could? However, the very first question in the Shorter Catechism comes fairly close to posing just that query when it asks what is the main purpose, what is the "chief end," of humanity? In other words, what are people for anyway? What is the meaning of life? In one of the best-known and most often-quoted phrases in *The Book of Confessions*, the catechism, unlike the cartoon clerk, answers that question confidently and clearly: Humanity's "chief end is to glorify God, and to enjoy him forever" (7.001).

To glorify and enjoy God—that answer is so beautiful, so compelling, that we are halfway down the street whistling a merry tune before the obvious follow-up question hits us between the eyes: Wait a minute—how? How can human beings glorify and enjoy God? The Shorter Catechism is ready for this question too, and it answers just as confidently: "The Word of God which is contained in the Scriptures of the Old and New Testaments is the only rule to direct us how we may glorify and enjoy him" (7.002).

In sum, the first answer tells us that we are at our most human when we glorify and enjoy God, and the second answer informs us that we need the Bible to know how to do that. The fact that many Presbyterians and others can quote the first answer but few can cite the second answer is quite revealing. As the title of a recent book would have it, Americans tend to want to be "spiritual, but not religious,"[5] so glorifying and enjoying God has a nice, positive spiritual ring to it, while the idea of the Scriptures ruling and directing us has a heavier, more negative, religious footstep. Glorifying and enjoying God sounds like something that can be done on a mountaintop, watching a glorious sunset, or out on the golf links, but discovering the provisions and patterns of the Bible sounds more like dreary church work.

But this is one place where the confessional documents confront our culture head on. The confessions are not really interested in making us either spiritual or religious; instead, they are interested in making us human. The first two questions of the Shorter Catechism have to be taken together. How does one become a full human being? By glorifying and enjoying God. And how do we do that? We cannot do that, thus we cannot be fully human, without the guidance of Scripture.

Why is this so? Why is engaging a long, complex, ancient, and often obscure book full of recipes for cereal offerings, parables with surprise endings, and visions of dragons and beasts necessary for us to be human? Taken together, the confessional documents give two main responses to that question. First, we need the Bible to be human because of what is in the Scripture, and second, we need the Bible to be human because of the One who meets us there.

With regard to the content, the confessions affirm that the Bible tells us who God is and what it means to be in faithful relationship to God. John Calvin opened his magisterial *Institutes of the Christian Religion* by claiming that almost all human wisdom can be divided into two kinds of knowledge—knowledge of God and knowledge of ourselves—and then went on to say that it was hard to figure out which of these was the chicken and which was the egg. "Which one precedes and brings forth the other," said Calvin, "is not easy to discern."[6] On the one hand, thinking about ourselves, Calvin observed, inevitably leads to transcendent thoughts about the God in whom we live and move, but on the other hand, thinking about ourselves can be an exercise in vanity; we do not really understand ourselves until we have first beheld the face of God.

The Bible is necessary because it provides the essential and truthful versions of both kinds of knowledge. Of course, the Bible is not the only place to get knowledge about God and ourselves. Aunt Myrtle, the op-ed section of the *New York Times*, or a fortune cookie in a Chinese restaurant may say some true things about God or life, but the confessions insist that all other sources of wisdom must be measured against the norm of Scripture.

Even though the confessional documents are bold to say that in the Bible we have "the true Word of God . . . and . . . the most complete exposition of all that pertains to a saving faith" (Second Helvetic Confession 5.001–.002), the confessions are not naive about how the Bible conveys its wisdom. They recognize that not everything in the Bible is of equal importance, that some parts of the Bible are downright difficult to understand, that some things we want to know are not in the Bible at all and need to be inferred, and that the inspired words of the Bible are still human words "conditioned by the language, thought forms, and literary fashions of the places and times at which they were written" (Confession of 1967, 9.29).[7] Taken together, however, the Scriptures present the great and sweeping story of God's interaction with creation, a framework for rightly seeing God and ourselves. The Bible is, as the Confession of 1967 puts it, "the witness without parallel" (9.27).

In a famous metaphor, John Calvin compared the Scriptures to a pair of eyeglasses. Just imagine, said Calvin, what would happen if you were to put a beautiful book in front of "an old or bleary-eyed" man. He could perhaps recognize that he was looking at a book, but he could not read the words. If he put on a pair of spectacles, though, the words would come into clear focus. That is akin to the way the Scripture clarifies our vision of God. "So Scripture, gathering up the otherwise confused knowledge of God in our minds, having dispersed our dullness, clearly shows us the true God."[8]

But as important as the content of the Bible is, the Presbyterian catechisms, creeds, and confessions refuse to limit the Bible to being a textbook full of true ideas about God and life. The Bible is also a meeting place, a place of encounter. As we go to the Bible, God comes to us and speaks to us, becoming for us a living presence.

Episcopal priest and preacher Barbara Brown Taylor remembers the early days of her ministry when she served as the coordinator of a congregation's Christian education program. Members of the church would tell her that they wanted to know more about the Bible, so she would arrange for professors to come from a nearby seminary to teach classes in the Old and New Testaments. The problem was, even though people said these Bible courses sounded like just what they wanted, hardly anybody came. Courses on topics such as parenting and religion and the arts were oversubscribed, but people stayed away from the Bible classes in droves. This was curious, because every quarter the congregation would tell Taylor again that they wanted more Bible, that they were not getting enough, but few showed up for the courses. "Finally," she said, "I got the message. 'Bible' was a code word for 'God.' People were not hungry for information about the Bible; they were hungry for an experience of God, which the Bible seemed to offer them."[9]

It is indeed the experience of God that the Bible offers. In fact, when we study the Bible we are not ultimately trying to master the history of the Hittites, count the number of porticoes on the pool of Bethesda, or figure out whether the Bible approves of drinking wine. We are trying to hear God, know God, and experience God today, here and now. The Larger Catechism spends a paragraph lauding the majesty, purity, unity, literary sweep, and persuasive power of the Bible, but then confesses that what ultimately matters is that God is present there: "But the Spirit of God, bearing witness by and with the Scriptures in the heart of man, is alone fully able to persuade it that they are the very word of God" (7.114).

Theologian Stephen H. Webb has observed that mainline Christians like Presbyterians get so fearful of fundamentalist claims to "hear God speaking in the Bible" that we start listening more for other voices in Scripture than for God's voice:

> Some theologians suggest that we should always hear the voice of the poor in the biblical text, or the voice of women, or the voice of whoever happens to be reading it at the time, since all reading is contextual and thus socially constructed. While it is true that the Bible is full of many voices—it is the paradigmatic example of what postmodernists call a "multivocal' text"—the one voice that is silenced by these theologians is the very voice of God.[10]

The affirmation that the living Spirit of God indeed speaks in Scripture is not only a sign of faith and hope, it is also a sign of humility. We may carry around a thumb-indexed Bible and a concordance, we may be able to read the Bible in Hebrew and Greek, we may even have memorized every word of the Bible, but we cannot claim thereby to possess the Word of God. Human beings do not have and hold God's Word, and it is not captured between the leather covers of a Bible. God freely speaks, God freely comes to us, and there is an unexpected quality to God's Word, an elusiveness that defeats all human attempts to control it. We go to the Bible and bow our heads, praying in the words of the old hymn, "Beyond the sacred page, I seek Thee, Lord; My spirit pants for Thee, O living Word."

THE BIBLICAL DANCE

So how do the Presbyterian creeds and confessions imagine that the Bible can move from being a book on the shelf to becoming a power in our lives? How do the words printed on the "sacred page" become the "living Word" for us? The confessional documents are quick to let us know that, in one sense, this is not our business; it is God and God alone who transforms the written words of the Bible into the living voice of revelation. The confessions are keen to keep the equation straight: The Bible's authority is from God and not from human beings or even from angels. The Scots Confession is quite colorful on this point: "We affirm, therefore, that those who say the Scriptures have no other authority save that which they have received from the Kirk are blasphemous against God and injurious to the true Kirk, which always hears and obeys the voice of her own Spouse and Pastor, but takes not upon her to be mistress over the same" (3.19).

In other words, when it comes to hearing the Word of God in Scripture, the authority flows from God, through Scripture, and toward us—not in the other direction. We are the student and not the teacher, the servant and not the mistress of the biblical house. The Westminster Confession of Faith could hardly be clearer: "The authority of the Holy Scripture, for which it ought to be believed and obeyed, dependeth not upon the testimony of any man or church, but wholly upon God . . . , the author thereof; and therefore it is to be received, because it is the Word of God" (6.004).

If this were all the confessions said about the authority of Scripture, it would sound a bit like the prickly bumper sticker: "God said it, I believe it, and that's that." But the confessions are more nuanced than any such slogan. Having firmly articulated the freedom and authority of God to speak in Scripture, the confessional documents are equally firm in declaring that the church and faithful Christians have an active part in this too. Like a good center fielder racing to catch the line drive, the church moves faithfully to position itself where it can hear God speaking in Scripture. We don't hit the ball—that is God's part— but if we don't move, we'll miss it. To be submissive before Scripture is not to be passive; there are things the church is called to do and be that better enable it to hear God speaking in Scripture. To employ another image, the engagement with Scripture is like a dance. We are not supposed to try to lead, but we are supposed to get out onto the dance floor.

One of the ways the church gets out on the scriptural dance floor is by taking a certain posture, a certain attitude, toward the Bible, namely, by choosing to grant to it the position of authority. If we walk into a bookstore, there is nothing magic about the shelf of Bibles that says, "Treat us as more authoritative than books on gardening, psychology, or European history." The Bible does not glow in the dark or grab us by the throat and demand our allegiance. If the Bible actually functions as the living Word of God for us, it is in part because we have chosen to turn toward it in expectation and obedience, and the confessions at least tacitly acknowledge this.

One of the places we can see this tacit awareness of the church's role in the Bible's authority is in the listing of the sixty-six canonical books in the Westminster Confession of Faith. After listing each of these books by name and then claiming that they are "given by inspiration of God, to be the rule of faith and life," Westminster turns its guns on the Apocrypha: "The books commonly called Apocrypha, not being of divine inspiration, are no part of the canon of Scripture; and therefore are of no authority in the Church of God, nor to be any otherwise approved, or made use of, than other human writings" (6.003). How does Westminster know this? If the Apocrypha is not inspired and not a part of the real Bible, this point has been missed by a goodly number of the world's Christians. So how did the Westminster divines get the message? Did Jesus list the sixty-six truly inspired books in his Sermon on the Mount? Did Paul, like the original Mormon Joseph Smith, find golden plates of the authentic canon buried under a tree in Damascus? No, of course not.

The Reformed tradition's decision to view these sixty-six books and not any other as Scripture is just that—a church decision. It is not an arbitrary decision—there are historical and theological reasons to describe the canon this way—but it is a decision nonetheless.[11] As Luke Timothy Johnson states,

> The decision to regard the canon of the Old and New Testaments as normative—as providing a sort of measure for authentic life before God—does not result from scientific inquiry, or from historical research. The decision to regard these historically conditioned documents as having a normative force for every age of the church is a decision of faith. It is preeminently a church decision. In fact, it is one of the decisions that constitute the church in every generation. The canon and the church are correlative in this sense: Without the community regarding them as addressing it in an authoritative and normative way, these ancient writings would not be Scripture. On the other hand, without such a fixed frame of understanding, which mediates the identity of the community from age to age, there would not exist any historical community identifiable as the church in the first place.[12]

A second place the confessional documents spotlight the church's active role in engaging Scripture is in the task of forming doctrine and setting out the ethical responsibilities of the church. The confessions are strong in the view that all of the church's creeds, doctrines, and ways of living should conform to the pattern of Scripture. Especially those confessional documents that derive from the Reformed tradition agree that, as A Brief Statement of Faith phrases it, "The Spirit . . . rules our faith and life in Christ through Scripture" (10.4).

One could take this kind of statement to mean that the Bible already contains all the doctrine and all the ethical instruction we need, and so faithfulness consists in simply returning to the biblical gold mine over and over and digging out the nuggets. But as biblical scholar Benjamin Jowett said over a hundred years ago, it is "not easy to say what is the meaning of 'proving a doctrine from Scripture.'"[13] Theologian David Kelsey agrees: "A theologian who marshals his proposals under the emblem 'Let theology accord with scripture' does not thereby announce that he has made a methodological decision, but only that he has taken on an awesome array of methodological problems."[14]

In their own ways, the Presbyterian confessional documents recognize and respect these methodological problems, if in no other way than by refusing to enshrine any single method of biblical interpretation, leaving each new generation to find its own proper approaches to scripture. Even the Scots Confession, which may well be the most nervous of the confessional documents about mischievous theological innovation and the capacity of church councils to come up with "the doctrine of devils," recognizes that the church in each age has the responsibility to "refute heresies, and to give public confession of

[its] faith to the generations following" (3.20). In other words, the Bible is not some static repository of mathematical truths, but a place of encounter to which the church in every time must return again and again to correct its errors and to refresh its witness. As Kelsey puts it, "To say that biblical texts taken as scripture are 'authority' for church and theology is to say that they provide patterns determinate enough to *function* as the basis for assessment of the Christian aptness of current churchly forms of life and speech and of theologian's proposals for reform of that life and speech."[15]

A third place the church gets into the act of engaging Scripture is in biblical study and interpretation, or what the Larger Catechism calls Bible "reading" (7.265). What is remarkable about the confessional documents is the conviction that Bible study is an essentially communal event and their insistence that the Bible be translated into vernacular languages so that everybody could get in on the act. Yes, Christians read and study the Bible privately, but eventually Bible study should be done together in groups, families, and congregations.

There are several reasons for this communal emphasis. To begin with, group reading and study of Scripture mirrors the character of the Bible itself, which is a kind of miniature faith community. Just as group wisdom is sometimes to be valued over individual insight, just so separate biblical passages are to be best understood in conversation with the whole of Scripture: "When there is a question about the true and full sense of any scripture," states the Westminster Confession of Faith, "it may be searched and known by other places that speak more clearly" (6.009).

Another reason for group engagement with the Bible is that one of the primary functions of Scripture is the building up of the church, the community of Jesus Christ. It is through the Bible, states the Confession of 1967, that the church "hears the word of God and by which its faith and obedience are nourished and regulated" (9.27). Theologian Paul Janowiak points to the social character of the biblical texts themselves as one of the characteristics of Scripture that enables it to continue to "nourish and regulate" the life of the church: "We need to appreciate that sacred texts are social events that are negotiated, contested, and redefined in light of the contingent nature of social practices in which they are embedded. What endures in these works is their capacity as literary artifacts to convey a 'life' that was originally encoded in them and which continues to be refashioned in every encounter."[16]

Theologian and preacher William Willimon argues that the Bible should be read "politically," but he does not mean politics in the usual sense. "The Bible," he writes, "is political in the classic sense of the word politics—the formation of a *polis*, the constitution of a people through a discussion of what needs are worth having, what goals are good."[17] He points out that the New Testament was not just a devotional writing but was a manifesto in the midst of the Roman

Empire for a new way of understanding the way the world could be: "Scripture gave us a new story, a new narrative account of the way the world was put together, new direction for history, new purpose for being on earth. The world of Rome had many other stories which gave meaning to people's lives: eroticism, pantheism, polytheism, cynicism. To be a Christian was to be someone who had been initiated, by baptism, into this alternative story of the world."[18]

The deepest reason that the confessional documents give for communal engagement with the Scripture, however, is the human tendency to twist the Scripture to make the Bible say what we want it to say. The Second Helvetic Confession cites 2 Peter 1:20 to the effect that "the Holy Scriptures are not of private interpretation," then continues that in the Reformed tradition "we do not allow all possible interpretations" (5.010). Given his historical context, Bullinger was blasting away at the private and idiosyncratic interpretations of the medieval Catholic Church. What he says, though, applies equally to pseudobiblical tracts such as *The Prayer of Jabez*, *The Da Vinci Code*, *The Celestine Prophecy*, and the Left Behind series. Whenever anybody steals away with the Bible by himself or herself in a corner and then comes back with a secret interpretation of Scripture, Presbyterian confessions blow the whistle. One has to interpret the Bible in a public place, in humble prayer and in debate and conversation with other Christians. The Second Helvetic Confession had it right. The Scriptures can only be truly interpreted in "faith and love" (5.010), virtues that belong to the whole people of God.

But it is the fourth way that the Presbyterian confessional documents highlight the church's engagement with Scripture that most clearly marks the Reformed tradition. Scripture comes alive, the confessions vigorously announce, through preaching. No stronger statement of this conviction has ever been made than the Second Helvetic Confession's claim that "the preaching of the Word of God is the Word of God." Even if the preacher "be evil and a sinner," the preaching of the Word of God is still the Word of God (5.004). For anyone who has ever suffered through a rambling, dull, inarticulate sermon (or ever delivered one), the idea that preaching is to be equated with the very Word of God stretches credulity. Even the best of preachers are, after all, flawed and limited human beings. How can the sermon we heard last Sunday, regardless of whether it was inspiring or bumbling, be put up there with the Bible and with Christ as "the Word of God"?

Part of the answer lies in the confessions' notion of the "inward illumination of the Spirit" (Second Helvetic Confession 5.005), which is a way of describing what every preacher knows: God is always doing more in a sermon than can be accounted for by the preacher's abilities and efforts. But "inward illumination of the Spirit" is only part of the answer. If that were the full reason why preaching is the Word of God, then it would not matter much what preachers did or said. A preacher could read from the Yellow Pages, recite dialogue from old *Beavis and Butthead* shows, or speak gibberish in a hypnotic trance, and it would make little difference since the inward witness of the Holy Spirit could still communicate directly to people's hearts.

But the confessions will have nothing to do with such nonchalance or irresponsibility in terms of preaching. The "inward witness" does not erase the need for careful and faithful "outward preaching" (5.005). A question in the Larger Catechism puts it beautifully:

Q. How is the Word of God to be preached by those that are called thereunto?

A. They that are called to labor in the ministry of the Word are to preach sound doctrine, diligently, in season, and out of season; plainly, not in the enticing word of man's wisdom, but in demonstration of the Spirit, and of power; faithfully, making known the whole counsel of God; wisely, applying themselves to the necessities and capacities of the hearers; zealously, with fervent love to God, and the souls of his people; sincerely, aiming at his glory, and their conversion, edification, and salvation. (7.269)

In this one catechism question and its moving answer, we glimpse the key insight as to why the Reformed tradition identifies preaching as the Word of God. The faithful sermon is nothing less than a recapitulation of the incarnation. This description of the preacher and preaching could, with a word change here and there, be a description of the life and ministry of Jesus. Like art students sitting for hours before their easels, trying brush stroke by brush stroke to copy the work of the great masters, Christian preachers, frail as they are, devote themselves in their preaching to the attempt to enter into the world of their congregations with the wisdom, love, and saving intent manifested in Jesus. Even their sermonic failures, then, point, like the finger of John the Baptist, to the Christ who is in every way the Word.

STANDING ON THE PROMISES

Biblical scholar Markus Barth once said that the best Easter message he ever heard was a sermon where the preacher simply "fell down in front of the biblical text." The fact that the preacher was overwhelmed by the Easter story and could only stammer before it was a testimony to the amazement, the power, and the glory of the resurrection.[19] To read through the creeds and catechisms of the Presbyterian Church is to experience this same awestruck astonishment in the face of Scripture, this falling down before the biblical Word. In these documents, we do not saunter up to the Bible casually, but instead we take off our shoes, for we are on holy ground. Here we are drawn over and again to Scripture, not because we are religious types or out of habit, but because, as Peter said to Jesus, "Lord, to whom can we go? You have the words of eternal life" (John 6:68).

In his book *Shaped by the Bible*, William Willimon notes that in the Gospel of Luke, Jesus began his ministry in his hometown synagogue not by asking the congregation how things were going that week, spinning yarns from his youth, or by sharing his feeling. Instead, Jesus unrolled the scroll and read Scripture. Willimon observes, "There may be religions which begin with long walks in the woods, communing with nature, getting close to trees. There may be religions which begin by delving into the recesses of a person's ego, rummaging around in the psyche. However, Christianity is not one of those. Christianity is a people who begin with the action of taking up a scroll and being confronted with stories of God."[20]

The creeds, confessions, and catechisms of the Presbyterian Church offer a hearty *Amen!*

NOTES

1. See "The Bible," a Presbyterian Panel survey produced by the Office of Research Services of the Presbyterian Church (U.S.A.), February 1995.
2. Andre Malraux, *The Voices of Silence* (Garden City, NY: Doubleday, 1953), 468–91.
3. Hans-Reudi Weber, *Experiments with Bible Study* (Philadelphia: Westminster Press, 1983), vii.
4. Ibid.
5. Robert C. Fuller, *Spiritual, but Not Religious: Understanding Unchurched America* (New York: Oxford University Press, 2001).
6. John Calvin, *Institutes of the Christian Religion*, ed. John T. McNeill, trans. Ford Lewis Battles (Philadelphia: Westminster Press, 1960), 1.1.1 (LCC 1:35).
7. See also the Westminster Confession of Faith, 6.006–.009.
8. Calvin, *Institutes* 1.6.1 (LCC 1:70).
9. Barbara Brown Taylor, *The Preaching Life* (Boston: Cowley Publications, 1993), 47.
10. Stephen H. Webb, *The Divine Voice: Christian Proclamation and the Theology of Sound* (Grand Rapids: Brazos Press, 2004), 166.
11. The footnote for this section of Westminster in *The Book of Confessions: Study Edition* acknowledges as much, saying candidly that the canonical decision was a stool resting on several legs: "The Canon of Scripture is not established by explicit passages, but by the testimony of Jesus and His Apostles; of ancient manuscripts and versions; of ancient Christian writers and church councils, and by the internal evidence exhibited in the separate books" (*Book of Confessions: Study Edition* [Louisville, KY: Geneva Press], 217).
12. Luke Timothy Johnson, *Scripture and Discernment: Decision Making in the Church* (Nashville: Abingdon Press, 1983), 31.

13. Benjamin Jowett, *The Interpretation of Scripture and Other Essays* (London: Routledge & Sons, n.d.), 27–28.
14. David H. Kelsey, *The Uses of Scripture in Recent Theology* (Philadelphia: Fortress Press, 1975), 111.
15. Ibid., 194.
16. Paul Janowiak, *The Holy Preaching: The Sacramentality of the Word in the Liturgical Assembly* (Collegeville, MN: Liturgical Press, 2000), 165.
17. William H. Willimon, *Shaped by the Bible* (Nashville: Abingdon Press, 1990), 19.
18. Ibid., 21.
19. Markus Barth, "Introduction," in Leonhard Goppelt, et al., *The Easter Message Today: Three Essays* (New York: Thomas Nelson & Sons, 1964), 11.
20. Willimon, *Shaped by the Bible*, 17.

12

How Shall We Worship?

Martha L. Moore-Keish

In the classic 1978 film *The Muppet Movie*, Kermit the Frog and his friends trek across the country on their way to Hollywood to start their careers as rich and famous movie stars. At one point, exhausted, Kermit and Fozzie Bear stop outside a ramshackle country church to catch a little sleep. When they awaken, they hear music from inside the church, and they decide to investigate. They open the doors of the church to discover flashing disco lights and the raucous music of the rock band Dr. Teeth and the Electric Mayhem. Fozzie blinks, shakes his head, and says, "They don't look like Presbyterians to me."

Fozzie is, of course, right in his assessment. We Presbyterians have not been known for colored lights and rock bands in worship (though this is beginning to change in some places). The question is: Why is this the case? Should it remain so? Should we rule out certain styles of music and uses of technology as un-Presbyterian? What norms do we have to guide our liturgical preparation and leadership?

Before turning to the confessions to explore their responses to this question, let us consider how ordinary Presbyterians think about worship. What constitutes authentic and appropriate Presbyterian worship? When confronted with this question, we tend to respond either with the phrase "decently and in order" or with some portion of our identifying motto, "Reformed and always being reformed according to the Word of God." Each of these responses provides a helpful but incomplete picture of the fullness of Presbyterian worship.

Decently and in order. This phrase has been part of Reformed Presbyterian identity at least since the Scots Confession, which proclaims that "good policy and order should be constituted and observed in the Kirk where, as in the house of God, it becomes all things to be done decently and in order" (3.20).

Presbyterians frequently offer this description in a sly, self-deprecating tone, but as a description, it is not entirely untrue. Since the sixteenth century, Presbyterians have had a strong affection for orderliness in worship: not too much pomp and circumstance, not too much emotional display, just the well-prepared and articulately proclaimed gospel delivered by someone in a black gown in a simply furnished room to a gathering of well-dressed faithful. Not Dr. Teeth and the Electric Mayhem. We Presbyterians are fond of order and, as I will say later, this maxim still has something to teach us. But if it is the only thing we say, or even the first thing we say about worship, we risk becoming stodgy characters in someone's forgotten play rather than living worshipers of the living God.

Reformed . . . Depending on the local context, a Presbyterian may emphasize that Reformed means "not Roman Catholic" (and therefore includes minimal ritual, longer sermons, and less frequent celebration of the Lord's Supper) or "not Baptist" (and therefore includes more emphasis on educated clergy and celebration of infant baptism). Some comparison of the Presbyterian Church with surrounding Christian churches is inevitable, and it is even necessary at times to define what makes us a distinctive Christian tradition. But if it is the only thing we say, or even the first thing we say about worship, we portray ourselves in an entirely negative fashion rather than articulating a positive vision of how we worship. We also risk ignoring what we share with the wider community of Christian worshipers.

. . . and always being Reformed . . . Sometimes Presbyterians emphasize the adaptability of worship to particular places and times. As a tradition without fixed forms, we celebrate the fact that local congregations can and do worship in a variety of ways in response to the leading of the Spirit. The passive voice here reminds us that we do not reform ourselves, but we are *being* reformed by God. But if this is the only thing we say, or even the first thing we say about worship, we give the impression that there is nothing enduring through our liturgical shifts, no recognizable structure undergirding our adaptations.

. . . according to the Word of God. Finally, Presbyterians sometimes emphasize that we worship according to God's Word, claiming that our worship does not change according to human whim, but is shaped according to the more durable revelation of God. This claim contains a measure of truth, for since the sixteenth century, Reformed Christians have appealed to biblical warrant for the form and content of worship. Presbyterians have believed that in Jesus Christ the Word of God incarnate and through the witness of Scripture, God has provided not only everything necessary for salvation but also good and reliable guidance for how we are to live and pray. So, for instance, Presbyterians have traditionally preached sermons founded on careful biblical exegesis and have provided biblical warrants for the sacraments of baptism and the Lord's Sup-

per. But if this is the only thing we say, or even the first thing we say about worship, we fail to give a full account of what it means to worship according to God's Word, and we risk giving the impression that Scripture provides a clear and unequivocal set of liturgical rules requiring minimal translation into a local context.

If we put all of these partial responses together, we gain a somewhat more adequate response to the question "How shall we worship?" We worship in a way that is decent, orderly, reformed, and always being reformed according to the Word of God. Here we have a certain style, a distinctive identity, and an openness to change together with an objective norm guiding such change. Yet even this does not constitute a full answer, because it does not tell us what has been reformed, what is the stuff of worship that is subject to reform according to God's Word. We need a still better answer.

What do the confessions have to say about how we shall worship? At the outset it is important to acknowledge that the bulk of *The Book of Confessions* consists of documents from the sixteenth and seventeenth centuries, and therefore much of the direct discussion of worship is dominated by anti–Roman Catholic rhetoric: no priests, no ceremonies, no saints, no women performing baptisms, and so forth.[1] This polemical treatment of worship has even more weight because three of the confessions—the Nicene Creed, Apostles' Creed, and Barmen Declaration—have virtually nothing to say directly about worship.

But behind the negative rhetoric of the Scots, Heidelberg, and Second Helvetic Confessions, and Westminster Confession and Catechisms, and in and through the remaining five documents, we can discern a positive, constructive account of human worship. Discussions of worship in *The Book of Confessions* tend to approach the subject in one of three ways: in relationship to the Holy Spirit, in relationship to Jesus Christ, and in relationship to the one God. Specifically, according to the broad consensus of the confessions, worship is directed to and empowered by the Holy Spirit; directed to and mediated by Jesus Christ; and directed to and authored by God alone. This trinitarian pattern should not surprise us, but it does represent a way into the worship discussion that is different from our usual approaches. I will unpack each of these points and then ask what the confessions have to contribute to some of our most pressing worship discussions today.[2]

Directed to and Empowered by the Spirit

Let us begin at the beginning. The first mention of worship in the confessions is in the third article of the Nicene Creed, which asserts that together with the Father and the Son, the Holy Spirit is "worshiped and glorified" (1.3). From this we know at the outset that we worship a triune God, and that the third person of the Trinity is no less worthy of worship than the first two. The Second Helvetic and Westminster Confessions also voice the claim that the Holy Spirit is worthy of our worship together with the Father and the Son (5.016; 6.051, 6.113, and 6.183). Before we have any hint about how we are to worship, the question itself is changed; it is no longer "How?" but "Whom?" *Whom* do we worship? The answer is that we worship a God made known to us in classic terms as Father, Son, and Holy Spirit. And the first thing we learn is that our worship should be directed to the Holy Spirit.

The Spirit is not just the object of worship, however. Much more frequently, the confessions describe the Spirit as the one who makes it possible for us to worship at all. "The cause of good works, we confess, is not our free will," proclaimed the Scots in 1560, "but the Spirit of the Lord Jesus, who dwells in our hearts by true faith, brings forth such works as God has prepared for us to walk in" (3.13). This Spirit makes possible all of humanity's good works, both works to the honor of God and works to the profit of the neighbor. "To have one God, to worship and honor him, to call upon him in all our troubles, to reverence his holy Name, to hear his Word and to believe it, and to share in his holy sacraments, belong to the first kind" (3.14). In other words, the Spirit empowers our worship of the one God, since "by ourselves we are not capable of thinking one good thought" (3.12).

Such an assertion of human incapacity may sound insulting to our ears. How can those impudent Scots say that we cannot think one good thought by ourselves, that we are incapable of any sort of worship without the aid of the Holy Spirit? Before we object, however, we do well to remember that this statement comes from an age when new Protestant believers saw all around them evidence that humans left to their own devices did not worship God rightly. In their judgment, this was simply a factual observation. The wonder is that God does not abandon us to our own free will but continues with the work of sanctification through the power of the Holy Spirit, enabling us to worship rightly "to the praise and glory of his undeserved grace" (3.12). The proclamation that the Spirit enables our worship is not first and foremost bad news about our shortcomings; it is good news about God's grace.

We should note here that the emphasis on the work of the Spirit, not only in the Scots Confession but in all of the sixteenth- and seventeenth-century documents, is never an excuse to avoid worship preparation. None of the confessions suggests that the Spirit fills in when I have not had time to finish my sermon, for instance. This "God of the gaps" strategy has emerged more recently, implying that liturgical preparation and the work of God's Spirit are mutually exclusive.[3] By contrast, what we have in the Scots and other confessions is a way of preserving perpetual humility with regard to our own efforts in worship. We can never manufacture authentic worship of God through proper technique. Even when we have done all we can to plan a faithful and engaging worship service, we truly worship God only in and through God's own activity in the person of the Holy Spirit.

The Scots Confession, then, asserts that the Spirit makes possible all worship of God. Yet the confessions offer us more than simply this general observation about the Spirit's role in worship. All of the Reformation confessions and the Westminster Standards concur that the primary areas of the Spirit's work are the Word and the sacraments: the two "marks of the church" and the two major elements of Christian worship.[4] The Spirit makes both the Word and the sacraments effective. The Shorter Catechism summarizes the work of the Spirit with regard to the Word: "The Spirit of God maketh the reading, but especially the preaching, of the Word an effectual means of convincing and converting sinners, and of building them up in holiness and comfort, through faith unto salvation" (7.089).[5] It is because of the Holy Spirit that the reading and preaching of the Word reaches and changes the listeners.

The Confession of 1967 also affirms reliance on the Holy Spirit to make the words of Scripture God's word today: "God's word is spoken to his church today where the Scriptures are faithfully preached and attentively read in dependence on the illumination of the Holy Spirit and with readiness to receive their truth and direction" (9.30; cf. 9.49). When a worship leader prays for illumination before reading Scripture, calling on the Spirit to make these words into the Word of God for these people, she is embodying this affirmation of the confessions. Even the words of Scripture do not bring illumination on their own, but require the action of the Holy Spirit to make a difference in the lives of the hearers.

The Spirit makes the sacraments effective as well as the Word. With regard to the Lord's Supper, the Scots Confession explains, "This union and conjunction which we have with the body and blood of Christ Jesus in the right use of the sacraments is wrought by means of the Holy Ghost" (3.21). The Heidelberg Catechism gives one account of how this happens. In answer to the question "What does it mean to eat the crucified body of Christ and to drink his shed blood?" this catechism responds, "It is to be so united more and more to his blessed body by the Holy Spirit dwelling both in Christ and in us that, although he is in heaven and we are on earth, we are nevertheless flesh of his flesh and bone of his bone, always living and being governed by one Spirit, as the members of our bodies are governed by one soul" (4.076).[6] The sacraments are not effective in and of themselves, but only through the action of the Spirit.

Although this is not the place for an extended reflection on various strands of sacramental theology in the confessions, it is worth noting that the understanding of the Holy Spirit's role in relation to the sacraments shifts from the sixteenth to the twentieth century. In their discussions of the sacraments, the sixteenth-century confessions try in various ways to balance their horror at idolatry with an insistence that through the work of the Holy Spirit, the sacraments are truly effective. They are not "naked and bare signs" (3.21) or "common signs" (5.181), for they convey the real presence of Jesus Christ. They do not do this by their own power or because of the intention or action of a priest, however, but by the power of the Holy Spirit.

The Westminster documents are a bit more cautious in their claims for the ability of the sacraments to convey Christ's presence. Still, they insist that worthy receivers of the Lord's Supper "outwardly partaking of the visible elements in this sacrament, do then also inwardly by faith, really and indeed, yet not carnally and corporally, but spiritually, receive and feed upon Christ crucified, and all benefits of his death" (6.167). Significantly, the Spirit is not mentioned in this paragraph. Even so, Westminster's general statement on the sacraments does affirm that the efficacy of the sacraments depends on the work of the Spirit together with the word of institution (6.151).

A curious thing happens, however, when we get to the Confession of 1967 (C67). Though the basic confession affirms that Christ "is present in the church by the power of the Holy Spirit to continue and complete his mission" (9.07), and though the Scriptures become God's Word today through the work of the Holy Spirit (9.30), C67 does not state that it is the work of the Spirit that makes the sacraments effective. Why is this? Had the writers of C67 lost the rich Reformation sense of the power of the Holy Spirit working in and through the sacraments as well as the proclaimed Word? I suspect this is a clue that through the centuries we Presbyterians lost our early conviction that in baptism and the Lord's Supper we truly encounter the presence of God in Christ through the power of the Holy Spirit. We have been more willing to proclaim God's action in and through the Word, and less willing to proclaim that action in and through bread, wine, and water.

In A Brief Statement of Faith (1993) the Spirit's connection with the sacraments was restored: "The same Spirit who inspired the prophets and apostles rules our faith and life in Christ through Scripture, engages us through the Word proclaimed, *claims us in the waters of baptism, feeds us with the bread of life and the cup of salvation* . . ." (10.4). Yet it is worth asking whether current Presbyterian practice embodies the conviction that the Holy Spirit brings us into Christ's presence in the sacraments. When we celebrate baptism and participate in the Lord's Supper, do we call on the Spirit to unite us with the risen Christ, or is the Spirit an afterthought? What difference would it make to our sacramental life if we trusted the Spirit's presence and action in our corporate actions?

I suggested earlier that when we Presbyterians call ourselves "Reformed," we are often defining ourselves over against Roman Catholic and Baptist churches. Perhaps, in contemporary North America, we are also distinguishing ourselves from Pentecostalism, the most rapidly growing force in Christianity today. Pentecostal theology and worship are built on the affirmation that the Holy Spirit is powerfully present and active in the world today, manifesting itself through the same gifts of healing, prophecy, and tongues that the New Testament records were present in the earliest churches. Could it be that part of our reluctance to claim the presence and power of the Spirit in our worship is due to our suspicion of "those people" who embrace the gifts of the Spirit so readily?

If we listen to the confessions as we think about worship today, we are confronted by the fact that our sixteenth-century forebears placed enormous stress on the the Holy Spirit's role in empowering worship. Though the confessions do not address the gifts of the Spirit, they do speak of the Spirit working, quickening, empowering, enabling our worship, and uniting us with the living Christ. According to the Larger Catechism, the Spirit enables us to pray, "We not knowing what to pray for as we ought, the Spirit helpeth our infirmities, by enabling us to understand both for whom, and what, and how prayer is to be made; and by working and quickening in our hearts . . . those apprehensions, affections, and graces, which are requisite for the right performance of that duty" (7.292). While this may not be glossolalia, it does represent a firm reliance on the Holy Spirit to lead our prayers, never relying on our power alone to address God. We could benefit from the wisdom of our forebears by trusting the Holy Spirit in our preparation and leading of Presbyterian worship today.

One major theme in a conversation with the confessions on the subject of worship, then, is the Holy Spirit, both as worthy of worship and as the one who makes our worship worthy.

Directed to and Mediated by Jesus Christ

The confessions also approach the subject of worship through the role of Jesus Christ, who both receives our worship and mediates our worship to God. The Westminster Confession sums up both of these aspects of Christ: "Religious worship is to be given to God, the Father, Son, and Holy Ghost; and to him alone . . . and since the Fall, not without a Mediator; nor in the mediation of any other but of Christ alone" (6.113; cf. 7.146–.152). Just as the Holy Spirit both receives and enables right worship, so also Jesus Christ both receives and mediates our worship.

The focus on Christ as sole mediator grew out of the sixteenth-century polemical context, in which the Reformers saw the late medieval Western church relying on other mediators, particularly saints and their relics (5.024–.026). This they repudiated, insisting that Christ alone intercedes for us before God and shows us the way to God. In our own time and place, thanks to deepened ecumenical understanding, we need not condemn the worship of our Roman Catholic sisters and brothers. Yet the understanding of Christ as mediator of our worship offers a word we need to hear, teaching us that in Christ we have a pattern for how we are to worship, and that a member of our family is already in the very presence of God, offering up prayers on our behalf.

Christ's act of mediation has two directions: from God to us, and from us to God. Both of these directions appear in the confessions: Christ reveals God to us, and he brings us before God. The Barmen Declaration clearly voices the revelatory character of Christ when it asserts, "Jesus Christ, as he is attested for us in Holy Scripture, is the one Word of God which we have to hear and which we have to trust and obey in life and in death. We reject the false doctrine, as though the church could and would have to acknowledge as a source of its proclamation, apart from and besides this one Word of God, still other events and powers, figures and truths, as God's revelation" (8.11–.12). Barmen's strong declaration that Christ is the revelation of God to us also affirms the integral relationship between Christ and the Scriptures as the Word of God. Both Christ and the Scriptures reveal God to us, giving us a pattern for all of life, including the way we should worship.

The Reformed emphasis on worship according to the Word of God in Scripture should be understood in relation to Christ's mediating role. The same Word in both is what brings God to us. When the Second Helvetic Confession opens with the affirmation that Scripture is the Word of God (5.001) and goes on to affirm that "the preaching of the Word of God is the Word of God" (5.004), its claims presuppose the mediating character of Jesus Christ as the Word of God. Because Scripture bears witness to Jesus Christ, Scripture itself can be called the Word of God.

The Westminster Confession offers a classic statement on Scripture as the norm for worship: "The acceptable way of worshipping the true God is instituted by himself, and so limited by his own revealed will, that he may not be worshipped according to the imaginations and devices of men, or the suggestions of Satan, under any visible representation or any other way not prescribed in the Holy Scripture" (6.112).[7] Presbyterians lift up this strand of the Reformed tradition when we emphasize worship "according to the Word of God." Although the Westminster statement may sound restrictive, it is important to understand its relation to Christ's mediating role.

Scripture is the Word of God because it bears witness to Christ the Word of God, and if part of Christ's mediating role is the revelation of God's will to us, then the Scriptures also reveal God's will to us. This does not mean that every detail of our life and worship is prescribed; even Westminster admits that "there are some circumstances concerning the worship of God . . . which are to be ordered by the light of nature and Christian prudence, according to the general rules of the Word" (6.006). The point is that the Word of God in Jesus Christ and in Scripture as it witnesses to Jesus Christ is the mediator of our worship, and we are on dangerous ground if we reject or neglect this Word of God.

A problematic outcome of this line of thinking is that too much emphasis on worship according to the Word of God can lead to wordiness in worship. The sixteenth- and seventeenth-century confessions present us with a tension. On the one hand, they emphasize both Word and sacraments as chief elements in worship; the sacramental sections help to balance the focus on the Word alone. On the other hand, they are at pains to emphasize the authority of Scripture and preaching as the Word of God. In general, Presbyterians have most often adopted the latter rather than the former emphasis.

If it is assumed that Christ as the Word of God is attested only in and through Scripture as the Word of God, words can quickly become the primary (or only) medium of worship. The Heidelberg Catechism, the Second Helvetic Confession, and the Westminster Confession exacerbate this danger by explicitly forbidding any use of images in worship (4.096–.098; 5.020–.021; and 6.112), in effect equating "worship according to the Word alone" with "worship by words alone." We rightly question this unrelenting emphasis on words in worship today, adopting C67's greater appreciation for the use of the arts in worship (9.50) as a way of receiving the Word of God incarnate. Nevertheless, as we seek to expand our use of visual and other arts in worship, we do well to maintain the positive emphasis of the earlier confessions on the Word of God as mediator, revealing God's will to us and graciously providing a pattern for our worship.

Christ as mediator reveals God to us, and as mediator he also brings us to God. This second direction of Christ's mediation appears in the Second Helvetic and Westminster Confessions especially. For instance, the Second Helvetic Confession insists that we call on God alone "by the mediation of our only mediator and intercessor, Jesus Christ" (5.024). We may not pray to God in any way other than through the mediation of Christ. The Westminster documents offer a variation on this theme with their emphasis on Christ as priest and intercessor (e.g., 7.154). In his priestly role, Christ offers continual intercession to God on our behalf. Whether we offer prayers through Christ or Christ offers prayers in our place, the movement is the same: Jesus Christ our Mediator enables our prayers to come before the throne of grace.

The Barmen Declaration offers a fitting conclusion to this discussion of Christ's role as mediator. It suggests that we not only receive the benefits of Christ's mediation, but as the church we also participate in Christ's mediating role to all the world: "The church's commission, upon which its freedom is founded, consists in delivering the message of the free grace of God to all people in Christ's stead, and therefore in the ministry of his own Word and work through sermon and Sacrament" (8.26). In and through the Word and sacraments, Christ not only offers us to God, but extends the offer of God to the world.

The confessions' emphasis on Jesus Christ as the mediator of our worship presents two challenges to current Presbyterian worship practice. First, it challenges patterns of proclamation, prayer, and sacramental practice that do not witness to Christ's life, death, resurrection, ascension, and return. In our proclamation, do we welcome the stranger, feed the hungry, lift up the lowly—and do these things in the name of Christ? In our prayer, do we frankly acknowledge the powers of sin in the world and in ourselves and receive forgiveness through Christ? Do we give thanks and intercede for the needs of the world after the pattern of Christ? In our celebration of the Lord's Supper, we know better than to try to duplicate Jesus' last meal—or any of his meals—in a mechanical fashion, as if merely repeating a formula counted as celebrating the Supper in the manner of Christ. But as we come to the table, we ought to ask ourselves how this meal leads us into the life-giving and life-changing presence of our Savior.

Second, this emphasis on Christ's mediation challenges us to question how we participate in Christ's mediating role to all the world. Although we should ask this of all our worship practices, we should ask specifically how our baptismal practice manifests the "message of the free grace of God to all people." Do we welcome people of all ages joyfully to the font, nurturing them both before and after to live into the fullness of the new life they are entering through the waters? Do we preach regularly on living the baptized life after the pattern of Christ? Do we come to the table understanding it as a reaffirmation of the baptismal promises of God's abundant grace? Do we baptize in a way that proclaims our oneness in Christ?

In all of these ways and more, Presbyterian worship can witness to and participate in the mediating role of Jesus Christ.

Directed to and Authored by God Alone

Finally, say the confessions, right worship is not only enabled by the Spirit and mediated by Jesus Christ, but is directed to and authored by God alone. The Creator of heaven and earth formed humanity in such a way that our chief end is to glorify and enjoy God forever (4.006; 7.001). God is therefore both the author of worship and the only true object of our worship. As the Westminster Confession puts it, "religious worship is to be given to God, the Father, Son, and Holy Ghost; and to him alone" (6.113). God is both source and goal of right worship.

God is not only the author of human worship in general, but of the sacraments in particular. As the Second Helvetic Confession puts it, "The author of all sacraments is not any man, but God alone. Men cannot institute sacraments. For they pertain to the worship of God, and it is not for man to appoint and prescribe a worship of God, but to accept and preserve the one he has received from God" (5.172). The point here is similar to the point about Christ's work of mediation. We do not decide how to worship God; the pattern for worship is revealed to us. Therefore, we are not free to institute any sacraments other than the ones God has provided: baptism and the Lord's Supper. God alone provides the particular means for us to reach our "chief end": glorifying and enjoying God forever.

Several of the confessions present the law (particularly articulated in the Ten Commandments) as a support of this "chief end" of humanity. In its discussion of the law, the Scots Confession lists as "works to the honor of God" (also cited above in the discussion of the Holy Spirit): "to have one God, to worship and honor him, to call upon him in all our troubles, to reverence his holy Name, to hear his Word and to believe it, and to share in his holy sacraments" (3.14). These "works" of worship are intended to help us live out our original purpose in creation.

This is even clearer in the Heidelberg and the Westminster Catechisms, both of which include lengthy discussions of the Ten Commandments. The Shorter Catechism includes the following question and answer:

Q. What is required in the First Commandment?
A. The First Commandment requireth us to know and acknowledge God to be the only true God, and our God, and to worship and glorify him accordingly. (7.046–.047)[8]

The answer deliberately echoes the opening question and answer of the catechism: "What is the chief end of man? Man's chief end is to glorify God, and to enjoy him forever" (7.001). Clearly, the law coheres with God's original intention in creation: We are directed to joyful worship of the one true God because such worship is part of the hard-wiring of our created being!

The Reformation confessions share a grave concern about idolatry, the offering of worship to anything other than the one true God. We have already seen how the concern about idolatry is related to an emphasis on the Word of God as that which alone reveals God to us and bears us to God. But it is also important to note that idolatry is understood as a fundamental rejection of our created nature and a transgression of the law. Idolatry simultaneously repudiates God's work of creation, Christ's work of redemption, and the law as a good guide for the life of the redeemed. No wonder idolatry occupies such a prominent place in the confessions of the sixteenth and seventeenth centuries![9]

Our question is how to understand idolatry in contemporary North America. We may easily agree with the confessions that idolatry is a bad idea, but how do we know it when we see it? How do we know when we are worshiping someone other than the Holy One of Israel, revealed as Jesus Christ and present as the Holy Spirit? In the United States, our nation sometimes sneaks into worship as an idol! Processing the American flag and singing triumphal national hymns in worship can too easily eclipse the praise of the God of *every* nation. While we affirm that the state can serve God's purposes, we must also hear the prophetic words of the Barmen Declaration: "We reject the false doctrine, as though the State, over and beyond its special commission, should and could become the single and totalitarian order of human life, thus fulfilling the church's vocation as well" (8.23). The state is not the church, and it is certainly not God. Nothing in our worship should lead people to adoration of this or any other nation.

In sum, the confessions situate our question "How shall we worship?" in the context of the question "Whom shall we worship?" The answers fall into a trinitarian pattern: We worship a God called Father, Son, and Holy Spirit, who not only receives but also authors, mediates, and enables our worship. Worship, then, can be understood as our entrance into this trinitarian life: learning to recognize the end for which we were created, conforming our worship to the pattern given in Jesus Christ, and opening ourselves to the Spirit who gives life to our worship today.

Worship's trinitarian pattern may help us to think through some of the questions that currently confront Presbyterian worshipers. The following issues are not exhaustive, but they address some of the most frequent questions about worship in our church.

Is Worship Primarily for the Already Churched or the Not Yet Churched?

Should we adapt our forms of worship to welcome those who were not born and raised in a Christian, much less a Presbyterian, environment? The confessions do not address this issue directly, for worship is usually assumed to be for the faithful and their children, a gathering of the covenant community for the purpose of hearing the Word, receiving the sacraments, and offering praise and thanksgiving to God. This discloses a difference between the contexts of most of our creeds and confessions and our own post-Christian context. Until recently, the church simply was not aware of large numbers of "unchurched" people who might wander into worship.

C67, however, adopts a slightly different approach, emphasizing that the church's role is to continue Christ's reconciling mission to the world. This confession displays a greater awareness of and openness to the world outside the church than did the sixteenth- and seventeenth-century documents. C67 states, "Jesus Christ has given the church preaching and teaching, praise and prayer, and Baptism and the Lord's Supper as means of fulfilling its service of God among men. These gifts remain, but the church is obliged to change the forms of its service in ways appropriate to different generations and cultures" (9.48). In this summary, C67 acknowledges that worship is part of the church's service of God among all people, suggesting that it is at least partly intended for public proclamation. Furthermore, the call to adapt the "forms of service" to different generations and cultures implies that worship necessarily varies with its context. This outward-directed aspect of worship honors the "always being reformed" part of our identity, for when the church finds itself in a largely unchurched context, as do many Presbyterian congregations today, worship leaders have a responsibility to take this missional context into account.

Even the sixteenth- and seventeenth-century confessions imply that there is a dimension of worship that is for all the world, not just for those born and raised in the faith. Heidelberg and Westminster affirm that all of humanity is created to glorify God (4.006; 7.001). Could we not take this one step further and argue that the church should welcome and empower all people to fulfill their chief end? The Second Helvetic Confession states that faith comes through preaching and prayer (5.113).[10] Could we not interpret this for our time to mean that at least these elements of worship should be adapted to a congregation that includes those who do not yet believe?

Yet the confessions consistently affirm that some elements of worship are more intended to distinguish the church from the world than to speak directly to those who have not yet joined themselves to Christ. This is particularly true of baptism and the Lord's Supper. For instance, the Scots Confession states that one of God's purposes in instituting the sacraments was "to make a visible distinction between [God's] people and those who were without the Covenant" (3.21). Although the sacraments, according to confessional consensus, communicate the good news of the gospel to the world (e.g., 9.51), they are not given directly to the entire world, but to the believing community.

How Formal Should Our Worship Be?

As we become more aware of generational differences, the increasingly marginal role of the church in our culture, and the shift of American culture as a whole toward greater informality, we wonder how formal or informal our worship should be. Should we maintain a greater formality, to distinguish ourselves from the surrounding environment and suggest the mystery and transcendence of God? Or should we strive for a more casual, accessible style, to communicate directly with younger generations, or with our cultural context in general?

On the one hand, the confessions' vision of worship as authored by God alone, mediated by Christ, and empowered by the Spirit suggests the need for a certain gravity. It is hard to imagine how a congregation could enter into the fullness of trinitarian worship when the worship leaders are unfailingly flip and chatty. On the other hand, the confessions counsel simplicity and modesty in worship, suggesting that an abundance of formal gesture may detract from rather than enable authentic worship (3.20; 5.215, 5.240).

This is an appropriate place to discuss the favorite Presbyterian phrase "decently and in order." It appears twice in the confessions, once in the Scots Confession with regard to general church councils (3.20) and once in the Second Helvetic Confession with regard to ornamentation in the church (5.216). In the first instance, the point is that good order helps to instill common practice and belief among various congregations; in the second, the point is that decoration of churches should focus attention on the virtues of those gathered, not on luxury and pride. Both the Scots and the Second Helvetic Confessions employ this phrase to contend that the best way to form Christian worshipers is through simple, unpretentious attendance on the Word of God that is shaped in common with other Christian communions.

The use of "decently and in order" reminds us that nothing should distract from the Word of God and that Christians should rightly attend to the worship practices of other Christians, so that we all proclaim the gospel to the world in a consistent manner. Therefore, those who prepare and lead worship ought to ask themselves regularly: Does this worship direct people toward, or distract them from, the Word of God? What does this worship have in common with other manifestations of Christian worship? Are we as local worshiping churches offering a common gospel to the world?

Finally, the confessions express concern that worshipers understand what they are doing in worship. Worship must be comprehensible in order to facilitate full participation, because worship is intended for the "edification" of the church (see, e.g., 5.216–.217; 6.008). Those who prepare and lead Presbyterian worship today need to consider whether worshipers are able to follow what is happening in worship. Are they able to pray the words that are put in their mouths? Are they able to sing the songs? Do words and gestures engage them in full participation, or are they alienated from the worship leadership because it is either unduly casual or overloaded with arcane terminology and opaque ceremony? This is not a plea for explaining the liturgy as we go. Presbyterians do not need any more excuses for making worship into a didactic exercise. But we ought to strive for worship that engages, invites, illuminates, "edifies"—which means avoiding the extremes of overly casual or overly formal liturgical style.

What Style of Music Should We Use?

Many conversations about worship in the church revolve around tensions over the question of what kind of music to use in worship. Unfortunately, the confessions offer little help. In all ten documents, there are a total of three direct references to music. The Second Helvetic Confession cautions that "moderation is to be exercised where singing is used. . . . For all churches do not have the advantage of singing" (5.221). The Westminster Confession endorses the singing of psalms (6.116). The Confession of 1967 affirms that music can contribute to the praise and prayer of a congregation when it directs the people to God and to "the world which is the object of his love" (9.50). Taken together, these passages provide minimal guidance on the question of musical style.

But the silence of the confessions on this issue is itself instructive; it calls into question whether musical form and style are really central issues after all. Far more central, as far as the confessions are concerned, is the object of worship—is our worship directed to the triune God? Does our music, as C67 recommends, direct the people to "look beyond themselves to God" and to God's beloved world? Or does it encourage preoccupation with self, or with the community of faith, or even with ecclesiastical institutions?

How Often Should We Celebrate the Lord's Supper?

Since the middle of the twentieth century, many Protestant churches have begun observing the Lord's Supper more frequently, moving from quarterly Communion services to celebrations of the Supper on each major festival of the church year, or once a month, or even every week. The Presbyterian *Book of Common Worship* itself presents weekly celebration of the Supper as the norm. Do the confessions have any wisdom to offer Presbyterians on the frequency of Eucharistic celebration?

Again, the confessions offer no direct advice on this particular question, but it is noteworthy that from the Scots Confession forward, the two major elements of worship discussed in each confession are the Word and the sacraments.[11] Word and sacraments appear to be the basic pattern for Christian worship. This suggests that the Lord's Supper ought to be celebrated frequently enough to be understood as normative.[12] It also suggests that baptism should be practiced as a central part of our worship life and Christian identity.

The Westminster documents offer more than just this general pattern of worship as a suggestion. The Westminster Confession offers firm admonition that the sacraments are not to be neglected as God's ordinary means of grace (6.158). And both catechisms counsel "diligent use of all the outward means whereby Christ communicateth to us the benefits of redemption," naming the "outward means" as Word, sacraments, and prayer (7.085–.088; cf. 7.263–.264). Surely no Presbyterian would question that the "diligent use" of preaching and prayer translates into the inclusion of sermons and prayers in worship each week. Why then fail to include the celebration of the Lord's Supper? There is nothing in any of the confessions to suggest that it is less of an outward means of grace than prayer or the proclamation of the Word. For our confessional documents then, the Word and sacraments constitute the normal basic pattern of worship for Presbyterians. Those who wish to omit the Lord's Supper on some Sundays must find extraconfessional reasons for doing so.

Who Participates in the Lord's Supper?

If the celebration of the Supper is regarded as normative, we have to ask who is invited to participate in this meal. The basic answer of the sixteenth- and seventeenth-century confessions is that all who are members of the church, who have examined themselves and have a desire to strengthen their faith should come to the table. The sacraments are not to be neglected, but neither are they to be treated carelessly. Those who wish to come to the table, argue the Scots, Second Helvetic, and Westminster Confessions, as well as the Shorter and Longer Catechisms, ought to examine themselves with regard to their faith in Jesus Christ and love of neighbor and engage in fervent prayer as preparation for the meal.[13]

Does this mean that children should not participate in the Lord's Supper? The emphasis on self-examination in preparation for the Supper for centuries led the church to conclude that children should not come to the table until they were "of years and ability to examine themselves" (7.287). So while baptism was extended to the children of believers, the Lord's Supper was reserved for those of more mature faith. The understanding and practice of our church has shifted since the seventeenth century, however. In the twentieth century, Presbyterians and many other churches gained a new appreciation for the link between baptism and the Lord's Supper, so that now baptized children who are being nurtured in the faith (but have not yet made a mature profession of faith) are welcomed to the Supper. This helps to restore the ancient pattern of the church, which maintained a close connection between baptism and entrance to Communion. It also helps embody the joyful character of the feast, as we welcome even wiggly little ones to the Lord's Table.

But even as we celebrate the inclusion of children in the sacrament, we do well to hold on to the confessions' emphasis on the need for preparation. What the confessions teach us well is that simply receiving the elements alone, without ongoing nurture in faith, makes a mockery of the Supper. Self-examination may have been overly emphasized by an earlier generation, but what Westminster and other confessions had right was the notion that we should not approach the Lord's Supper the way we approach a McDonald's drive-through window. If this is an encounter with the living Christ, we ought to treat it with joyful reverence, and raise our children to do the same.

What about those who are not part of the church but desire to participate in the Lord's Supper? This question would baffle the writers of most of the Confessions. In the view of these documents, preaching and prayer are the ordinary means God uses to bring people to faith, and once people come to faith, baptism joins one to God and the covenant family (5.187). Once baptized, participation in the Supper nourishes one in faith. There is no approach to the table except by way of baptism. We need to appreciate the logic of this order: Baptism joins us to the body of Christ, and the Lord's Supper nourishes that body. But in our context, nonbaptized persons are often present at celebrations of the Lord's Supper. Should they be welcomed to the table? Here too, as with the question about children, we can benefit from the confessions' emphasis on preparation for coming to the table. We rightly emphasize that this is the joyful feast of the people of God, a "foretaste of the kingdom" (9.52), but this proclamation is hollow without the formation of the Christian community. Our welcome to the table, therefore, should be paired with baptism and ongoing nurture in the faith, ministries that cannot be divorced from one another. The feast becomes more holy and joyful the more we understand what we are doing: eating and drinking the body and blood of Jesus Christ and thus being formed into the body of Christ.

How Do We Speak to and about God?

In addition to issues of style, music, and the sacraments, the Presbyterian Church continues to wrestle with the use of language in worship, especially language about God. The confessions help to shape this discussion by explicitly affirming a close relationship between the Word of God and our words. The most dramatic statement of this relationship is the Second Helvetic Confession's affirmation that "the preaching of the Word of God is the Word of God" (5.004). The words we use to describe and address God are not a matter of casual choice or personal preference. What language shall we use to describe and address God? The confessions offer three guidelines:

1. *Language about God needs to reflect language about God in Scripture.* We need to attend to the ways Scripture itself has named God. A good example of this is found in A Brief Statement of Faith: "We trust in God, whom Jesus called Abba, Father" (10.3). This directly acknowledges a central way Scripture names God. The same confession also refers to "the Lord Jesus Christ," "the

Holy Spirit," "the Holy One of Israel," and "the God of Abraham and Sarah"— all names for God drawn from Scripture. In our prayers, hymns, and proclamation, our naming of God should reflect language for God in Scripture.

2. *Language about God needs to reflect the range of God's acts in salvation history.* Our words to and about God ought to grow out of our encounter with the wide sweep of divine activity in Scripture: from creation to exodus to exile to the first coming of the Christ to the expectation of Christ's return. Both the Nicene and the Apostles' Creeds include the range of salvation history in brief scope, while A Brief Statement of Faith does it in slightly more extended fashion. By examining these statements, we may be led back to the biblical narrative in a way that allows us to expand our language for God even as we respect the biblical norm.

3. *Language about God needs to attend to the local context.* C67 helpfully reminds us that "all acts of public worship should be conducive to men's hearing of the gospel in a particular time and place" (9.49). This coheres with the earlier confessions' concern that worship needs to be in a language that the gathered people understand (5.217). So with our language about God: Even holding up Scripture as a norm, our language will be sensitive to time and place in order to engage the people who are present.

Of course, even these guidelines do not provide a lexicon of appropriate terms to use when praying and preaching. In fact, from the Scots to C67, the confessions declare that the particularities of worship will and should change according to context in order to communicate the Word of God with the people of God in each time and place. But these do offer critical questions that worship leaders need to consider when crafting language for worship: Is it rooted in the biblical witness? Does it reflect the broad sweep of salvation history, as attested in both Old and New Testaments? Does it communicate with the people in this time and place? Does it edify?

Conclusion

The confessions do not offer final judgments on how we ought to worship in our time and place. What they do offer is a broad vision of what constitutes right worship: directed to the triune God, enabled by the Holy Spirit, mediated by Jesus Christ, and authored by God alone. If we keep our eye on this broad vision, it can help us situate some of our divisive arguments about worship. When we approach questions of style, we remember that style in and of itself is not the issue; the issue is how this particular word, gesture, or piece of music enables us to participate in genuine worship of the Holy One. When we approach the celebration of the Lord's Supper, we remember that this is not a meal we grab nor a door prize that we offer, but the Table of the Lord, which we receive with holy joy. When we approach issues of God-language, we remember that the words we use for God are themselves given by God, the author, mediator, and power behind our speech.

From the Council of Nicea to the Westminster Assembly to Dr. Teeth and the Electric Mayhem, people have praised God in a variety of ways. How shall *we* worship God? We should prepare and lead worship in a way that opens us up to divine encounter. We should attend with utter seriousness to the liturgical details, not for their own sake, but so that the *how* of worship may become transparent and we may encounter the *Who* at the heart of it all.

NOTES

1. Contemporary readers may be perplexed by this stern admonition in the Second Helvetic Confession: "We teach that baptism should not be administered in the Church by women or midwives" (5.191, cf. 3.22). This represents a reaction to the practice that had grown up in the medieval church of allowing anyone (even women!) to baptize infants in emergency situations. Infants who might die before reaching a priest could be baptized by anyone in order to cleanse the newborn of the stain of original sin. Because of high infant mortality and fear of dying without the benefit of baptism, it became more and more common for women present at childbirth to baptize newborn infants. The Reformers of the sixteenth century forbade that practice, arguing that it went against biblical teaching for women to have ecclesiastical duties (5.191), and also that although it was wrong to neglect the sacrament, "yet grace and salvation are not so inseparably annexed unto it as that no person can be regenerated or saved without it" (6.158).
2. For a related discussion of John Calvin's trinitarian understanding of divine action as applied to worship, see John D. Witvliet, "Images and Themes in John Calvin's Theology of Liturgy," in *Worship Seeking Understanding: Windows into Christian Practice* (Grand Rapids: Baker Academic, 2003), 127–48.
3. The Westminster Directory, however, did reject written prayers on the grounds that using written texts interfered with the work of the Spirit. This marks the beginning of the notion that the work of the Spirit is incompatible with advance preparation (Tom Trinidad, private communication, June 2004).
4. In the sixteenth century, the Protestant Reformers had to develop means of identifying the true church. Luther was the first to propose that the church is found where the Word is rightly preached and the sacraments administered according to Christ's institution. Calvin adapted this phrase to read that the church is found "wherever we see the Word of God purely preached *and heard*, and the sacraments administered according to Christ's institution" (*Institutes* 4.1.9 [LCC 2.1023], emphasis added). Since Calvin, these *notae ecclesiae*, or marks of the church, have been important to Reformed ecclesiology, and Word and sacrament have constituted the two major elements of worship addressed by the confessions. See 3.18; 4.065; 5.134–.135; and other references at note 5.
5. Cf. 6.186; 7.265.
6. Cf. 6.054, 6.151, 6.186; 7.091, 7.271.
7. Cf. 6.006–.008; 7.051, 7.219.

8. Cf. 4.094; 7.213–.216.
9. For discussions of idolatry in the confessions, see 3.05; 4.094–.095; 5.015ff.; 7.046–.047 and 7.213–.216.
10. Cf. 6.058, 6.190; and 9.49.
11. See, e.g., 3.18; 4.065; 5.134–.135; 6.116; 7.264; 8.17; 9.48; 10.4.
12. There is a great deal of scholarship on Word and Table as the normative pattern of Christian worship from the early church, a pattern that has been recovered in many quarters in the twentieth century. One accessible volume written especially for a Presbyterian audience is Ronald P. Byars, *Christian Worship: Glorifying and Enjoying God*, Foundations of Christian Faith (Louisville, KY: Geneva Press/Office of Theology and Worship, 2000).
13. See 3.23; 5.207; and 7.281ff.

13

How Shall We Live?

Charles A. Wiley

So what?

The question comes easily from adolescents, skeptics, and realists of all ages. *So what? What difference does it make?* Even when the question is asked dismissively or cynically, it may be difficult to answer. It may be particularly hard for Christians to answer, for the real effect of our beliefs may not be apparent to others—or to ourselves. Discussion of core beliefs, fine points of doctrine, or ecclesiastical politics may seem self-evidently important until the troubling question comes up. Does any of this make a difference?

You believe that Jesus is the savior of the world. *What difference does this make in the world?*

You believe that Jesus Christ is both human and divine. *What difference does this make to the living of human life?*

You believe that the Godhead is an eternal communion of three consubstantial persons? *So what?*

The question is not new. "You believe that God is one," wrote the apostle James. "Even the demons believe—and shudder" (Jas. 2:19). Unless belief that God is one makes a difference in the life of the believer, *so what?* The Presbyterian Church has recognized the necessity of linking right belief and right consequences to belief. At the first General Assembly in 1788, the new national church declared, "That truth is in order to goodness; and that the great touchstone of truth, its tendency to promote holiness, according to our Savior's rule, 'By their fruits ye shall know them.'"[1] Unless truth is accompanied by goodness, *so what?*

Yet when we look honestly at the life of the church, it appears that what Christians believe does not always make a difference in how they live. Vicious denominational fights, scandals involving ministers, petty quarrels in congregations, and churchly indifference to suffering in the world seem all too characteristic. Life in the church is a confounding affair, filled with both glorious experiences and the same pettiness that we find everywhere else in the world. "We believe in one holy catholic and apostolic Church." *So what? What difference does it make?*

When Christians are pressed on the question, they may take some comfort from the often quoted words of G. K. Chesterton: "The Christian ideal has not been tried and found wanting; it has been found difficult and left untried."[2] We hear Chesterton and then breathe a sigh of relief. Perhaps the problem is not that Christian faith makes no difference, but only that Christians have failed to live out the difference that Christian faith makes. We can say that the affirmations and convictions of the faith are true, then, even though Christians do not live the new life that Christian faith proclaims. But it is cold comfort to defend the credibility of the faith by saying that Christianity has been left "untried" for two thousand years. Chesterton's words should neither give false comfort nor discourage, however. Instead, they can challenge us to take the implications of the Christian faith seriously—to see what difference faith does make when it is "tried."

HOW DO WE LIVE AS CHRISTIANS?

Perhaps we lack clarity about the Christian life because there have been so many versions of it. It seems as though there are more opinions about how Christians should live than there are Christians: Christians are countercultural, working nonviolently for peace in the world. Christians transform culture, taking responsibility for government and society. Christians try to live out the Sermon on the Mount. Christians follow the lead of the Holy Spirit. Christians are solid citizens. Christians live lives of personal holiness. Christians are free from simplistic codes of personal living that require abstinence from alcohol and swearing. Christians are to avoid the appearance of sin and thus scrupulously avoid anything considered unsavory by the wider culture. Christian living leads naturally to success in life. And, of course, the ever popular, Christians do what Jesus would do.

No wonder we're confused. What *would* Jesus do? And if we knew what Jesus would do, is that what we should do? How should what we believe shape our lives? There is no need for us to engage these difficult questions on our own. The church's *Book of Confessions* makes it possible to join in a conversation about the shape of the Christian life with those who have lived it before us. Our forebears give us the wisdom of years that we should not ignore.

This particular conversation with the confessions will engage two primary documents in *The Book of Confessions*. One of them has the least to say about the Christian life; one has the most to say. One does not mention Christian living at all; the other one goes on for pages and pages about how we are to live. One emerged over a number of centuries as the Christian faith developed; one was written relatively quickly as the church tried to understand its new place in the world. Our primary conversation partners will be the Apostles' Creed and the Westminster Larger Catechism.

APOSTLES' CREED

Oddly enough, we turn first to a creed that includes no direct statement about living the Christian life. Instead of specifying the shape of the Christian life, this baptismal creed sets the context for it. Baptism's words ("I baptize you in the name of the Father, and of the Son, and of the Holy Spirit") and its actions (water bath, touch, and sign) frame the Christian life. In the waters of baptism, we are claimed by God, in Christ, through the power of the Holy Spirit. We die to ourselves and are raised with Christ. We confess our faith with the words of the whole church through time and space in the words of the Apostles' Creed. As our identity is formed within this new reality, we make and receive promises that shape our life.

Too often in the American context, a discussion of baptism quickly devolves into a discussion of the mode of baptism and the age at which it is received: immersion versus sprinkling, infants versus adults. However, in whatever way we are baptized—as a child of believers or as a believer, by immersion or by sprinkling—we are baptized because God loves and calls us before we call upon God or respond to God in love.

The sacrament's powerful reality can be obscured when the baptism of children takes on an overly sweet character. Unfortunately, many Presbyterian churches focus baptismal attention on the precious child, or on the endearing quality of the welcoming congregation. It is almost impossible to understand baptism as dying and rising with Christ when the central image is the adorable nature of the young one. Everything is so cute and cuddly that nothing of eternal significance would be going on. Sacramental reality can also be obscured in the baptism of a believer behind an overemphasis on the faith of the person being baptized. It can appear as though baptism is only a response to the believer's faith—after all, a believer is baptized only because she requests it. The creed's "I believe" can appear to be the faith of the isolated individual.

The French Reformed Church developed a liturgical element for the baptism of children that emphasizes Christ's initiative, expressing this deep conviction liturgically in words spoken by the pastor to the newly baptized infant. (I wonder if we speak similar words to adults who are baptized as well.)

> Little one, for you Jesus Christ came into the world:
> for you he lived and showed God's love;
> for you he suffered the darkness of Calvary
> and cried at the last, "It is accomplished";
> for you he triumphed over death and rose in newness of life;
> for you he ascended to reign at God's right hand.
> All this he did for you,
> though you do not know it yet.
> And so the word of Scripture is fulfilled:
> "We love because God loved us first."[3]

This marvelous statement locates the life of a Christian within the narrative of salvation. For each one of us Jesus came into the world to show us God's love. For each of us he suffered on the cross and accomplished our salvation. For each of us he triumphed over death, rose and ascended. Naturally, infants (and many adults) do not know yet these great truths, yet we can only love God because God loved us first. Even those of us who respond in faith as mature people, though we grasp in some measure the wonderful story of salvation, only see through a glass darkly. None of us knows it fully. All of us love because God loved us first.

I AND *WE*

We respond with "I believe." Almost all analyses of the current state of Christianity in the West have an obligatory segment decrying the toxic effects of individualism. This consistent refrain is sounded for good reason. We tend more and more toward atomistic individualism, particularly in the religious realm. Do-it-yourself faith is the norm for many Americans. This ancient creed likewise begins with the individual: It is *I* who believe. Christian faith is a personal faith. But *personal* does not mean *private*. Personal faith is not individual faith, much less individualistic faith. "I believe" is communal in two very important ways. First, it is declared in public worship, in the community of faith. Far from being the act of an isolated individual, it is precisely the act of a person within a larger community. I confess *my* belief even as I am incorporated into a larger body where all confess a shared belief. Within this community, a baptized believer or the believing parents of an infant make promises, but the community makes promises to the baptized as well. Confession of faith within the baptismal community is a decidedly corporate activity.

The community of faith extends beyond the walls of the particular congregation, for the faith confessed is the faith of the church everywhere and in all times.[4] We use not our own idiosyncratic formulations of the faith, but a shared creed that links us to the faith of Christians throughout the ages. As we confess the Apostles' Creed, we confess the same faith that millions have before us (and millions with us, and millions after us). Some of the creed's formulations may sound odd to our modern ears ("he shall come to judge the quick and the dead"), but even unfamiliar words may highlight the reality that although it is *my* faith that *I* confess, it is a faith that encompasses the "communion of saints" throughout time and space.

LIVING IN LIGHT OF JUDGMENT

We live our lives as Christians, affirming the story of salvation in the life, death, and resurrection of Jesus Christ. We claim this faith as our own, but in the context of the Christian community, both local and universal. The significance of the way we live our lives is thunderously announced when we confess that Christ "shall come to judge the quick and the dead."

Judgment is not on the top-ten list of things contemporary Christians want to hear about. Judgment elicits the image of a stern-looking preacher clad in black and proclaiming hellfire and brimstone, frightening us to heaven by fear of hell. Most of us would rather dispense with talk of judgment. Yet in our most basic statement of faith, we affirm that we live in expectation of judgment—a judgment that comes from the Christ who was born of the Virgin Mary, suffered under Pontius Pilate, was crucified, dead, and buried. We live in expectation of judgment by the same Christ who descended to the dead, was raised again, and ascended into heaven. The Christian life is located within these acts of God revealed to us in the life, death, resurrection, and ascension of Christ that simultaneously reveal to us the shape of the present and the horizon of the future. This same Christ to whom we have pledged our lives will come to judge all human beings. Because it is *this* Jesus who will judge us, the Savior who called us and claims us in the waters of baptism, we need not fear. Nonetheless, this horizon of judgment reminds us that the shape of life matters. How we live is not a matter of indifference to our Lord. God's judgment is real, but even so our acknowledgment that Christ will come to judge the living and the dead is embraced by faith in the forgiveness of sins and the resurrection of the body.

PROMISES TO KEEP

Because God has claimed us in Jesus Christ in the power of the Holy Spirit, and because we give our very selves to God in the light of Jesus' coming again, we make specific promises in baptism. We commit ourselves wholly to faith in Jesus Christ. This is no mere moral imperative, for we are enlivened by the Spirit to live faithful lives. In gratitude for all God has done for us, in response to the hope we have been given, we prepare to confess the creed as we renounce the old life and promise to be faithful to Christ:

> In embracing that covenant, we choose whom we will serve,
> by turning from evil
> and turning to Jesus Christ.
> Do you renounce all evil,
> and powers in the world
> which defy God's righteousness and love?
>
> **I renounce them.**
>
> Do you renounce the ways of sin
> that separate you from the love of God?
>
> **I renounce them.**
>
> Do you turn to Jesus Christ
> and accept him as your Lord and Savior?
>
> **I do.**
>
> Will you be Christ's faithful disciple,
> obeying his Word and showing his love,
> to your life's end?
>
> **I will, with God's help.**
>
> Will you be a faithful member of this congregation,
> share in its worship and ministry
> through your prayers and gifts,
> your study and service,
> and so fulfill your calling to be a disciple of Jesus Christ?
>
> **I will, with God's help.**[5]

This is a simple and straightforward account of the Christian life, at least while the water is still dripping from the new believer's head. The Apostles' Creed, the New Testament, and the character of Jesus' call to the new kingdom all exhibit the "already but not yet" character of the gospel life. But what is *already* and what is *not yet*? What does this mean in our ordinary lives? What does this vision of the Christian life look like? The framers of the Larger Catechism deeply desired that this vision of the Christian life have a specific shape in the lives of ordinary believers. It is to the particular shape of Christian living that we now turn.

THE WESTMINSTER LARGER CATECHISM

If the Apostles' Creed is a little thin on guidance for living, the Westminster Larger Catechism may be all too specific for our modern tastes. The confessions and catechism that arose during the Reformation and its aftermath are quite different from the early creeds. Instead of stating simply the basics of the faith, these later statements are confessional and catechetical testimonies that go into elaborate detail about issues that were not even covered in the early creeds. What accounts for the Reformation era's extensive, specific consideration of the Christian life?

Two Kinds of Christians

There has been tension throughout the church's life between the affirmation that all Christians are to live to the glory of God and the notion that some Christians are called to live distinctive lives that are especially holy. Think about how ministers are sometimes described as "holy" people. There is a widespread assumption that holy living is only possible for people who live restricted lives, free from family responsibilities and worldly cares.

In the early church there was a widespread conviction that Christians should not marry in anticipation of the coming of Christ.[6] This instinct was later transformed into the presumption of celibacy for those answering a "higher calling." A legacy of Augustine that came to mark the medieval church was the notion that there were essentially two forms of the Christian life: a higher calling and a lesser calling. The higher calling was the monastic life, the lower calling was what we might call the ordinary life. Why choose the monastic life? In order to live a disciplined existence fully committed to the spiritual life that brings one closer to God. Why shouldn't everyone choose the monastic life? Because one cannot live the spiritual life if one must engage in base behaviors such as procreation, the rearing of children, secular vocations, and the like. Such activities might be a tragic necessity in this world but are not to be preferred over the more spiritually pure life of monastic brotherhood or sisterhood. Ordinary life was to be marked by discipline, of course, but not the same level or breadth of discipline that characterized monastic life. Monks or other members of monastic orders were freed from worldly cares in order to devote themselves fully to the spiritual life. Without the encumbrances of secular life, monastics could truly live in the spiritual life, taking on disciplines unsuitable, even impossible, within ordinary life. The monastic ideal was held up before all persons as a sign of the life they should lead but could not because they lived within secular vocations.

Worldly Monastics

Perhaps the most revolutionary aspect of the Reformation era confessions and the Westminster Catechisms is the affirmation that *common* life is the arena for holiness. The affirmation that holiness is not the sole province of monks and ministers signified a turning point in church history. The Larger Catechism rejects the idea that there are essentially two kinds of Christians, those given a higher calling and those given a lesser calling.

John Calvin rejected monasticism, but not because the calling of the monk was too strict. Calvin argued that monasticism was too limited. In Calvin's view, Augustine "cheated" by artificially dividing spiritual and secular life. The division limited the vocations of both the monk and the ordinary person, for neither was held to the wholly disciplined life called for by the Bible. Thus, the church leaders in Geneva instituted practices that emphasized that all of life was to be lived in creedal faith. The establishment of the consistory, its attendant discipline of the sacramental life, and the catechesis of all Christians, especially children, indicate a monastic-like call to *all* in the church. However, this monastic call was to be lived out in the ordinary life: in family, vocation, business, and state. There is a sense in which Calvin does not call for the end of monastic life, but for its extension to all of life. By its very nature, such an extension changes the character of what one would think of as monastic life: It is not an escape from ordinary life, but rather an embrace of all ordinary life within the disciplined life of Christian faith.[7]

Such reasoning helps us understand why the descriptions of the Christian life were so detailed in the Reformation era. They were, in a sense, manuals of monastic discipline for ordinary life. If one will allow such a disciplined life within the secular life, monastic life is recast. The strict keeping of the hours, celibacy, and other monastic disciplines are transmuted. However, descriptions of the secular life must be recast because it is no longer a strictly secular life. It is now understood as the life in which holiness can be lived out in its fullness, even while trading, marrying, and even fighting for the state. In the terms of Edmund Morgan's well-known book on the Puritans, this was a vision of "visible saints."[8] Sainthood was to be lived out in everyday life, not in the cloister.

LAW AS A GIFT FOR LIVING

How then do Christians live holy lives in secular vocations? By following the law of God. This may appear to be a limiting answer, for contemporary Christians often think of the law as restrictive. However, Calvin and the subsequent Reformed tradition has understood that the most important use of the law is not as a *mirror* that shows us our sin (though it does that), or as a *fence* to protect us from the sinful behavior of others (though it does this as well), but as a *guide* to teach forgiven sinners how to live.[9] As people who are forgiven by Christ's merits, not our own, we can receive God's law as a gift to show us how to live, not as a straightjacket to confine our living. The Westminster Confession tells us that the law is of "great use" to Christians, "informing them of the will of God and their duty, [and] it directs and binds them to walk accordingly" (6.106). Understood this way, the law is neither condemning nor a burden, but is, in the words of the psalmist, more to be desired "than gold, even much fine gold; sweeter also than honey, and drippings of the honeycomb" (Ps. 19:10). The Spirit of Christ enables us to "sweetly comply" with the law "freely and cheerfully" (6.107).

The leaders of the emerging Reformed tradition believed that this law of God is most clearly set forth in the Ten Commandments. Contemporary Christians, on the other hand, may think that the Ten Commandments as a helpful guide to living the Christian life rings a bit hollow in a complicated era such as ours. While there are still debates in the United States over displaying the Ten Commandments in public spaces, their guidance seems limited at best. Of course we should honor God and not kill other people or steal their goods or spouses. These are solid guidelines, to be sure, but not really the helpful and specific guidance we are looking for in the living of our lives.

But the authors of the Larger Catechism see the commandments with different eyes. The genius of Westminster's exposition of the commandments is that they always begin by what each commandment calls us *to do*, only then discussing what it *prohibits* (see 7.209). The law is a gift to guide us, not a stricture to confine us.

A good example is the first commandment: "You shall have no other gods before me." We normally read this as a straightforward prohibition against worshiping other gods. But the catechism teaches us that much more is called for:

> The duties required in the First Commandment are: the knowing and acknowledging of God to be the only true God, and our God; and to worship and glorify him accordingly; by thinking, meditating, remembering, highly esteeming, honoring, adoring, choosing, loving, desiring, fearing of him; believing him; trusting, hoping, delighting, rejoicing in him; being zealous for him; calling upon him, giving all praise and thanks, and yielding all obedience and submission to him with the whole man; being careful in all things to please him, and sorrowful when in anything he is offended; and walking humbly with him. (7.214)

Although the language is somewhat archaic, the call is clear: Our lives are to be lived in the worship of God as we give our whole lives in faithful response to the wondrous love of God.

Similarly, the second commandment's prohibition of graven images is not limited to the production of wooden or metal representations of God. Positively, the commandment calls us to the worship of God, "particularly prayer and thanksgiving in the name of Christ; the reading, preaching, and hearing of the Word; the administration and receiving of the sacraments . . ." (7.218).

The Reformed tradition has often focused on Old Testament law instead of New Testament ethical codes such as the Sermon on the Mount. Mennonites, for example, have understood Jesus' words in the Gospels as a radical deepening of the older tradition. Jesus took the sixth commandment, "You shall not kill," and extended it to "You have heard that it was said to those of ancient times, 'You shall not murder'; and 'whoever murders shall be liable to judgment.' But I say to you that if you are angry with a brother or sister, you will be liable to judgment" (Matt. 5:21–22). Thus, Mennonites and others have criticized Reformed emphasis on Old Testament law as an avoidance of the more radical dimensions of Christ's call. (Most of us are able to go through life without committing murder, but few manage to avoid anger!) The criticism may be justified at certain points, but it does not apply to this magnificent Reformed catechism.

The Larger Catechism's exposition of the sixth commandment sounds like an expansion of the Sermon on the Mount, calling on us to shape our lives in a far more fulsome way. Note how the duties of the commandments are lined out: "The duties required in the Sixth Commandment are: all careful studies and lawful endeavors, to preserve the life of ourselves and others, by resisting all thoughts and purposes, subduing all passions, and avoiding all occasions, temptations, and practices, which tend to the unjust taking away the life of any." We are even to be careful in our eating and drinking lest we put ourselves in places where the taking of life is more likely: "a sober use of meat, drink, physic, sleep, labor, and recreation." When these are practiced, we treat others not simply by avoiding the negative ("You shall not kill"), but by "forbearance, readiness to be reconciled, patient bearing and forgiving of injuries, and requiting good for evil; comforting and succoring the distressed, and protecting and defending the innocent" (7.245).

Likewise, the command not to steal goes far beyond the duty not to take that which is not lawfully ours. We are enjoined to look out for the good of others. For those looking for the *So what?* of Christian living, the catechism provides a stunning answer. "What are the duties required in the Eighth Commandment?" In the "common" world of contracts and commerce, we are to render "truth, faithfulness, and justice." We are to give to everyone their due. And beyond that, we are to be generous to those in need, "giving and lending freely, according to our abilities, and the necessities of others." There are more subtle ways in which we take what is due others, so we are to avoid "unnecessary lawsuits." And it is our calling to actually "further the wealth and outward estate of others" (7.251).

Wow! What would our lives look like if we lived out "You shall not steal" in the manner of the catechism? Unexpectedly, the Larger Catechism delivers a radical answer to the weary question, *So what?*

LIVING THE CHRISTIAN LIFE

This vision of the Christian life founded in God's claim in baptism and described in detail in the Larger Catechism receives beautiful and poetic interpretation under the ugliest of circumstances in the Theological Declaration of Barmen. In the 1930s, National Socialism began to dictate all forms of life in Germany, including the church. As different sectors of German society became dominated by the Nazis, only one group organized to resist. In a heroic act, the Confessing Church stood against Nazi co-option of the church:

> "I am the way, and the truth, and the life: no one comes to the Father, but by me." (John 14:6.) "Truly, truly, I say to you, he who does not enter the sheepfold by the door but climbs in by another way, that man is a thief and a robber. . . . I am the door; if anyone enters by me, he will be saved." (John 10:1, 9.)
>
> Jesus Christ, as he is attested for us in Holy Scripture, is the one Word of God which we have to hear and which we have to trust and obey in life and in death.
>
> We reject the false doctrine, as though the church could and would have to acknowledge as a source of its proclamation, apart from and besides this one Word of God, still other events and powers, figures and truths, as God's revelation. (8.10–.12)

Protestants have been suspicious of naming saints. We are impoverished, however, when we do not have the lives of saints to guide us: "Remember your leaders, those who spoke the word of God to you; consider the outcome of their way of life, and imitate their faith" (Heb. 13:7). The relatively small group of people in the Confessing Church provide an example for us to imitate in living out this Christian life. Martin Luther King, Jr., said that until we are ready to die, we are not worthy of living. By proclaiming faithfulness to the gospel in the light of a totalitarian regime that threatened to turn the church from its Savior, the signers of Barmen proved worthy of living.

Yet the story of the Barmen Declaration is also a cautionary tale, for the final text was only able to pass when specific references to the persecution of Jews were omitted. Even our best attempts at living the Christian life are marred by the sin that so easily besets us. But the fact that we sin does not cancel out our authentic attempts at faithfulness.

IF IT IS TO BE . . .

A few years ago, supporters of Robert Schuller's television ministry were rewarded with coffee mugs sporting the saying, "If it is to be, it is up to me." Perhaps unwittingly, Schuller reinforced the notion that the Christian life is primarily an exercise of effort. But the Scots Confession first mentions the Christian life—the most practical of doctrines—in its article on the ascension. If there is any doctrine not associated with human effort, it is the ascension! The ascension extends and confirms the work of Christ in incarnation, death, and resurrection. God's work in Christ did not end with the resurrection, but God raised up this same Christ to reign in glory. For the authors of the Scots Confession, it is the power of Christ that underlies our lives as Christians.

A few years ago a person mentioned to me that most sermons could be summarized as variations on "more": Do more, pray more, give more. It was a stinging indictment of my own preaching. Soon after, I was assigned the text of Luke 24:13–35, Jesus and the disciples on the road to Emmaus. In this story, Jesus appears to disciples on the day of resurrection. But they do not recognize him, even after he explains the Scriptures to them. But at the table that evening, Jesus "took bread, blessed and broke it, and gave it to them. Then their eyes were opened, and they recognized him" (Luke 24:30–31).

As I worked with this text to prepare my sermon, I tried to think of how it applies to our lives. The disciples' eyes had been closed, they could not recognize Jesus, and then their eyes were opened and they saw him. So the goal is to have our eyes open, and of course, the question is, "How can we open our eyes?" Then it hit me. In the Gospel narrative, the disciples do *nothing*. They do not open their eyes—their eyes *are opened*. This is a story of grace, not of effort. Jesus did not tell them to do more or to pray more or to open their eyes wider. He took bread, blessed it, broke it, and gave it to them. Then their eyes were opened, and they knew who he was.

The foundation of the Christian life is what Christ does for us, not what we do for Christ. This does not mean that our response is only passive, but that our active response is grounded in God's profound work in Christ by the power of the Holy Spirit. It is not "up to me," but neither is it "up to God" if that means I do nothing. While the words will not fit on a mug, our faith tells us, "If it is to be, it is because we have been forgiven, made whole, called, filled, strengthened, and directed in our response to God in Christ."

LIVING TODAY

So what?

By framing a discussion of the Christian life around this question, I have made an implicit promise to be practical. However, while we have looked at the way the Apostles' Creed frames our baptism and how the discussion of the Westminster Larger Catechism gives specific shape to our lives, I have not worked through some of the crucial, practical questions of our day. How do we balance work, family, and church? How do we answer the difficult questions raised by the promise and misuse of biotechnology? How do we manage the other ways that technology is becoming an increasing factor in our lives? How are we to be engaged in the political life of our country? How do we work for peace in a world of violence?

Perhaps there's not much *so* in the *what*.

I have passed over these issues in part because they are exceedingly complex and there is not enough space in this brief chapter even to begin addressing them. There is also a more substantial reason. A danger in the Reformed tradition generally, and the Larger Catechism in particular, is the latent implication that the Christian life is primarily a process of thinking, of reflecting on the issues and then relating our conclusions to our lives. Thinking is important. (If not, you have wasted some time working your way through this book!) But thinking itself is insufficient, and thinking by ourselves is inadequate; we need a community of lived faith and faithfulness.

The Christian life is a way of life, not just an intellectual pursuit for disembodied minds. We are whole people baptized into a community. Faithful living demands a community of people that form us within a culture of faithfulness, shaping habits that can sustain us over time. Our lives cannot be made up of a series of discrete decisions, each of which demands analysis, reflection, and decision. Christian habits of life are essential to how we shall live as Christ's people. My wife and I have taught our children to develop the habit of saying "Thank you" when someone does something for them. That the words now come reflexively does not cheapen them; it means that gratitude has been woven into their lives.

In the past, Christians have often relied on the generically Christian character of American culture to sustain the habits of a Christian, or at least a religious, life. American values and Christian values were often thought to be compatible, if not synonymous. We now live in a different social situation. American culture is changing at an increasingly rapid pace, becoming more religiously pluralistic. This cultural shift is not necessarily bad news for Christians, for the easy alliance between American and Christian culture has had some corrosive effects on the church. The new situation of religious pluralism puts in bold relief the new situation of the church within the culture. We need the sustaining nourishment of a community that forms us and nurtures us in faithful living within a perplexing culture. In other words, we need friends.

But not just any friends will do. We need friends who have also been bathed in the waters of baptism and formed in a baptismal community, friends with whom we can live out our baptismal vocation. We need friends who embody the serious reflection of a Christian life that is lived in the manner of the Larger Catechism. We receive help from friends, and give help to friends, within a community that practices discernment and makes faithful judgments. Instead of simply "obeying" the Larger Catechism, we work our way through it, together. It is in the context of a community of discipleship that we live the Christian life.

This provides us with a new opportunity for faithfulness. As communities of Christians, shaped and sustained by Word and sacrament, who live lives of shared fidelity to the gospel, one thing will be guaranteed: We will look odder and odder to the wider culture. Discipleship is a hard calling, and its cost is high. But as Chesterton noted a century ago, the only movements that have a chance at being truly faithful are those that seem impossible to achieve.

The Apostles' Creed and the Larger Catechism do not represent a minimal and maximal account of the Christian life. The Apostles' Creed provides a comprehensive call to a faithful life, but without specific shape to that life. The Larger Catechism gives specific shape to that life in the context of seventeenth-century England. What may be most impressive is the breadth of the call from both documents. We are to give our *whole* lives. *Nothing* is exempt. And if nothing is exempt, then there is indeed a compelling Christian answer to the key question, *So what?*

NOTES

1. *The Constitution of the Presbyterian Church (U.S.A.)*, Part II, *Book of Order* (Louisville, KY: Office of the General Assembly, 2004), G-1.0304.
2. G. K. Chesterton, *What's Wrong with the World* (Amazon Press, 2000), 28, Adobe e-book.
3. From the baptism liturgy of the French Reformed Church, as adapted in the Church of Scotland's *Book of Common Order* (Edinburgh: Panel on Worship/ Saint Andrew Press, 1996), 83–84.
4. In the case of the Apostles' Creed this is not entirely true. The Apostles' Creed is not used in the Orthodox churches (who confess the Nicene Creed at baptisms) or in the noncreedal churches such as Baptists, Churches of Christ, and Pentecostals.
5. "The Sacrament of Baptism," *Book of Common Worship* (Louisville, KY: Westminster/John Knox Press, 1993), 407–8.

6. "To the unmarried and the widows I say that it is well for them to remain unmarried as I am. But if they are not practicing self-control, they should marry. For it is better to marry than to be aflame with passion" (1 Cor. 7:8–9).

7. There has been a lot of work done in the past few years to correct mischaracterizations of monasticism. My point here is not so much to be critical of monasticism as to note that the kind of discipline that was most characteristic of monasticism Calvin applied to all Christians, including those who participated in marriage, governance, commerce, and the emerging business sector.

8. Edmund Sears Morgan, *Visible Saints: The History of a Puritan Idea* (New York: New York University Press, 1963).

9. John Calvin, *Institutes of the Christian Religion*, ed. John T. McNeill, trans. Ford Lewis Battles (Philadelphia: Westminster Press, 1960). See 2.7.6–13 (LCC 1:354–62) for Calvin's description of the law as a mirror, a fence, and a guide.

14

Essential Tenets?

Joseph D. Small

Presbyterian churches are characterized by a distinctive understanding of ministry. Basic to this understanding is the conviction that all Christians are called to ministry in their baptism. Baptismal vocation is more than vague hope showered on a squirming infant; it is a divine calling to new life in communion with God and neighbor. The Presbyterian Church (U.S.A.)'s Directory for Worship affirms that "Baptism is God's gift of grace and also God's summons to respond to that grace. Baptism calls to repentance, to faithfulness, and to discipleship. Baptism gives the church its identity and commissions the church for ministry to the world."[1] There is a sense, then, in which baptized persons are not only *called* but also *ordained* to ministry. Baptism is the inauguration of a way of being in the world that is to be shaped by faithfulness to the One who came not to be served, but to serve.

The ministry of the whole people of God is foundational, for the triune God graces each member from a rich variety of gifts, services, and activities, all of which work together for the common good. *All* the saints are equipped for the work of ministry, and *all* are called to build up the body of Christ. The lists of gifts, ministries, and actions found in 1 Corinthians 12, Romans 12, and Ephesians 4 are not intended as an exhaustive catalog, much less as a hierarchy of charismata. Rather, the biblical lists are simply distinct expressions of God's lavish blessings bestowed on the whole community of faith: "To each is given the manifestation of the Spirit for the common good" (1 Cor. 12:7).

Within the foundational ministry of the whole people of God, some members are called to particular forms of service that are considered vital—indispensable to the faith and faithfulness of the church. The precise shape of these services is understood differently by various churches, but most are variations on a threefold pattern. Presbyterians identify three "ordered ministries" that are needed in each congregation: minister of the Word and sacrament, elder, and deacon. This is not to say that other formal ministries such as educator, musician, and counselor are unimportant or second-rate. But while congregations can live faithfully without trained educators, musicians, and counselors, they must incorporate ministries of proclamation and sacramental life, discernment and oversight, and righteous service to those in need. Ordinarily, these ministries are performed by persons called, trained, ordained, and installed to ecclesial office. Because these ordered ministries are essential in every congregation, the whole church has a stake in their right ordering. Thus, certain churchwide requirements are set forth for ordination, including levels of understanding and obedience that are not required for church membership.

When persons become members of a Presbyterian congregation, they are asked to profess their faith in Jesus Christ as Lord and Savior and to express their intention to live in faithful discipleship. When persons are ordained as ministers, elders, and deacons, however, more is required. The *Book of Order* states, "Their manner of life should be a demonstration of the Christian gospel in the church and in the world," and they are to "lead a life in obedience to Scripture and in conformity to the historic confessional standards of the church."[2] Furthermore, they are required to make ten vows that express a high level of theological and ecclesial commitment. With the exception of the final vow concerning the different ministries of the three offices, the ordination vows are identical for ministers, elders, and deacons. The forms of the three ministries differ, but requirements for faith and faithfulness are the same. Two of the ordination vows make explicit reference to the church's confessions:

- Do you sincerely receive and adopt the essential tenets of the Reformed faith as expressed in the confessions of our church as authentic and reliable expositions of what Scripture leads us to believe and do, and will you be instructed and led by them as you lead the people of God?
- Will you fulfill your office in obedience to Jesus Christ under the authority of Scripture, and be continually guided by our confessions?

The second of these two vows seems fairly straightforward. In their ordered ministries, persons are called to be obedient to Jesus Christ, to place themselves under the authority of Scripture, and to be guided by the confessions. It is important to note that the three elements of the vow are not separate, but fundamentally interrelated. Obedience to Christ is primary, but since we do not have direct, unmediated access to Christ's will, the shape of obedience to Christ is most reliably known in and through Scripture. In turn, the confessions are dependable guides to the understanding of Scripture. Thus, obedience to Christ is linked to Scripture and confessions (tradition); apart from the regulative function of Scripture and confessions, it would be far too easy to imagine that our own inclinations are Christ's will.

If the second vow seems clear, the first seems almost incomprehensible. Complex syntax and adverbial/adjectival qualifiers combine to render the vow impenetrable, so that it is routinely ignored or evaded. Why the qualifier "sincerely"? Is there an assumption that some ordinands will receive and adopt the tenets deviously? Why pile "receive" on top of "adopt"? Surely the latter encompasses the former. Similarly, "authentic and reliable" appears to be an unnecessary doublet. Is there a danger that confessions might be received as authentic but unreliable, or reliable but inauthentic? Perhaps most tellingly, what are the "essential tenets" of the Reformed faith that ministers, elders, and deacons are supposed to "sincerely receive and adopt" as "authentic and reliable" expositions of Scripture?

The vow has an air of defensiveness about it, as if the authority of the confessions must be protected against persons who wish to evade their influence. Perhaps the almost compulsive need to ensure affirmation grows from an ambiguity at the heart of the vow. We are to affirm the "essential tenets" of the Reformed faith, and yet there seems to be no shared understanding of what those essential tenets are. How are we to receive and adopt an unknown, and how can the unknown be authentic and reliable expositions of Scripture? Little wonder that many in the church ask for a list of these essential tenets.

AS IT WAS IN THE BEGINNING

From the beginning, American Presbyterianism has embodied two tendencies, two poles between which the theological history of the church has moved. On the one hand, some Presbyterians have stressed the more "objective" aspects of Christian faith such as theological precision, the distinct character of the ministry, and ordered church government. Other Presbyterians have placed less emphasis on elaborated, fixed theology and ordered ministry, valuing instead spontaneity, vital experience, and institutional adaptability. It would be misleading to label these tendencies "conservative" and "liberal," for both tendencies are found among conservatives and liberals alike, among both progressives and evangelicals.

It has been the good fortune of American Presbyterianism to embrace both tendencies, holding them in dialectical tension. The church is most faithful to the gospel when clarity of belief is accompanied by deep personal experience, when flexibility is joined to orderly process, when evangelical fervor and regulated justice come together.

But there have been times when the dialectic has been pressed to the breaking point, leading either to formal church schism or informal partisan alignment. The eighteenth and nineteenth centuries witnessed Old Side/New Side and Old School/New School splits that lasted for decades. Twentieth-century polarities produced both formal schisms and unofficial, competing structures. At times, then, tension between the more "objective, theologically precise, ordered governance" tendency and the more "experiential, pragmatic, experimental" tendency has led to church division. More often, however, the strain has produced diverse expressions throughout the "unified" church's life.

In the early eighteenth century, many Presbyterians believed that orthodoxy was being threatened throughout the colonial church by rationalist innovations from Europe. In an attempt to ensure theological integrity, the orthodox group demanded that all ministers and candidates for ministry be required to subscribe to the Westminster Confession of Faith. Predictably, other Presbyterians opposed the imposition of such theological constraint. Church division was averted by a "compromise" agreed to in 1729. The "Adopting Act" consisted of four interconnected stipulations:

1. All ministers and candidates for ministry were required to accept the Westminster Confession of Faith, together with the Shorter and Larger Catechisms, as the church's doctrinal standard and as the expression of their own theological views. Acceptance entailed both negative and positive elements.
2. Negatively, ministers and candidates were not required to accept Westminster "categorically and verbally," that is, in every detail and in each articulation.
3. Positively, ministers and candidates were to declare "agreement and approbation" of the Westminster Standards "as being in all the essential and necessary articles, good forms of sound words and systems of Christian doctrine."
4. Any minister or candidate who could not accept a particular part of the confession or catechisms was to identify the point of compunction or hesitation, stipulating his "scruple." The presbytery would then decide whether or not the scruple concerned "essential and necessary articles of faith." If the scruple did touch upon a necessary and essential article, the presbytery would then decide whether or not the scruple was serious enough to call theological agreement into question.

The Adopting Act was a compromise in the best sense. It regularized confessional standards but did not require adherence to every confessional articulation, opting instead for acceptance of the confessional core—the essential and necessary articles. But the Adopting Act did not identify the essential and necessary articles. Rather, it balanced personal and corporate responsibility: Ministers and candidates were expected to declare their differences with the church's standards, while the church was expected to determine whether or not the differences concerned articles of doctrine that were essential and necessary to the church's faith and faithfulness.

The skillful compromise of the Adopting Act did not avert schism, however. The Great Awakening led to a split between those who welcomed the wave of conversions and deepened experience, and those who wished to sustain church order and theological orthodoxy. The New Side/Old Side division of 1741 weakened American Presbyterianism by separating the two complementary tendencies. The Old Side lost a measure of spiritual vitality, deep commitment, and evangelical ardor. The New Side became vulnerable to judgmentalism, ministerial idiosyncrasy, and theological aberration.

The 1758 reunion of the two factions built upon the Adopting Act by incorporating the best elements of the Old and New Sides. Old Side values were affirmed by stipulating that in the case of any Christian conviction or action deemed essential by the church, "every member shall actively concur . . . or passively submit . . . or peaceably withdraw." New Side values were affirmed by providing that presbyteries examine candidates on their "religious experience" as well as their theological views. The value of unity was affirmed by making it a censurable offense to irresponsibly accuse other ministers of inadequate theological orthodoxy or insufficient religious experience.

Among the five questions now asked at the ordination and installation of ministers was one that embodied the two tendencies: "Do you sincerely receive and adopt the confession of faith of this church as containing the system of doctrine taught in the holy Scriptures?" Old Side values were preserved by adoption of the confession, while New Side values were preserved by sincerity of reception. Old Side values were affirmed by highlighting the importance of doctrine while New Side values were affirmed by stipulating the *system* of doctrine rather than each and every article of doctrine. The new language of "system of doctrine" was interpreted in the spirit of the Adopting Act's "essential and necessary articles."

The church continued to live in the tension between the two tendencies. At times the tension stretched to the breaking point, while at times it eased. The Old School/New School division in the nineteenth century was an expression of the continuing force of the opposing tendencies, while reunions and openness to revision of the Westminster Confession signaled the whole church's capacity to combine confessional accountability and limited confessional flexibility. At the dawn of the twentieth century, Westminster was amended by adding chapters on the Holy Spirit and missions, and by clarifying the confession's teaching on God's eternal decree. The opening rationale of the new "Declaratory Statement" demonstrated a way in which confessional subscription and confessional flexibility could be held together:

> While the ordination vow of ministers, ruling elders, and deacons . . .
> requires the reception and adoption of the Confession of Faith only as
> containing the system of doctrine taught in the Holy Scriptures, nev-
> ertheless, seeing that the desire has been formally expressed for a dis-
> avowal by the Church of certain inferences drawn from statements in
> the Confession of Faith, and also for a declaration of certain aspects
> of revealed truth which appear at the present time to call for more
> explicit statement, therefore . . . (6.191)

The 1903 amendments to the Westminster Confession did not resolve tensions between the church's two tendencies, of course. Actually, the years leading to confessional revision may have given new impetus to each inclination:
on the one hand, openness to confessional revision; on the other hand, openness to doctrinal definition. In the first decade of the twentieth century, each
tendency seemed to gather strength.[3]

In response to a complaint against the Presbytery of New York for licens-
ing candidates for ministry who allegedly refused to affirm belief in the virgin
birth of Jesus, the 1910 General Assembly of the Presbyterian Church in the
United States of America declared that the Adopting Act of 1729 called upon
church judicatories to determine which articles of faith are "essential and necessary." The General Assembly then named five doctrines as essential: the
inerrancy of Scripture, the virgin birth, sacrificial atonement, bodily resurrection, and Christ's miracles. These doctrines were virtually identical to the five
fundamentals of the 1895 Niagara Bible Conference, although the General
Assembly added to its list of essential doctrines the puzzling notation that
"others are equally so." The General Assembly was clear that candidates who
did not declare their agreement with these essential and necessary articles of
the Westminster Confession could not be ordained.

Although the 1910 deliverance was challenged repeatedly in subsequent
assemblies, it was not repealed. In fact, it was reaffirmed by the 1916 and 1923
assemblies. These actions had the effect of shifting the issue of confessional
subscription away from the Westminster Standards themselves and toward a
brief, shorthand list of doctrines. Perhaps more tellingly, assembly actions
were instances of broader battles being fought in what has come to be known
as "the fundamentalist-modernist controversy."

Opposition to the five-point deliverance built, reaching a dramatic public
level in the 1924 "Auburn Affirmation," signed by over 1,200 ministers, which
confronted the 1910-1916-1923 doctrinal deliverance head on. The Auburn
Affirmation challenged the five-point deliverance by asserting that it

> attempts to commit our church to certain theories concerning the Inspi-
> ration of the Bible, and the Incarnation, the Atonement, the Resurrec-

tion, and the Continuing Life and Supernatural Power of our Lord Jesus Christ. We all hold most earnestly to these great facts and doctrines. . . . Some of us regard the particular themes contained in the deliverance of the General Assembly of 1923 as satisfactory explanations of these facts and doctrines. But we are united in believing that these are not the only themes allowed by the Scriptures and our standards as explanations of these facts and doctrines of our religion, and that all who hold to these facts and doctrines, whatever theories they may employ to explain them, are worthy of all confidence and fellowship.[4]

If the Auburn Affirmation was an acute instance of one of the church's historic tendencies, an overture to the 1925 General Assembly was an intense representation of the other. The overture asked that "all who represent the church on Boards, General Council, Theological Seminaries, and every other Agency of the Church be required to re-affirm their faith in the Standards of the Church, together with the historic interpretations contained in the doctrinal deliverance of 1910, 1916, 1923."[5] What the church, at its best, held in creative tension had now become opposing forces.

In an attempt to bridge the distance between the two positions, the 1925 General Assembly appointed a Special Commission "to study the present spiritual condition of our Church and the causes making for unrest."[6] The Special Commission reported to the 1926 General Assembly and delivered its final report in 1927. Among its wide-ranging and influential observations and recommendations, the section on "essential and necessary articles" directly addressed the old question of subscription and its limits. The Special Commission put the question starkly: "*What authority, if any, does the General Assembly possess for declaring any article to be an essential and necessary one* in a sense which renders its statement mandatory and applicable in all cases?"[7] The answer, played out historically, theologically, and constitutionally, amounted to "None." The Special Commission affirmed the right of the presbytery to determine the fitness of a candidate, restricting a General Assembly's authority to decide questions of this kind to the review of a specific ordination decision made by a presbytery. A General Assembly could hold in a particular case that "the opinions which the candidate holds are not such as fit him for the office of the ministry in the Presbyterian Church; but this is quite different from deciding, as a general proposition, that certain articles, when considered abstractly and logically, are essential and necessary to the system of doctrine contained in the Holy Scriptures."[8]

The final nail in the coffin of the 1910 Doctrinal Deliverance was the Special Commission's note that even if a limited authority were granted to a General Assembly to identify an article as essential and necessary, "it would be required to quote the exact language of the article as it appears in the Confession of Faith. It could not paraphrase the language nor use other terms than those employed within the Constitution, much less could it erect into essential and necessary articles doctrines which are only derived as inferences from the statements of the Confession."[9] The authority of the General Assembly to set forth universal, binding designations of essential and necessary doctrines was denied.

ORDINATION QUESTIONS

Responsibility for determining the adequacy of candidates' reception and adoption of the Westminster Confession's system of doctrine was lodged firmly in presbyteries, but the 1927 General Assembly had not settled the "subscription" issue. Although judging the adequacy and sincerity of a candidate's avowals was the right and responsibility of the presbytery, the church continued to require affirmation of ordination vows that called for fidelity to the core of the confession, yet without a demand for subscription to a catalog of specific doctrines. Presbyterians sought to craft ordination questions that would maintain a creative tension between theological precision and theological latitude. It is instructive to note how the questions have been articulated and altered at critical points in the church's life.

Prior to the 1958 union of the Presbyterian Church in the United States of America (PCUSA) and the United Presbyterian Church of North America (UPCNA), the two churches had different ways of stating what in the confessional standards was to be professed and what the implications of that profession were:

> UPCNA: "Do you believe and acknowledge the doctrine professed by the United Presbyterian Church, contained in the Confession of Faith, the Larger and Shorter Catechisms, and the Confessional Statement, as agreeable to, and founded on, the Word of God, and do you engage to adhere to and maintain them against all opposing errors?"

> PCUSA: "Do you sincerely receive and adopt the Confession of Faith and catechisms of this Church as containing the system of doctrine taught in the Holy Scriptures?"

Following union, the new United Presbyterian Church in the United States of America (UPCUSA) adopted the briefer question of the PCUSA. "Receive and adopt" may have been stronger than "believe and acknowledge," but the newly united church softened confessional fidelity by deleting the obligation to adhere to and maintain the confessional standards "against all opposing errors."

The Presbyterian Church in the United States (PCUS), an original partner in efforts to achieve Presbyterian unity, declined reunion. It struggled with the same issues as its northern partners, however. The PCUS asked a first question identical to that of the UPCUSA, but added a second: "Do you promise that if at any time you find yourself out of accord with any of the fundamentals of this system of doctrine, you will on your own initiative make known to your Presbytery the change which has taken place in your views since the assumption of this ordination vow?"

The 1967 adoption of *The Book of Confessions* by the UPCUSA necessitated changes in the ordination vows. Two new questions replaced the older "receive and adopt" and "system of doctrine." Ordinands were now asked, "Will you perform the duties of a minister of the gospel in obedience to Jesus Christ, under the authority of the Scriptures, and under the continuing instruction and guidance of the confessions of this Church?" and "Do you promise to be zealous and faithful in studying the Scriptures, the Book of Confessions, and the Book of Order, in maintaining the truths of the gospel, and in furthering the peace, unity, and purity of the church, whatever persecution or opposition may arise onto you on that account?" In 1970, the first vow was altered slightly, the second was abandoned, and a new vow was added: "Will you be instructed by the Confessions of our Church, and led by them as you lead the people of God?" This form of the questions remained until reunion in 1983.

Meanwhile, attempts at enlarging the church's confessional standards led to revisions in the PCUS ordination questions. Although the church did not adopt a new confession—"A Declaration of Faith"—and a proposed *Book of Confessions*, discussion of confessional standards prompted new vows. PCUS vows incorporated the UPCUSA question and added, "Do you sincerely receive and adopt the Confession of Faith and Catechisms of this Church as, in their essentials, authentic and reliable expositions of what Scripture leads us to believe and do, and will you be instructed and led by them as you lead the people of God?" The 1983 reunion brought together UPCUSA and PCUS questions to give us the present, familiar vows concerning the church's confessional standard.

Throughout the American Presbyterian experience, the church has sought to balance the need for adherence to confessional standards and the need to avoid strict subscription to every doctrinal point. The current ordination vows attempt to assure confessional fidelity by requiring sincere reception and adoption while avoiding doctrinal nit-picking by confining reception and adoption to essential matters. The questions of 1729, 1910, and 1983 remain, however. Which articles of doctrine are "necessary and essential"? What are the "essential tenets"? Who decides which elements of Christian faith and faithfulness are essential, necessary to the church's life?

ESSENTIAL TENETS

It is not surprising that calls for an account of the "essential tenets" are heard regularly. Yet even those most eager for a definite list are aware that an agreed upon catalog would be difficult to produce. When the 1910 General Assembly concluded its list of essential and necessary articles of faith with the tag line "others are equally so," it was in good company. John Calvin was not indifferent to doctrinal precision, but he recognized that "not all the articles of true religion are of the same sort. Some are necessary to know that they should be certain and unquestioned by all men as the proper principles of religion." What are Calvin's "necessary" doctrines? "Such are: God is one; Christ is God and the Son of God; our salvation rests in God's mercy; and the like."[10] Calvin's three essential tenets, like the 1910 Assembly's five, needed "and the like" because no short list is adequate. Nevertheless, Calvin, General Assemblies, and the ordination vow all assume that some Christian truths are more central, foundational, necessary, essential than others.

The issue of doctrinal essentials is not unique to the Reformed tradition. A study document on the "hierarchy of truths" was recently produced by a joint World Council of Churches and Roman Catholic working group. Although the term itself is distinctly Catholic, the document notes that churches of the Reformation also observe a kind of "hierarchy" in dealing with the truths of the Christian faith: "These churches hold that the gospel of God's saving action in Jesus Christ, witnessed to normatively by holy scripture, is the supreme authority to which all Christian truths should refer. It is in relation to the gospel as the center of the faith that these churches have summarized the truths of the faith."[11] Widespread recognition that not all Christian truths are on the same level suggest that attempts to distinguish "essential tenets" are not necessarily perverse or quixotic.

Some Presbyterians suggest that essential tenets can be inferred from the ordination vows themselves. The list of necessary doctrines would then include (1) the Trinity, (2) several christological affirmations, (3) the authority of Scripture, (4) the reliability of the church's confessions as guides to belief and action, (5) adherence to the church's polity and discipline, (6) obedient discipleship, (7) an ecumenically principled ecclesiology, and (8) a particular understanding of ministry. Others propose that the catalog of the confessions' salient characteristics in chapter II of the *Book of Order* yields a constitutionally credible list of essential tenets: (1) the Trinity, (2) the incarnation, (3) grace alone, faith alone, Scripture alone, (4) the sovereignty of God, (5) election, (6) covenantal ecclesiology, (7) stewardship, and (8) the necessity to transform societies.

Each of these potential lists of essential tenets has the advantage of being constitutional; neither is the product of personal viewpoint, party preference, or momentary enthusiasm. Yet the ordination questions and the *Book of Order*'s paragraphs were not composed for the purpose of delineating authentic and reliable confessional expositions of what Scripture leads us to believe and do, or identifying the essential tenets that ordinands must sincerely receive and adopt. Moreover, most Presbyterians would object either that one or more essentials is missing or that one or more nonessentials is included. Where is cross and resurrection? Why is the Holy Spirit absent? Faithful stewardship and adherence to the church's polity are important, of course, but are they at the heart of the confessional witness?

Even though the two lists are problematic, we can undertake a brief thought experiment by imagining how a specific list might work in the church. If the *Book of Order* list in G-2.0300–.0500 were to comprise "the essential tenets of the Reformed faith," all candidates for the offices of minister, elder, and deacon would have to sincerely receive and adopt the Trinity, several christological affirmations, the authority of Scripture, and so on. But surely the question is not *whether* one believes "the doctrine of the Trinity," but *what one believes about* the doctrine of the Trinity, *how* one understands, receives, and adopts the confessions' Trinitarian teaching. Similarly, the mere assertion that one accepts the authority of Scripture is insufficient, for the real issue is the character and extent of Scripture's authority. While a list of essential tenets might serve to identify (and limit) the scope of the third ordination question, it would not help with the central task of determining what candidates believe, and whether the beliefs they receive and adopt are consistent with the church's confessional faith.

Perhaps that is why the Special Commission of 1925 insisted that even if a General Assembly were to stipulate essential and necessary doctrines, "it would be required to quote the exact language of the article as it appears in the Confession of Faith. It could not paraphrase the language nor use other terms than those employed within the Constitution, much less could it erect into essential and necessary articles doctrines which are only derived as inferences from the statements of the Constitution."[12] Quoting the full text of G-2.0300–.0500 would provide little help, however, for "the mystery of the triune God and of the incarnation of the eternal Word of God in Jesus Christ" do not take us much beyond the shorthand list derived from the exact language of the *Book of Order*. An alternative procedure—providing a compendium of every confessional reference to the authority of Scripture, for example, and requiring assent—would be a mechanical exercise that would trivialize confessional integrity.

CONVERSATION WITH THE CONFESSIONS

Even if the whole church could agree on a catalog of essential tenets, the list would provide candidates and examining bodies with little helpful guidance, for it would not address doctrinal substance, the manner of reception and the character of adoption, an understanding of implications for belief and action, or consequences for ministry. The intention of *The Book of Confessions* is not merely to provide raw material for a doctrinal digest or a theological précis. A primary intention of *The Book of Confessions* is captured in the abandoned ordination question from 1967–1969: "Do you promise to be zealous and faithful in studying the Scriptures, the Book of Confessions, and the Book of Order, in maintaining the truth of the gospel, and in furthering the peace, unity, and purity of the church, whatever persecution or opposition may arise onto you on that account?" Although elements of this short-lived vow were transferred to other questions, something important was lost. The question made it clear that study was central to the vocation of ministers, elders, and deacons in the church. Furthermore, study of Scripture, theological tradition, and ecclesial order was not expected for its own sake, but because it is essential in sustaining fidelity to the gospel, integrity of witness, and the wholeness of the body of Christ. (The question was also honest in implying that fidelity, integrity, and ecclesial wholeness are not ingredients in a recipe for success, but might bring opposition, if not persecution.)

Continual study of the church's confessions is necessary to maintaining a conversation with the confessions about matters of faith and faithfulness. It is this ongoing conversation that enables distinctions to be drawn between central and derivative doctrines, between enduring insights and transitory concerns. Conversation with the confessions is not only an individual concern, however, and the discernment that grows from the conversation is not merely personal insight. As ministers, elders, and deacons answer the call to study the confessions, even though it is no longer expressed in an ordination question, they would create a *community* of conversation within which discriminating judgments could be made about the character of foundational matters. Presbyteries and sessions in which ministers and elders converse with the church's confessions would become collegiums that engage in conversations about Christian faith and life, developing shared understandings of the identity, meaning, and significance of tenets that are essential to the gospel. Persons who are called to ministry as deacons, elders, and ministers of the Word and sacrament would then become candidates within a community of conversation that invites them to join the discussion. Preparation for ministry, whether the relatively brief period for elders and deacons or the protracted period for ministers of the Word and sacrament, would include significant exchanges about the confessional witness of the church and the convictions of candidates. "Examinations" would be less like true/false quizzes and more like concluding tutorials in which reception and adoption of central doctrinal elements are explored and assessed.

Would different presbyteries and sessions have different understandings of what constitutes essential tenets? Probably. Yet the differences should not be divisive, for the task is to recognize essential tenets of the Reformed faith as expressed in the confessions of our church, not to devise personal or communal preferences. Because genuine conversation gives the confessions full voice and honors the church's commitment to them, agreement about essential tenets would be broader and deeper than the distinctive emphases that might emerge. It is likely that differences would reflect the variety of cultural and ecclesial situations, and thus would draw on the diversity of confessional expressions emerging from the diversity of the confessions' origins.

Conversation with the confessions—confessional conversation within presbyteries and sessions, and conversations between governing bodies and candidates—might be deeper if the spirit of another discarded ordination question were revived. At one time, PCUS candidates for ministry were asked, "Do you promise that if at any time you find yourself out of accord with any of the fundamentals of this system of doctrine you will on your own initiative make known to your Presbytery the change which has taken place in your convictions since the assumption of this ordination vow?" The question harkens back to the Adopting Act's stipulation that candidates and ministers should declare their "scruples," that is, their sense of departure from the church's confessional standards. The presbytery was then responsible to determine if the scruple concerned an essential and necessary matter, and if the departure was significant or minor. A contemporary ecclesial understanding echoing the former PCUS question would balance personal and corporate accountability among us, making both governing bodies and candidates responsible for discernment and honest communication. If ministers and their presbyteries were mutually responsible for the articulation of their faith, the confessions would be less like minefields and more like living instances of the church's search for shared faith. If elders, deacons, and their sessions were mutually responsible for the articulation of their faith, the confessions would be less like ordination souvenirs and more like living instances of the church's search for shared faith.

Are there essential tenets of the Reformed faith expressed in the confessions of our church as authentic and reliable expositions of what Scripture leads us to believe and do? Surely there are essential tenets. And surely we are responsible for making appropriate distinctions between center and periphery, between what is necessary and what is not required, between essential and discretionary. However, our responsibility is not fulfilled by devising an abstract list of doctrines. Instead, we are called to a deeply communal conversation with the whole confessional witness, inquiring about the eternal and the timebound, the catholic and the parochial. Essential tenets emerge from a dialogue between us and our forebears in faith; they are not a template to be imposed upon the confessions and us.

The church's confessions are contextual articulations of faith that comes to us from various times and places. No contextual interpretation can claim to be absolute, as if it fully expressed every element of Christian truth. Yet each of the confessions, in its own time and place, intends to formulate the truth of the gospel. Because no single confession says all that we need to hear, we have a confessional collection: individual expressions of the apostolic faith handed down from generation to generation within the communion of churches in all particular places and ages. Because each confession bears witness to the truth of the gospel, the confessions within the collection speak to our own time and place. *The Book of Confessions* is the gift to us of our forebears' witness to the grace of the Lord Jesus Christ, the love of God, and the communion of the Holy Spirit. *The Book of Confessions* is also our calling to join in the church's ongoing conversation about the truth of the gospel. We now bear responsibility to join with "colleagues in ministry" to "be zealous and faithful in studying the Scriptures, the Book of Confessions, and the Book of Order."

> Hold to the standard of sound teaching that you have heard from me, in the faith and love that are in Christ Jesus. Guard the good treasure entrusted to you, with the help of the Holy Spirit living in us. (2 Timothy 1:13–14)

NOTES

1. *The Constitution of the Presbyterian Church (U.S.A.)*, Part II, *Book of Order* (Louisville, KY: Office of the General Assembly, 2004), W-2.3006.
2. *Book of Order*, G-6.0106a, b.
3. The complex history of the Presbyterian Church in the last decades of the nineteenth century and the early decades of the twentieth century is fully related in a number of important books. Among the best are Lefferts Loetscher, *The Broadening Church* (Philadelphia: University of Pennsylvania Press, 1954); Bradley Longfield, *The Presbyterian Controversy* (New York: Oxford University Press, 1991); and William J. Weston, *Presbyterian Pluralism* (Knoxville: University of Tennessee Press, 1997).
4. "Auburn Affirmation," accessed at http://www.mlp.org/resources/auburn.html.
5. *Minutes of the 137th General Assembly (1925) of the Presbyterian Church in the U.S.A.*, Part I, *Journal*, 25.
6. Ibid., 88.
7. *Minutes of the 139th General Assembly (1927) of the Presbyterian Church in the U.S.A.*, Part I, *Journal*, 78.
8. Ibid., 81.
9. Ibid.

10. John Calvin, *Institutes of the Christian Religion*, ed. John T. McNeill, trans. Ford Lewis Battles (Philadelphia: Westminster Press, 1960), 4.1.12 (LCC 2:1026).

11. "The Notion of 'Hierarchy of Truths': An Ecumenical Interpretation," in *Joint Working Group between the Roman Catholic Church and the World Council of Churches, Sixth Report*, Appendix B (Geneva: World Council of Churches, 1990), 40.

12. *Minutes* (1927), 81.

Index

context for, 61, 74–75
double grace of God, 77–78
elements missing in, 78–79
on fighting idolatry, 76
final words, 65
imperative to confess the faith, 71
Jesus Christ as center and source of
faith, 75–77
rejecting false doctrines, 73, 129–30
on role of the state, 198
tension between authority and freedom, 71–72
unifying role of, 22
yes and no of, 12
theology, province of the church, 3–4
Tillich, Paul, 124
Timequake (Vonnegut), 2
total depravity, 39
tradition, distinguished from
traditionalism, 5
trinitarian structure, of ancient creeds,
55
Trinity, 101–2
avoiding modalism in describing,
105–6
in creation, 102–3
economic and immanent, 103–4
oneness of, distinguishing God from
humans, 105
three persons always in mission, 151

Unbearable Lightness of Being, The, 2–4
United Presbyterian Church in North
America, 155, 230
United Presbyterian Church in the
United States of America, 52, 53,
81, 84–85, 230, 231
United States, handling religious diver-
sity in, 22–23. *See also* American
Presbyterianism
Ursinus, Zacharias, 35

Voices of Silence (Malraux), *The*, 173–74
Vonnegut, Kurt, 2

Warfield, Benjamin B., 57
weakness, 115–17
Webb, Stephen H., 177–78

Weber, Hans-Reudi, 174–75
Western attitudes
individualism of, 18–19
modernity, achievement of, 118
Westminster Confession of Faith, xii, 34,
36, 51–52, 54, 125
Adopting Act relating to, 226–27
allegiance to, 9
amending, 52–53
authority of Scripture in, 57–58
on being reconciled to God in Christ,
165
on canon and Apocrypha, 179–80
communal character of new creation,
118–19
on creation, 102–3, 112
on ecclesial unity, 160
final words, 65
God's nature, 107
God's self-revelation, 93
God's simplicity, 99
on invisible and visible church, 161
Jesus Christ, role of, in receiving and
mediating worship, 193–94, 195
law of great use to Christians, 215
method for understanding Scripture,
181
on music in worship, 201
necessity of God's existence, 99
new Declaratory Statement, 227–28
predestination in, 63–64
Scripture as norm for worship, 194
starting point, 55, 60
worship of a triune God, 190
Westminster Directory of Worship,
prayer for illumination, 59
Westminster documents, on Christ's
presence in the sacraments, 192
Westminster Larger Catechism, 49 n.15,
51, 52, 54, 59
baptism, 61
benefits of redemption, 62
duties and sins resulting from first
commandment, 128
expanding scope of fifth commandment, 145
glorifying and enjoying God, 65–66
God's nature, 106